CCAR Journal
The Reform Jewish Quarterly

Contents

CONTENTS

CONTENTS

At the Gates — בשערים

It's not every day, or even every year, that the *CCAR Journal: The Reform Jewish Quarterly* introduces a new section! So I'm excited about the debut of *Maayanot* (Primary Sources), to which we give pride of place for this occasion.

Bernard Mehlman's presentation of *Maaseh Avraham Avinu Alav HaShalom* represents a coming together of the broadly scientific with the spiritually imaginative. Through his translation, introduction, and annotations, Mehlman grants us direct access to a document we might well have missed otherwise, while contextualizing it through the tools of modern scholarship. We are in his debt for making this unusual text accessible to *Journal* readers and a wider audience.

Two members of the *Journal's* editorial board get credit for the new *Maayanot* rubric: Michael Shire for suggesting it, and Daniel Polish for refining the concept and assuming responsibility as section editor. With the entire editorial board, they welcome further submissions that bring readers in touch with primary sources from all periods of Jewish civilization.

As if to demonstrate that scholarship and imagination, prose and poetry can nicely coexist, this issue includes two poems by Dan Polish. It also includes both an article and two poems by Reeve Brenner. These four poems, like all poetry submissions, are read blind—without identifying marks of the author—by our poetry editor. Other rabbi-poets have been published within these, as within other published, pages. We encourage rabbis to send us their poetry, along with primary-source studies and articles.

Speaking of articles, this issue includes a wide range of topics and approaches—some with common threads. Several authors challenge prevailing practice and received wisdom. I direct your attention to Jeffrey Brown's "Preaching against the Text: An Argument in Favor of Restoring Leviticus 18 to Yom Kippur Afternoon," Reeve Brenner's "Shabbat Weddings Revisited: The Pro Side for a Change," David Kline's *"Sh'ma Echad,"* Stephen Passamaneck's "An Eye for an Eye—Indeed!" and Farhad Arbab and Daniel

Berry's "Why Jews Wear Costumes on Purim." I hope that these carefully reasoned pieces will stimulate your thinking, whether or not you wind up agreeing with their authors.

As for common threads, that of our first Patriarch connects the *Maayanot* piece to Naomi Graetz's provocative "Trauma and Recovery: Abraham's Journey to the *Akeidah*." At the same time, the Persian background of *Maaseh Avraham* links to Arbab and Berry's study of dressing up on Purim. Admiel Kosman gives us Alexander of Macedon "dressed up" in fool's motley as he encounters the wisdom of women. And in another article where gender and public presentation figure importantly, Darren Kleinberg grants us access to the world of "Orthodox Women (Non-)Rabbis." In their article chronicling the transformational leadership of the late Rabbi Eric Bram, Samuel Joseph and Jeffrey Schein invoke the Dutch theologian Jans Huzinga's *Homo Ludens,* which rejects the characterization of human beings as *Homo sapiens* (the wise species) in favor of *Homo ludens* (the playful creature)—the sort of creature that dons costumes and creates midrash. And finally, Ilana Grinblat's "Parent's Torah" is both playful and serious, modeling for us an ability to find Torah in the ordinary moments of parenting. Her article concludes with a poem that draws on traditional sources to create seven similes for Torah, beginning with "Torah, you are like a prince,/You have the power to give life."

In addition to all these riches, four striking book reviews offer insight into a wide range of scholarly works. All these reviews, and the books upon which they focus, are worth our consideration.

Writing of Rabbi Bram, Jeffrey Schein says that he knows of "few other rabbinic colleagues who combined playfulness, skill, and wisdom in the same way Eric did." Playfulness, skill, and wisdom seem to me a special, almost magical combination—a combination from which life-giving nourishment is likely to issue, a *maayan*, as is Torah. Hopefully, this publication too provides such nourishment. Drink deeply!

Susan Laemmle, Editor

Maayanot (Primary Sources)

The *Maaseh Avraham Avinu Alav HaShalom*: Translation, Notes, and Commentary

Bernard H. Mehlman

Sefer Ben Sira,[1] a late midrashic compilation published in Constantinople in 1580, contains the first printed edition of the *Maaseh Avraham Avinu Alav HaShalom*. The *Maaseh*, a late medieval work, was probably written in Persia and dispersed widely among Jews in the Muslim world, particularly in the Ottoman Empire. Two fragmentary manuscripts of the *Maaseh* at the Jewish Theological Seminary of America of Kurdustani provenance were copied no later than the first printed edition.[2]

Jews in medieval Persia and in other lands dominated by Islam confronted a theological conundrum. Islam laid claim to Abraham, the founder of the Jewish religion through the line of Ishmael. It further claimed that Muhammad's prophetic revelation superseded both Judaism and Christianity. How did Jews respond to this expropriation of Abraham and Islam's supersessionist theology? The *Maaseh* responds to this question and reasserts the primacy of Abraham in Judaism and God's covenant with the people of Israel.

Literary, historic, theological, linguistic, social, and folkloristic elements inhere in the text of the *Maaseh Avraham Avinu Alav HaShalom*. Scholars have long contended that this midrash was originally written in Arabic and was later translated into Hebrew. As such, language itself becomes one of the most intriguing aspects of the text. Other literary features influenced its composition. The

RABBI BERNARD H. MEHLMAN (C63) is senior scholar of Temple Israel, Boston, Massachusetts, and teaches Midrash and Homiletics at the Hebrew Union College in New York City.

fabulous royal court described in the midrash is on one hand like the courts of the *Arabian Nights* and on the other hand like the courts of the biblical kings, Ahasuerus and Nebuchadnezzar. The *Maaseh* draws upon a range of religious literature known to medieval Jews: the Hebrew Bible, the *Targumim*, the Talmud, the classic midrashim, the siddur, and the Koran.

The author (or authors) of the *Maaseh* used the classical *B'reishit Rabbah* (38:13 and 44:13) midrashim as the starting point for a new iteration of the tale. The author(s) sets out to reclaim Abraham, the first monotheist, the enemy of all forms of idolatry, and the faithful emissary of the One God. The *Maaseh* opens with a description of Nimrod as a cunning astrologer, who used magical arts to gain divine power over his people. The *Maaseh* closes with Nimrod's last-gasp effort to accuse Abraham of sorcery. This structure of the *Maaseh*, from the opening to the closing scene, serves as a large inclusio, encompassing its underlying message: to deny validity to idolatry and to proclaim the truth of the one incorporeal God of the universe.

The *Maaseh* uses Moses and Abraham as central figures in the struggle for freedom, which has resonance in the Babylonian Talmud (*P'sachim* 116a) and on the pages of the Passover Haggadah. Moses leads the Jewish people in its struggle for physical emancipation from bondage in Egypt. Abraham is emblematic of the struggle of the Jewish people to liberate itself from the spiritual bondage of Babylonian idolatry. In this recounting, Pharaoh and Nimrod, considered divine by their people, become archetypes of the usurpation of the divine prerogative.

The author(s) of the *Maaseh* was familiar with the Arabic language, the Koran, and some Hadith tradition. The oft repeated phrase "the Maggid said" is a translation of the Arabic, *q'al al-qa'il*. Segments of the Koran, Sura 6:76 and 21:69, are incorporated into the body of the narrative. The depiction of Abraham, derived from the Hadith tradition, tying a rope around the heads of the idols and dragging them face down through the market, is deftly woven into the text.

The environment and flavor of the Books of Esther and Daniel, set in the courts of absolute eastern potentates, fit the reality of the Jews in Islamic lands. It may also explain why these historically late biblical works are frequently cited in the *Maaseh*. True believers, Esther/Abraham, in perilous circumstances faced destruction.

Esther's noble behavior parallels that of Abraham. The biblical Book of Esther, like the *Maaseh*, was set in Persia, making its characters more real and accessible to its audience.

In every era we Jews endeavor to make our sacred literature relevant. We recreate our heroes, clothe them in contemporary garments, focus on their virtues, and make them responsive to our quotidian reality. The *Maaseh Avraham Avinu Alav HaShalom* is one notable example of that creative process. This apologue is an imaginative, passionate, and engaging effort by the author(s) to reconnect their contemporaries to the biblical Abraham. The *Maaseh* demonstrates how Jews, integrated in some measure in Muslim society, responded to the influence of Islam and how they educated their listeners/readers to Abraham's foundational role in Judaism. In reading this translation, the reader is invited to consider how this iteration of the Abraham story can be reshaped and applied in our age.

Translation

They said[3] that before Abraham was created, Nimrod[4] [A] denied belief in God, Blessed Be God, vaunted himself, and then asserted that he was a god. The ancients in his time used to worship and prostrate themselves to him. Now this king [Nimrod] was a cunning astrologer, who saw through the science of astrology that a man would be born in his day and would arise against him, dissuade him of his faith, and defeat him. "And he was seized with violent trembling."[5] What did he do? He sent for his princes and governors and told them of the matter. He asked them, "What do you advise me to do about this child who is yet to be born?" They responded, "The counsel which we agree upon is that you should build a large house, set a guard at its entrance, then decree throughout your realm that all the pregnant women shall come there. After they arrive, they

Commentary

[A]
Nimrod and Astrology

The *Maaseh* opens with astrology as its central theme. Nimrod uses it to exert his power. His reputation is well established in the biblical text where he appears four times: Genesis 10:8, 10:9; Micah 5:5; and I Chronicles 1:10. He is known as the hunter and lord of Babylon, Erech, Accad, and Calneh (?). He is connected to Ninurta, the Assyrian god of hunting and warfare. His power is epitomized in I Chronicles 1:10, "the first mighty one on earth." At the end of the *Maaseh* this ancient, fabled warrior is bereft of his shall also bring the midwives so that they are with the pregnant women at the time of their delivery. Now when a woman's time to deliver arrives, the midwives will see, and if it is a boy, they will kill him at the womb, but if it is a girl they will let her live.[6] Then they shall give gifts to her mother and clothe her in regal raiment and call out before her, "Thus shall you do to a woman who bears a daughter."[7]

When the king heard their counsel he was overjoyed. Then he decreed in all the provinces of his realm that all artisans should gather to build a large house for the king, sixty cubits high and eighty cubits wide. When the building of the house was completed, he decreed that all the pregnant women come to that house to be there until they gave birth. He appointed officials to bring them there and he also set guards over the house to guard the doorway that they do not escape. He also appointed midwives over them to help deliver them. He ordered them to kill a male child on his mother's bosom; but if it was a female child, they were to clothe her mother in "raiments of fine linen, silk, and embroidery."[8] Then they led her out from the house of confinement and gave her great honor, for thus did the king order. And so they led her to her home in honor.

The Maggid[9] said that more than seventy thousand male infants were slain in this manner. When the angels on high saw the slaying of these children, they said before the Holy One Blessed Be God, "Have you not seen that which the sinner and blasphemer, Nimrod son of Canaan did? For he slew so many children and spilled their blood on the ground although they had done no harm!" God answered them, "Holy angels, I know and I see, 'for I neither slumber nor sleep,'[10] for I see and know 'the hidden and the revealed things.'[11] But you will see what I will do to this sinner and blasphemer, for 'I will set my hand against him and chastise him.'"[12]

The Maggid said that at that time the mother of Abraham, our father of blessed memory, went and married a man named Terah.

advisors and his power. He stands helpless, stripped of his divinity and his realm.

Astrology and astrologers play a key role in predicting the birth of Nimrod's and Pharaoh's nemeses. Astrologers announced to Pharaoh the precise day the redeemer of Israel will be born. See BT *Sotah* 12a–b; *Tanchuma Bet II* 122; *Tanchuma Vayak'heil* 4; *Sh'mot Rabbah* 1:18; Josepheus, *Antiquities*, vol. 2, 9:2. In the *Maaseh* the parallel is clear.

[B] She conceived with him and at the end of three months of pregnancy, her stomach grew large[13] and her face became pale. Terah, her husband, said to her, "My wife, what is wrong with you? Your face is pale and your stomach is big." She answered him, "Every year this illness befalls me and they call it *Qolasni*."[14] Terah responded, "Show me your belly for it seems to me that you are pregnant. And if you are, it is not fitting to transgress the command of Nimrod our god." Now when he placed his hand on her belly, God performed a miracle on her behalf. The child moved up under her breasts. He felt with his hands and found nothing. He said to her, "You spoke honestly." Thus nothing showed nor became known until the period of gestation finished.

Out of her great fear she left the city and went through the desert on the edge of a valley.[15] She found a large cave there and entered it. The next day birth pangs seized her and she gave birth to a son. Then she saw the whole cave illuminated as if by the sun, by the face of the infant and she was overjoyed. [C] And he was Abraham, our father of blessed memory.

Then she opened her mouth and said, "I am the one who bore you at the time that king Nimrod killed seventy thousand male infants because of you. Now I greatly fear for you, for if he learns about your existence he will kill you! Therefore, it is better that you die in this cave so that my eyes do not see you slain upon my bosom." So she took her own clothing and swaddled him. Then she abandoned him in the cave

[B]

Marriage and the Birth of a Child

The *Maaseh* uses the motif of finding a mate but reverses the order of the biblical prototype. Abraham's unnamed mother goes out and marries Terah. This detail is modeled on the Moses birth story: A certain man of the house of Levi went and married a Levite woman (Exod. 2:1). Both stories reflect perilous times for the people of Israel ruled by cruel monarchs who claimed to be divine. In each instance the birth of an infant marks the reversal of Israel's fortunes.

[C]

Great Light

Light plays a central role in the birth story of Abraham. Earlier midrashic accounts depict the birth of heroes accompanied by great light. At Noah's birth the house was filled with light (*Sefer Derashot Rabbi Yehoshua Shu'aib*, vol. 1, 13). Similarly the Sages relate that at the hour of Moses's birth the house was completely filled with light (BT *Sotah* 12a; Avigdor Shinan, ed., *Sh'mot Rabbah*, 71).

Light in this story adumbrates the dawning light of monotheism, which will be brought to light by this newborn child.

and said, "May your God be with you. May God not fail you or forsake you."[16]

[D]

The Maggid said that when Abraham, our father of blessed memory, was in the cave and yet a child, he had no wet nurse to suckle him. He wept, and God, Blessed Be God, heard his cry "where he is."[17] God sent the angel Gabriel to sustain him and give him milk.

He [Gabriel] [E] made milk flow from the right finger of the baby's right hand and Abraham suckled from it until he was ten days old. Then he began to walk about, left the cave, and walked alongside the edge of the valley.[18] When the sun set and the stars came out, he said, "These are the gods."[19] Later when dawn came, he could not see the stars. He said, "I shall not worship these because they are not gods." Later he saw the sun. He said, "This is my god and I will worship it."[20] But when the sun set he said, "This is no divine being." He saw the moon and said, "This is my god and I will worship it." When

[D]

Abandonment

The story of Abraham's unnamed mother in the *Maaseh* parallels the story of Moses's unnamed mother in the Tanach and Hagar and Ishmael in Genesis 21:15. Each woman is unable to bear seeing her infant son die. One abandons her son on the banks of the Nile (Exod. 2:2–4), one swaddles him and leaves him in the cave, and one abandons her son under a bush. These women leave the destiny of their infant sons to God's will.

This short midrashic unit ends with a citation expressing Abraham's mother's prayerful hope. But there is another literary twist to this story in parallel versions of the *Maaseh*. In the *Tanach*, Hagar casts her son Ishmael out of her sight in order not to see him die. She leaves his destiny to God's will. In the biblical story God's messenger reassures Hagar that God will attend to the child, *baasher hu sham*, "where he is" (Gen. 21:17). In two other printed versions of the *Maaseh* and in the Jewish Theological Seminary Manuscript #33 the identical words, "where he is," are applied to Abraham's mother in the moment that she abandons him in the cave, swaddled in her own clothing. Although these words are anachronistic, they heighten a mother's anguish and reassure her of divine protection.

[E]

Gabriel

The angel Gabriel appears first in Daniel 8:16, 9:21 and in later Rabbinic literature as a defender of Israel. In this, his first appearance in the *Maaseh*, he provides nourishment for the abandoned infant, Abraham. Gabriel will deliver Abraham in several encounters he has with Nimrod. In the end, Gabriel delivers Abraham from death in the fiery furnace.

Gabriel also plays a role in Christian and Muslim Scripture. He is the herald of the birth of John the Baptist (Luke 1:19) and Jesus (Luke 1:26). Gabriel is known as it turned dark, he said, "This is not a deity—they have a force which moves them."[21] While he was still speaking[22] the angel Gabriel came and said, "Peace be unto you Abraham." He responded, "Unto you peace." Abraham asked, "Who are you?" The angel replied, "I am Gabriel, a messenger of the Holy One Blessed Be God." At that time Abraham went to a spring which he found there, washed his face, his hands, and his feet and worshiped God, Blessed Be God, bowing down and prostrating himself.

Ruh-ul-amin, the Spirit of Faith (the faithful), attesting to his role in delivering the word of God to Muhammad.

The Maggid said that the mother of Abraham our father remembered him, wept greatly, and left the city to seek her son in the cave in which she abandoned him, but did not find him. She cried even more for him, and said, "Woe is me, for I bore you to become prey for the wild animals, for the bears, for the lions, and the wolves." She walked to the edge of the valley[23] and found her son but did not recognize him because he had grown greatly. She said to him, "Peace unto you." He responded to her, "Unto you peace. Why are you walking in these wastelands?" She answered him, "I left the city to seek my son." He asked her, "Who brought your son here?" She answered him, "I was pregnant with child by my husband, Terah. At the time of delivery I was fearful for my son who was in my belly. I did not want our king, Nimrod son of Canaan, to kill him as he killed seventy thousand male infants. As soon as I came to one cave in this valley, then birth pangs came over me and I bore a son. And I abandoned him in the cave and went to my home and now I came to seek him out but I cannot find him."

Abraham said to her, "These things that you related to me concerning the child that you abandoned, how old was he?" She replied, "About twenty days old." He said to her, "Is there [really] a woman in the world who would abandon her infant child, all by himself in the desert, and come to see him after twenty days?" She responded, "Perhaps God will have mercy." He said to her, "I am your son, Abraham, for whose sake you came to the valley."[24] She replied,

"My how you have grown my child! [F] Only twenty days old and you are able to walk and talk!" He answered, "Yes, my mother, you know that there is in the world

[F]
Rediscovery

After twenty days Abraham's mother

a great and awesome God,[25] living[26] and ever-existent,[27] who sees but is not seen. God is in the heavens and God's presence fills all the earth."[28] She inquired, "My son, is there another god besides Nimrod?" He answered, "Yes my mother, the God of heaven and the God of earth is also the God of Nimrod, son of Canaan. Now you go to Nimrod and inform him of this."

So she went to the city and told her husband, Terah, how she found her son. Now Terah was "a prince and leader"[29] in King Nimrod's house. He went to the palace, to the place where the king was to be found. He prostrated himself before the king with his face to the ground. In that time it was the rule that anyone who prostrated himself to the king could not raise his head until the king ordered, "Raise your head." The king commanded him, "Raise your head and state your request." He responded, "Long live my lord, the king.[30] I have come to notify you about that which you saw through the medium of astrology. [Through astrology you learned] that a male child would be born in your realm who would destroy faith in you. [In trying to eliminate such a child,] you slew seventy thousand male infants. I have come to notify you that he is my son. His mother conceived but I did not know of her pregnancy because she told me, 'I am ill with *Qolasni*.'[31] I examined her belly but I found no embryo. When she completed the period of gestation, she left the city for the valley[32] and there found a cave. She gave birth to a son and abandoned him to the wild beasts of the field. After twenty days she went [back] to him and found him walking along the edge of the valley,[33] speaking like an adult man. He told her that there was a God in heaven, who sees but is not seen, a single God with no second."[34] When Nimrod heard these things, "he was seized with a violent trembling."[35] He asked his advisers and princes what to do with this child. They answered, "Our king, our god, why are you frightened of a small child? There are thousands upon thousands of thousands of princes in your realm. 'You have commanders of thousands, commanders of hundreds, commanders of fifties, commanders of tens,'[36] and officers without number. Let the

returns to the cave to find her son. Abraham's moment of self-revelation in the midrash echoes Esau's response to his father, Jacob, "I am Esau your son" (Gen. 27:32), and Joseph's self-revelation to his brothers, "I am your brother Joseph" (Gen. 45:4). At this moment of rediscovery and self-revelation the midrash draws us to the theological center of the story. This wondrous child will now proclaim the One God.

least among your commanders go and bring him and put him in prison." He answered them, "Have you ever seen a child twenty days old walk and speak and with his own tongue announce that there is one God in heaven and has no second? That God sees but is not seen?"

The Maggid said, all the princes who were there were horror-struck at these words.[37] Meanwhile Satan[38] came disguised as a man, dressed in black silk. He entered and prostrated himself before King Nimrod until the king ordered, "Raise your head and state your request." Satan asked, "Why are you worried and why are all of you horror-struck by a small boy? I will advise you what to do." The king asked, "What is your advice?" Satan retorted, "Open all your arsenals and give [weapons] to all your commanders, adjutants, governors, and to all the warriors. Then dispatch them to Abraham [so that] he comes and worships you and is under your control."

The Maggid said that the king ordered all the princes and all the warriors to come and take weapons from the royal arsenals. Thus they went forth to take Abraham. When Abraham our father saw that a great [number of] people were coming for him, trembling and great fear seized him on their account. He cried out to the God of heaven to deliver him from their hand, for God is the one who "'Delivers the weak from one stronger than he.'[39] Now please deliver me from them." God heard his cry and saw his tears and sent the angel Gabriel to deliver him from their hand. The angel said to him, "What is the matter Abraham? Why are you crying?" He answered, "I was afraid of these men who are coming to slay me." Gabriel said to him, "Do not be frightened or afraid for, 'God is with you'[40] and will deliver you from the 'hands of all your enemies.'"[41]

The Maggid said that the Holy One Blessed Be God commanded Gabriel to place a "dense cloud"[42] [G] between Abraham and his assailants. When they saw the darkness and dense cloud they were frightened and returned to Nimrod their king and said to him, "Let us get away from this

[G]

Dense Cloud

Nimrod and his minions assail Abraham. Gabriel is dispatched to aid Abraham. He is commanded to place a dense cloud between the camps. The incident resembles the flight of Israel before Pharaoh (Exod. 14:19–20).

empire." When the king heard this he gave money to all his princes and courtiers and set out from there for Babylonia.

After they moved, God commanded the angel Gabriel, "Go tell Abraham to follow after the enemy Nimrod to Babylonia." Our father Abraham of blessed memory said to him, "I have no provisions for the road, no horse to ride upon and no soldiers to wage war with him." The angel Gabriel responded, "You need nothing: neither provisions for the road, nor horse to ride upon, nor soldiers to wage war; neither chariot nor horsemen because you will ride upon my shoulders and I will bear you up and bring you to Babylonia." In an instant Abraham arose and rode on Gabriel's shoulder and found himself within the gates of the city of Babylon. Then the angel said to him, "Enter the city and proclaim loudly, '*Adonai* is God in the heavens above and on the earth below there is none other';[43] God is unique with no second;[44] God has neither bodily form nor corporeality; is the only God, the God of Nimrod; and I am Abraham, God's servant, in God's house." Our father Abraham of blessed memory went and entered the city and proclaimed aloud to all the people of the city, "*Adonai* is God; God is unique and there is no second; God is God of the heavens; is the only God and the God of Nimrod! [H] Testify that this is the truth, all you men, women, and children. Testify also that I am 'Abraham, God's servant,' 'Trusted in

[H]
Acknowledgment of the One God

In this unit the theological heart of the midrash unfolds. Aided by Gabriel, Abraham enters the city of Babylon. He proclaims the nature of the one and only God: unique, without second, and incorporeal. He challenges Babylon's denizens to acknowledge the God he proclaims and his role as God's servant.

In a curious narrative twist, Abraham meets his parents and the angel Gabriel. Gabriel urges Abraham to proselytize his own parents. He scorns and derides their worship of a mere mortal. He uses biblical versets as barbs to disparage idolatry.

Finally, Abraham confronts Nimrod. He denounces him as a fraudulent deity and urges him to acknowledge the One God. Abraham's words, like the points of spears, demolish the idols in Nimrod's house. The images fall from their pedestals, broken into many pieces of shattered crockery.

The episode mirrors the biblical account of the Philistine's capture of the Ark of the Covenant. When the Ark was brought into the temple of Dagon the image of the god Dagon fell to the ground and broke into pieces (I Sam. 5:3–4). But it also resonates with the story of Abraham the idol-breaker found in the classic midrash, *B'reishit Rabbah* 38:13.

God's house!'" As he walked through the markets and the streets, proclaiming [this message], he found his father and his mother and also the angel Gabriel. The angel said to him, "Abraham, tell your father and your mother that they should also believe and attest to that which you are proclaiming, that '*Adonai* is God and there is none besides God.'" When Abraham heard the word of the angel, he said to his father and his mother, "You worship a mortal like yourselves. You prostrate yourselves to the image of Nimrod. Do you not realize that it has 'a mouth but does not speak, an eye but does not see, an ear but does not hear,' it cannot walk on its feet and it serves no purpose to itself or others?" When Terah heard his words, he persuaded Abraham to enter the house where he related how it happened that in one day he completed a forty-day journey. Upon hearing this Terah went to Nimrod and reported, "Know, our lord the king that the lad, my son from whom you fled, has arrived here." Nimrod asked him, "How much time did his journey take?" Abraham responded, "Last night I left there and today I arrived here." When Nimrod heard this, "He was seized with violent trembling" and ordered all his princes, counselors, and wise men to bring him advice on what to do with this child. They answered him unanimously, "May King Nimrod live forever!" So he issued a decree declaring that a feast and rejoicing take place for seven days throughout the city. Every person will celebrate at home, dress up, and go out in different kinds of clothes and ornaments. And there shall be "shouting and rejoicing."[45]

They shall also do this in the outer and inner courtyards of the royal house and in the provinces of your realm, and the force of your great power[46] will bring forth every person to worship you. The king ordered that this be done, "and a decree was issued"[47] in all the markets and streets. They all donned "raiments of fine linen, silk, and embroidery"[48] and all sorts of silver ornaments, each person acquiring what he could—and thus they did.

Afterwards, when King Nimrod was sitting on his royal throne, he sent for Abraham to come to him with his father, Terah. Abraham passed by the governors and prefects[49] until he reached the royal throne, the one on which King Nimrod was seated. He grasped hold of the throne and shook it, proclaiming these words in a loud voice, "O Nimrod, you loathsome man, who denies the unity of God, who does not believe in the living and ever-existent God,[50] nor in 'Abraham, God's servant,'[51] 'Trusted in God's house.'[52]

Attest and declare as do I, that *Adonai* is God, God is unique and has no second,[53] God has no body,[54] lives,[55] and is eternal, 'neither slumbers nor sleeps.'[56] Further testify against yourself that you are a mortal and aver that I am [God's servant] and that God created all the world in order that they would believe in God." While Abraham raised his voice with these very words, the idols which were standing there fell to the ground on their faces.[57] Now when the king and his princes saw how the idols had fallen [and heard] Abraham's outcry, they all fell face-down on the ground with their god Nimrod. Nimrod's heart melted within him[58] and he remained two and one half hours on the ground. His heart melted within him, his soul also fled from him. After two hours his spirit and soul returned to his body, "and he awoke from his sleep."[59] At that time the king asked, "Is this your voice, Abraham, or the voice of your God?" He answered, "This voice is the voice of the smallest of the creatures which the Holy One Blessed Be God created." Then King Nimrod said, "Indeed, your God, Abraham, is a great and mighty deity, the Sovereign of Sovereigns." Then he ordered Terah to take his son and remove him and go to his city, "Now the two of them went together."[60]

When Abraham reached the age of twenty years, his father, Terah, fell ill. He said to his sons, Haran and Abraham, "By your lives, my sons, sell these two idols for I have not the money to pay for our expenses." Haran went and sold the idols and brought the money to cover his father's expenses. Then Abraham went and took two other idols to sell. He placed a rope around their necks with their faces to the ground. In that manner he dragged them and he cried out, "Who wants to buy an idol that serves no purpose, either to itself or to the one who purchases it, in order to worship it? 'It has a mouth but does not speak, an eye but does not see, feet but does not walk, an ear but does not hear.'"[61] [I]

[I]

Abraham the Iconoclast

The *Maaseh* substantially enlarges one element of the *B'reishit Rabbah* tale. In that iteration an old woman brings a plate of flour as an offering to the idols. She becomes a more fully developed character in the *Maaseh*. Abraham is depicted as a more vigorous missionary. When his father falls ill, and the family's welfare is endangered, he takes two idols, ties ropes around their necks, and drags them through the market. Instead of promoting the sale of his goods, he mocks and scoffs at the idols. The old woman appears as a potential customer but Abraham berates her for thinking the idols can be of any help. He uses her own experience with her

When the people of the city heard Abraham's words, they were greatly surprised. As he went through the streets, he met an old woman who said to him, "By your life, Abraham, select an idol for me, a very good and large one, that I may worship and adore it." Abraham answered her, "Old woman, old woman, I don't know of any purpose in any of them, neither the big ones nor the little ones; neither by themselves nor for others." He went on, "What has become of the big idol which you bought to worship from my brother Haran?" She responded, "Thieves came that night while I was in the bathhouse and stole it." He retorted, "If this is so, how can you worship such an

stolen household gods to illustrate their worthlessness. Convinced by Abraham's arguments, the old woman abandons idolatry and professes her faith in the One God. She then goes out to urge the people in Babylon to embrace the God of Abraham. This element in the *Maaseh* serves as a paradigm for Abraham's larger mission. Abraham's monotheism set the standard for the new faith—to proselytize humanity.

Nimrod is dejected and his advisors propose a solution to his melancholy—make a great display of your power and wealth and Abraham and the people will abandon their infatuation with Abraham's unorthodox views and return to a true faith in the king. Nimrod, however, will soon learn that wealth and power are evanescent. The spiritual truth of Abraham's message will, in the end, prevail.

idol that was unable to save itself from thieves, let alone deliver others and you, you old, foolish woman from misfortune! And how can you say that the idol whom you worshiped is God? If it is God, why didn't it deliver itself from the hands of the thieves? It is but an idol. It has neither intrinsic worth nor value for the one who purchases it in order to worship it."

The old woman retorted, "If this is as you say, Abraham, whom shall I worship?" He answered, "'Worship the supreme God, the supreme Sovereign,'[62] Creator of 'heaven and earth, the sea and all that is in them'[63]—the God of Nimrod, the God of Terah, the God of the east and west, south and north. Who is Nimrod the dog, that he has made himself a divine worthy of worship?" The old woman answered, "From now on I shall not worship any god except your God, the God of Abraham. Now if I do worship God, what benefit will I have?" He answered, "All which was stolen from you will be restored to you and you will save your soul from Gehenna." The old woman asked, "What shall I do in order to save my soul from destruction?" He answered her, "Say,

'*Adonai* is God in the heavens above and on the earth below';[64] God is unique and has no second;[65] 'God deals death and gives life';[66] lives;[67] and will not see death;[68] also that I am Abraham, God's servant,[69] trusted in God's house."[70] The old woman said, "From now on I will affirm your words and attest that '*Adonai* is God in the heavens above and on earth below,'[71] and that you, Abraham, are God's prophet and I believe in God, may God be blessed, and in you."

The Maggid said that she repented and regretted that she had worshiped idols. He also reported that she found the thieves and they returned her stolen articles along with the idol. What did the old woman do? She took stone in hand and struck the head of the idol. She said, "Woe to you and the one who might worship you in the future, for you have no purpose and give no benefit to the one who worships you." Thus she went out of her house into the markets and streets and cried out, "Anyone who wants to save his soul from destruction and prosper in all his doings, let him worship the God of Abraham."

The Maggid said that the old woman would cry out every day until many men and women repented. The king heard this report, sent for her, and they brought her before him. He asked her, "What have you done? You have strayed from worshiping me. Why don't you worship me, for I am your god? 'I formed you and even uphold you with My right hand.'"[72] She answered, "You are a liar. You deny the unity of the unique God who has no second. You survive out of God's goodness, yet you worship another god, denying God, God's Torah, and Abraham, God's servant." When the king heard her words,[73] he gave the order to kill her. And they killed her, but, "his heart trembled and expanded"[74] because of her words. He wondered but did not know what to do about Abraham who undermined the people's faith in him [Nimrod], for most of the people believed in the God of Abraham. When his princes saw the grief in his heart[75] and when they heard his words, they said to him, "Arise quickly and go to the place where it is your custom to go on occasions and decree that all the people of the city make a seven-day feast, a rejoicing, and a holiday. Have them put on their finest robes of silk and embroidery, fine stones, and precious jewels—yellow emerald and jasper;[76] objects of gold and silver, food and drink, and all kinds of fine fruits." They argued that "by such a display of great wealth and power by the people of the city, people 'who glory in their great wealth,'[77] Abraham would return to the faith of the king."

When Nimrod heard this report he was overjoyed. He issued a decree that all the people of the city go to the place in the garden where they were accustomed to come each year. Let them bring their idols there and let them make a feast, a rejoicing, and a holiday greater than they were accustomed to previously. During the feast, the king asked Abraham's father, Terah, to bring his son to see his greatness, "and the vast riches of his realm,"[78] and the multitude of his officers and courtiers. Terah asked his son, "My son Abraham! Come with me to the assembly of King Nimrod our god." Abraham answered, "I am unable to go there." Terah responded, "If this is so, you stay with the idols until our return from there." He agreed and Terah went. Abraham stayed with the idols, the king's idols being among them. When Abraham saw that the king went to his assembly he took an ax in his hand and looking at the seated images of the king he said, "*Adonai* is God, *Adonai* is God," and cast them from their throne to the ground. He gave them a mighty blow beginning with the largest and ending with the smallest. He cut off the hands of one and beheaded another; he put out[79] this one's eyes and broke that one's legs, so that all were mutilated. Then Abraham left (but first he placed the ax in the hand of the largest idol).[80] [JJ]

[JJ]

Abraham the Iconoclast Redux

In *B'reishit Rabbah* 38:13 Abraham smashes his father's idols and places a stick in the hand of the largest statue. This ruse leads to a mocking disparagement of idolatry by Abraham to his father, Terah. The enduring popularity of the classical midrash is in part linked to the inversion of parental authority. The son teaches the father the worthlessness of idolatry. In the *Maaseh* version, Abraham is much fiercer. He cleaves the idols with an ax and then mutilates them. When he is finished, he leaves the ax in the hand of the largest icon. Abraham is hauled before Nimrod to explain his actions. Again, Abraham derogates idolatry as vanity. Nimrod, angry enough to die, throws Abraham into the prison and denies him food and drink.

When the feast[81] days ended the king returned home. When the king saw his idols broken, he asked, "Who was here? and Who dared to do this?" All the people weeping, answered, "Our lord the king, know that Abraham stayed with the idols and we heard that he smashed them." Then the king ordered that Abraham be brought before him. When they brought him, the king and his princes asked, "Why did you smash our gods?" He answered, "I did not smash them, but the largest among them did it. Don't you see the ax in his hand? And if you don't believe me, ask him and he will tell you." When Nimrod heard his words, "he was angry enough to die."[82] Then he ordered that they imprison Abraham[83] and he charged the commander of the prison to give him neither bread to eat nor water to drink.

The Maggid said that while Abraham our father of blessed memory was in prison,[84] he raised his eyes to heaven and prayed, "*Adonai* my God, You know the hidden things, You also know that I ended up here only because I worship You." The Holy One Blessed Be God hearkened to his prayer and sent the angel Gabriel to save him from the power of this dog. He said, "Peace to you, Abraham, 'Fear not, be not dismayed for *Adonai*, your God, is with you.'"[85] Immediately a well of fresh water appeared to him and he drank. Then the angel brought all kinds of food to eat and he dwelled with him there, serving as company for him for a complete year. At the end of the year, the king's commanders and advisers came to eat and drink with the king. They told the king to build a fence[86] and to decree in all the city that anyone who wants to serve the king bring a lot of wood to this house, until the whole place is totally filled with wood. Afterwards they will set the wood afire until the flames reach the heavens. Then they will hurl Abraham into its midst. Thus they will believe in you forever and not undermine your faith. The king was overjoyed by this advice. He ordered all the nation, every man, woman, youth, and old person who was in all the king's provinces to bring wood to this large house which he had built, until it was full. So all the people did this and they hastened to bring the wood to that house, for he gave them up to forty days' time to do it. During all this Abraham remained in the prison-house. The king further ordered them to prepare a large furnace within the house which he built. They ignited the wood in it and the flames reached the heavens so that all the people were terrified of the vastness of the fire.

Nimrod sent to the commander of the prison-house and ordered, "Bring me my enemy, Abraham, so that they may hurl him into this fiery furnace." The commander of the prison-house came before the king, prostrated himself before him and asked, "How can you ask me for such a man, who has just completed a full year in the prison-house, [during that time] nobody brought bread or water or any food known in the world?" He responded,

"In spite of this, you go into the prison-house and call out to him. If he answers, bring him and I shall hurl him into the fire. But if he is dead, the better! You will bury him 'and his name will be remembered no more.'"[87] The commander of the prison-house went to the entrance of the dungeon and called in a great, strong voice, "Abraham, are you alive or dead?" He answered him, "I am alive." He asked him, "Who gave you food and drink all this time?" He answered, "The One who is capable of all fed me and gave me drink; 'the supreme God, the supreme Sovereign,'[88] 'who alone does wondrous things.'[89] The God who is also the God of Nimrod, and the God of Terah, and the God of all the world. God sustains and supports everything.[90] God sees and is not seen. God is in the heavens above and is found in every place. God attends to every detail." Now when the commander of the prison-house heard his words, he also believed in the God of Abraham. He declared, "Your God, O Abraham, is God and I attest to this. Furthermore, you are in truth God's servant and prophet. And as for Nimrod, he is a liar!" After he spoke in this manner, they reported to the king, "The commander of the prison-house attests that the God of Abraham is the true God and that Abraham is God's truthful servant." The king was horror-struck[91] and sent after him. He asked him, "Commander of the prison-house, what is troubling you? How can you blaspheme against me and say that Abraham's God is the true God and that Abraham is God's truthful servant?" He replied to him, "For it is the truth, and you, King Nimrod, deny the truth." When the king grasped the words of the commander he was greatly grieved and he was filled with anger. He gave the order to strike him dead. The commander of the prison-house cried out when they struck him and declared, "*Adonai* is God, God of all the world and the God of Nimrod, the blasphemer."

The Maggid said that the sword did not cut into his neck, rather the one who smote with the sword, broke the sword.[92] The king was horror-struck[93] and gave the order to bring Abraham in order to hurl him into the fire. One of the princes was dispatched and brought him before the king. The king ordered, "Hurl him into the great fire." As he got up to cast him into the fire, a flame from the furnace leapt forward and consumed him. Then another prince left Nimrod's presence to cast Abraham into the fire but he too was consumed. Thus whoever would take hold of him to cast him into the fire was consumed, so that many died, "incalculable and without number."[94] Then Satan came along[95] masked as a human being and prostrated himself before the king.

The king asked, "What is it? Ask what you wish!"[96] He responded, "I shall give you counsel on how to hurl Abraham into the fiery furnace. [K] Bring me many trees, nails, and rope. Then I will make a catapult,[97] the movement of which will enable you to hurl him into the fiery furnace from afar. Thus the fire will not consume the man who operates the catapult. The king was overjoyed by this counsel. He gave the order to do this and they built a catapult. When they completed it, they tested it three times in the king's presence so that from afar, they hurled stones with it into the fire. (This is what is called a catapult.)[98] Then they took Abraham, tied his arms, hands, and feet together with a strong knot and placed him in the catapult to hurl him [into the fire]. When our father, Abraham of blessed memory, saw how they had bound him, he raised his eyes to heaven and prayed, "Adonai, my God, You see what this wicked man is doing to me!" Even the angels on high spoke before the Holy One Blessed Be God, "Sovereign of the universe, 'Your Presence fills all the earth.'[99] Have you not seen what Nimrod the blasphemer has done to Your servant and Your prophet Abraham?" The Holy

[K]

The Fiery Furnace

In prison Abraham is again aided by the angel Gabriel who earlier provided milk when Abraham was in the cave. He opens a well for him and supplies him with food and companionship during his imprisonment.

Nimrod's advisors hatch a plan. The king decrees that the people should bring wood to a fenced-off house and fill it to the hilt. Inside the house they prepared a huge furnace and ignited a massive fire. The commander of the prison was dispatched to bring Abraham to the house. The commander of the prison was amazed to find Abraham still living. He is convinced of the veracity of Abraham's teaching and returns to Nimrod professing the One God and denying the divinity of Nimrod. In a rage the king orders the executioner to decapitate the commander of the prison but his sword broke.

Abraham was brought forward and each prince who attempted to hurl him into the flames was consumed by the fire while Abraham remained unscathed. The image of the fiery furnace is no doubt connected to the *tanur 'ashan* (the smoking oven) (Gen. 15:17) in the *b'rit bein habetarim* (the covenant between the pieces).

The fiery furnace episode in the *Maaseh* has a close resonance with Daniel 3. In that account (Dan. 3:6) King Nebuchadnezzar threatens Shadrach, Meshach, and Abednego with execution in the fiery furnace unless they bow down to his golden

One Blessed Be God answered, "How is it possible for Me not to know, when I know all 'the hidden things.'[100] But I will show you vengeance against Nimrod the blasphemer, and I will deliver Abraham, My servant."

The Maggid said that Satan [L] came to Abraham masked as a man and said to him, "If you wish to deliver yourself from the fire of Nimrod, prostrate yourself before him and affirm your faith in him." When Abraham heard the words of Satan, he replied to him, "'May *Adonai* rebuke you, O Satan,'[101] repulsive, contemptible, accursed blasphemer!" Then he left his presence. At that time Abraham's mother came to kiss her son before they hurled him into the fiery furnace. She said to him, "My son, prostrate yourself before Nimrod and enter into his faith and save yourself from the fiery furnace." Abraham answered her, "My mother, my mother, go away." Then he pushed her away from himself and said to her, "My mother, that water can extinguish Nimrod's fire but the fire of my God is eternal, it is inextinguishable,[102] no water can put it out."[103] When his mother heard these truthful words she said, "May the God whom you worship deliver you from Nimrod's fire." Afterwards they placed him in the catapult to hurl him into the furnace.

idol. Their zealous obduracy parallels Abraham's adamant refusal to worship Nimrod as a god. In both narratives the heroes emerge from their ordeals whole and unscathed.

In addition to the motif of idolatry the *Maaseh* shares another important detail with Daniel 3. Both accounts have a miraculous concluding element. A stunned Nebuchadnezzar blesses the God of the Jews (Dan. 3:28) and Nimrod's advisors and courtiers embrace the One God of Abraham with these words: "*Adonai* is God, in heaven above and on earth beneath there is none else" (Deut. 4:39).

[L]

Satanic Proposals

Satan arrives and provides counsel to Nimrod: Build a catapult and propel Abraham into the fiery furnace. In order to accomplish this feat, Abraham's arms, feet, and hands are bound with a strong knot. The biblical imagery of the 'aqeda (Gen. 22:9), of Abraham binding his son Isaac, is a poignant example of intertextual artistry.

Satan comes to Abraham and urges him to recant his unorthodox beliefs and aver his faith in Nimrod as god. Abraham dismisses Satan. Abraham's mother pleads with her son to recant. He rejects her appeal and asserts that his God will deliver him. Gabriel attempts to intercede but Abraham rejects his offer with the claim that his God will save him. God orders the flames to cool off. God's spoken words are a Hebrew translation of Sura 21:69 in the Koran.

Satan in Rabbinic literature often dons a disguise to deceive the humans he visits. In the *Maaseh* we see this aspect of Satan most fully developed.

Meanwhile the ministering angels sought mercy from the Holy One Blessed Be God to go down to deliver Abraham from Nimrod's fire. The angel Gabriel came to him and asked him, "Well, Abraham, shall I save you from this fire?" Abraham answered, "The God in whom I trust, the God of heaven and earth will deliver me." When the Holy One Blessed Be God saw his sincere devotion, he turned to him in mercy. He commanded the fire, "Cool off and bring tranquility to My servant Abraham."[104]

The Maggid said that the fire was extinguished without water. The logs flowered[105] and all brought forth fruit, each tree producing its own fruit. The furnace turned into "the king's pavilion,"[106] and the angels sat in it with Abraham. When the king turned and saw the garden and the angels sitting with Abraham, he [Nimrod] said to Abraham, "Great sorcery! You know that fire does not have power over you, moreover, you show the people that you sit in a pavilion."

Then all Nimrod's princes in unison answered the king, "No, our lord, this is not sorcery! Rather, this is a great, divine power, the God of Abraham. Besides God there is none other. Furthermore, we testify to this and also that Abraham is truly God's servant!" In that hour all of Nimrod's princes and all the people believed in *Adonai*, the God of Abraham. They all proclaimed, "*Adonai* is God, in heaven above and on earth beneath there is none else."[107] [M]

[M]
The Doxology

The fire is extinguished. The brands flower into fruit bearing trees and the instrument of death, the fiery furnace, is transformed into an idyllic pavilion.

Nimrod launches into one last, fruitless claim: Abraham you engage in great sorcery. You know that fire has no power over you. At this moment all Nimrod's princes gainsay his assertion and affirm the great power of Abraham's God. They also testify that Abraham is God's servant. The irony here is unmistakable. The king's princes, counselors, and advisors, his most zealous supporters, repudiate him and affirm the truth about Abraham's God.

This version of the *Maaseh* closes with Nimrod's princes and all the people reciting a verse from Deuteronomy 4:39 as a doxology to the One God.

Notes

1. *Sefer Ben Sira* (Constantinople, 1580), 18b–23b; Abraham Yaary, *Hebrew Printing at Constantinople: Its History and Bibliography* (Jerusalem: Magnes Press, 1967), 129, #197.

2. Manuscripts, JTS Steinschneider Collection (Mic 4879); JTS *Ma'aseh Avraham Avinu* (Mic 5049).

3. This translation is based on the editions of *Maaseh Avraham Avinu Alav Ha-Shalom* found in J.D. Eisenstein, *Ozar Midrashim*, vol. 1 (New York: J.D. Eisenstein, 1915), 2b–6b and A. Jellinek, *Bet ha-Midrasch*, vol. 1 (Jerusalem: Wahrmann Books, 1967), 25–34.

4. The midrashic reading of Nimrod's name is important. It is linked to the Hebrew root, *mrd* (to rebel). He rebelled by denying a belief in the one God.

5. Gen. 27:33.

6. After Exod. 1:16.

7. This statement echoes Esther 6:8–9,11 with appropriate changes to fit the midrash. Such was the custom in medieval Muslim countries. I thank Dr. Ezra Spicehandler for bringing this custom to my attention.

8. See Ezek. 16:13.

9. A usage appearing thirteen times in this version of the *Maaseh*. It is one of the elements that led scholars to see an Arabic source for this midrash. See Adolph Jellinek, *Bet ha-Midrasch*, vol. 1 (Jerusalem: Wahrmann Books, 1967), 25 and n. 2; See Louis Ginzberg, *Legends of the Jews*, vol. 5 (Philadelphia: The Jewish Publication Society of America, 5728/1968), 212–213 n. 34; Joshua Finkel, "An Arabic Story of Abraham," *Hebrew Union College Annual* 12–13 (1937–1938): 288. See also my literary examination of this version of the *Maaseh* in *The Annual of Rabbinic Judaism* 2 (1999): 103–125.

10. See Ps. 121:4 The verb form has been modified to the first person to serve the purpose of the midrash.

11. See Deut. 29:28.

12. This is modeled on the story of Moses and not on the story of Jesus in the Greek Scripture. Ginzberg, *Legends*, vol. 5, 209 n. 8.

13. See BT *Nidah* 8b; *Tosefta, Nidah* 1:7; *B'reishit Rabbah* 85:10; *Targum Yerushalmi, Genesis* 38:24.

14. I follow Ginzberg's suggestion: See Ginzberg, *Legends*, vol 5, 209 n. 10. This malady was some sort of hardening of the stomach. See also Max Grunbaum, *Neue Beitrage zur Semitischen Sagenkunde* (Leiden: E. J. Brill, 1893), 128, who relates the word to a Spanish origin, which has the same meaning as the Italian word "*calcinaccio*," a tumor in the joints, a hard lump in the body that occurred annually,

15. I follow Ginzberg's suggestion. See Ginzberg, *Legends*, vol. 5, 209 n. 12.

16. See Deut. 31:6, 8; I Chron. 28:20.

17. Gen. 21:17.

18. See Ginzberg, *Legends*, vol. 5, 209 n. 12.

19. This coming to an awareness of God by Abraham is similar to the description in the Koran 6:76.

20. Exod. 15:2.

21. This element reflects Josephus's writings, Flavius Josephus, *Josephus IV, Jewish Antiquities*, trans. H. St. J. Thackeray (Loeb Classical Library) (Cambridge: Harvard University Press, 1958), book 1, 7, 1, p. 79.

22. This frequent biblical usage is found in Gen. 29:9; I Kings 1:22, 42; II Kings 6:33; Esther 6:14; and in other places.

23. See Ginzberg, *Legends*, vol. 5, 209 n. 12.

24. Ibid.

25. Deut. 7:21b; Ps. 99:3.

26. Josh. 3:10; II Sam. 22:47; Hosea 2:1; Pss. 18:47; 42:3; 84:3.

27. This term is found in the biblical Aramaic in Dan. 6:27 and occurs in Hebrew in the prayer book as it is found here. See also Michael Sokoloff, *A Dictionary of Jewish Palestinian Aramaic of the Byzantine Period* (Ramat Gan: Bar-Ilan University Press, 1990), 490.

28. Isa. 6:3.

29. II Sam. 3:38.

30. I Kings 1:31.

31. See note 14.

32. See Ginzberg, *Legends*, vol. 5, 209 n. 12.

33. Ibid.

34. This phrase יֵשׁ אֶחָד וְאֵין שֵׁנִי is used as a numerological form in Eccles. 4:8, 10 without theological implication. The same phrase assumes clear theological meaning in the hymn אֲדוֹן עוֹלָם where we read, וְהוּא אֶחָד וְאֵין שֵׁנִי. This theological note is the tone that the midrash wishes to strike. This may also be an adaptation of the Koran, Sura 2:255. See Finkel, "An Arabic Story of Abraham," 388–89.

35. Gen. 27:33.

36. Exod. 18:21, 25 and elsewhere.

37. Ginzberg, *Legends*, vol. 5, 211 n. 19.

38. See Shaye, J. D. Cohen, *From the Maccabees to the Mishnah* (Philadelphia: Westminster Press, 1987), 83.

39. Ps. 35:10; See J. F. Stenning, ed. and trans., *The Targum of Isaiah* (Oxford: Clarendon Press, 1949), 228. In this text the *Targum Jerushalmi, Isaiah* 10:23 (British Museum Or. MSS. 2211 and 1474) reflects Abraham's reaction to the advancing adversary as is depicted here.

40. I Sam. 10:17; I Chron. 17:2.

41. II Sam. 22:1; Ps. 18:1.

42. This image recalls, "the pillar of cloud," in Exod. 14:19–20. The expression "dense cloud" is found in the following biblical passages: Num. 14:14; Ezek. 34:12; Joel 2:2; Zeph. 1:15; Ps. 97:2.

43. Deut. 4:39.

44. See note 34.

45. Esther 8:15.

46. These words reflect philosophical usage and usually describe God's power. They are aptly applied to Nimrod who is depicted as a king/divinity in the midrash.

47. Esther 9:14.

48. Ezek. 16:13

49. This usage reflects the wording of Jer. 51:23; Ezek. 26:6, 12, 23.

50. See note 27.

51. Ps. 105:6, 42.

52. This attribute of Abraham is derived from Num. 12:7, where it is attributed to Moses.

53. See note 34.

54. Moses ben Maimon, *Mishneh Torah, Y'sodei HaTorah*, 1:7.

55. Josh. 3:10; II Sam. 22:47; Hosea 2:1; Pss. 18:47; 42:3; 84:3.

56. Ps. 121:4.

57. This incident reflects upon the biblical story in I Sam. 5:3, when the Philistines brought the captured Ark of God into Beit Dagon. In that episode, on the following morning the people of Ashdod entered Beit Dagon and found that the god Dagon had fallen face down on the ground (I Sam. 5:4). The parallel with its implication cannot be missed here in the midrash.

58. Isa. 19:1 reflects this idiom and shares an anti-idolatrous backdrop. Isaiah contends that God will come to Egypt, "Mounted on a swift cloud." Egypt's idols will tremble and "The hearts of the Egyptians will melt within them." Here Nimrod's heart melts as he realizes the truth about Abraham's God and the falsity of his own idolatry. Other biblical passages reflect the use of this idiom, especially Josh. 2:11; 5:1; 7:5.

59. Judges 16:14, 20; I Kings 3:15; Gen. 28:16.

60. Gen. 22:8.

61. The episode describing the dragging of the idols with ropes is discussed by Ezra Spicehandler, "Shahin's Influence on Babai ben Lotf: The Abraham-Nimrod Legend," in *Irano-Judaica II*, ed. Shaul Shaked and Amnon Netzer (Jerusalem: Ben-Zvi Institute, 1990), 161 nn. 11–12. The mockery of idolatry follows the tone and wording of Pss. 115:5–7; 135:16f, although the sequence mouth, eye, ear is somewhat different.

62. Deut. 10:17.

63. This passage resonates with the language of the fourth commandment as found in Exod. 20:11. I have supplied the fuller biblical text, which makes the point more sharply.

64. Deut. 4:39 and compare the Koran, Sura 7:158. See Joshua Finkel, "An Arabic Story of Abraham" in 388–89.

65. See note 34.

66. I Sam. 2:6.

67. See note 26.

68. The expression מות יראה ולא is used in Ps. 89:49 as descriptive of human mortality. The midrash turns this phrase aptly, arguing for God's deathlessness, hence God's eternality. Only such a God is worthy of worship.

69. There is great stress placed on Abraham's status as a trusted servant, prophet of God. This emphasis may reflect Islamic influence from the Shahada: "There is no god but God, and Muhammad is the messenger of God."

70. See note 52.

71. See note 43. The 1580 printed edition of *Ma'aseh Avraham Avinu* and the manuscripts JTS *Steinschneider Collection* (Mic 4879, p. 87b) and JTS Ma'aseh Avraham Avinu (Mic 5049, p. 9a) read, בורא שמים וארץ, reflecting other midrashic usage. See *Midrash B'reishit Rabbah* 30:3; *Ma'aseh Daniel Alav ha-Shalom*, in Jellinek, *Beit ha-Midrasch*, vol. 5, 122; *Baraita d'Mazalot*, in Eisenstein, *Otzar Ha-Midrash*, 281, col. 1; and Abraham Wertheimer, ed., *Batei Midrashot*, vol. 2 (Jerusalem: Mossad Ha-Rav Kook, 1953), 18, line 9.

72. This statement by Nimrod to the old woman reflects the combination and adaptation of three texts from the Book of Isaiah, 43:7; 44:21; and 41:10:

a) יצרתיו אף עשתיו

b) יצרתיך עבד לי

c) אמצתיך אף עזרתיך אף תמכתיך בימין צדקי

73. These words are an echo of I Kings 13:4, in which Jeroboam orders the execution of the faithful man of God. See also II Kings 6:30; 22:11; II Chron. 34:19.

74. The midrash cites Isa. 60:5 with an adjustment of the pronominal suffix to meet the context here.

75. This reflects the sense of Ps. 13:3.

76. "Emerald and jasper" may refer to the stones in the breastplate mentioned in the Torah. According to the accounts in the Book of Exodus, they were onyx and jasper. See Exod. 28:20; 39:13. They are also mentioned by the prophet Ezekiel (Ezek. 28:13). M. Jastrow cites שהם as a yellow emerald in his discussion of another gem בירלא. See Marcus Jastrow, *A Dictionary* (Berlin: Verlag Choreb, 1926), 166. He indicates that this stone was more dazzling and costly than onyx. This description fits this context best.

77. The printed text does not give the whole biblical allusion. By providing the full half verse as it appears in Ps. 49:7 the irony of the midrash is sharpened.

78. See Esther 1:4.

79. The idiom "put out the eyes" is more fitting than "broke his eyes," which is attested to in *Mishnah Bava Kama* 8:1. See Ginzberg, *Legends*, vol. 5, 211–12 n. 27.

80. I insert this sentence one sentence before it is found in the printed editions published by Jellinek and Eisenstein. It is consistent with the flow of the story.

81. The story now continues more smoothly.

82. Jon. 4:9.

83. This tradition is found in the Babylonian Talmud. See BT *Bava Batra* 91a.

84. Here near the conclusion of the *Maaseh*, Abraham is placed in a prison cell and is again closed off from life. The *Maaseh* began with Abraham in a similar circumstance. He was born in a cave, shut off from the world. These two instances form a large inclusio around this midrashic work. I am grateful to my colleague, Rabbi Daniel Polish, who made this observation.

85. After I Chron. 28:20.

86. According to Louis Ginzberg this is the preferred reading. See Ginzberg, *Legends*, vol. 5, 212 n. 29. The implication is that the fence enclosed the larger house which was to be set on fire.

87. Jer. 11:19.

88. Deut. 10:17.

89. Ps. 72:18.

90. These words are from the first blessing of the *Birkat HaMazon*. A discussion of these blessings may be found in BT *B'rachot* 48b.

91. Ginzberg, *Legends*, vol. 5, 211 n. 19.

92. A similar incident is related concerning Moses. See Ginzberg, *Legends*, vol. 5, 212 n. 30.

93. Ginzberg, *Legends*, vol. 5, 211 n. 19.

94. The phrase עד שממתו רבים אין חקר ואין מספר is much like Job 9:10 עשה גדולות עד אין חקר ונפלאות עד אין מספר and seems to be an adaptation here.

95. In the description of Satan's arrival at God's assembly, the same Hebrew verb is used as in Job 1:6; 2:1. One senses the author's focus on the Book of Job, for an idiom from that book is suggested by *The New Translation of the Holy Scriptures* (Philadelphia: The Jewish Publication Society of America, 5746/1985), 1339–40.

96. Esther 5:3

97. In translating the word טאבוק"ו by the English "catapult," I follow the work of Max Grunbaum. He translates this word with the German *die Wurfmaschine*, which I translate "catapult." See Grunbaum, *Neue Beitrage*, 129–30. I thank Dr. Isaac Yerushalmi

of Cincinnati for his help in confirming the meaning of this word from its use in the Spanish. See J. Corominas, *Diccionario Critico Etimolgogico de la Lengua Castellana*, vol. 4 (Bern: 1954 Editorial Francke), 522.

98. I believe this definition was originally a marginal note, which in the course of time was incorporated into the body of the midrash.

99. This represents a slight adjustment in the text of Isa.6:3 to suit the context. The biblical text reads, מלא כל הארץ כבודו and the midrash changes the third person, masculine, pronominal suffix to the second person, masculine singular, כבודך.

100. Deut. 29:28.

101. Zech. 3:2.

102, See Ginzberg, *Legends*, vol. 5, 212 n. 31 for this textual reading.

103. After Song of Songs 8:7

104. Grunbaum, *Neue Beitrage*, 129, indicates that this is a direct quote from the Koran, Sura 21:69, which reads, "We said, 'O fire! Be thou cool, And (a means of) safety For Abraham!'" Abdullah Yusuf Ali, trans., *The Holy Qur'an* (Washington, D.C.: The Islamic Center, 1978), 837. See further, Ginzberg, *Legends*, vol. 5, p. 212 n. 33.

105. This image is an adaptation from the story of Aaron's flowering staff. Num. 17:23.

106. These words are found in Esther 1:5. See also Esther 7:7, 8. "The *bitan* was a summer house, 'a small luxury structure, an independent architectural unit for the use of the king or his heir apparent . . . an open structure, probably a colonnaded open hall.'" A. L. Oppenheim, "On Royal Gardens in Mesopotamia," *Journal of Near Eastern Studies* 24 (1965): 330–31, as cited in Carey A. Moore, *The Anchor Bible: Esther* (New York: Doubleday and Company, Inc., 1971) 7, note to verse 5.

107. Deut. 4:39.

Trauma and Recovery: Abraham's Journey to the *Akeidah*[1]

Naomi Graetz

In the concluding paragraph of an article on the *Akeidah*, the late Tikva Frymer Kensky wrote that "in its stark horror and ambiguous statements, the story of the *Akedah* remains the central text in the formation of our spiritual consciousness."[2] In Genesis 22:1 it begins, "After these things, God tested (*nisah*) Abraham," in which God asks Abraham to sacrifice his son. As Wendy Zierler puts it, "Abraham offers no emotional or ethical response to the command. He simply sets out with his son to do God's bidding."[3] The *Akeidah* (Gen. 22:1–19), the binding of Isaac, is considered to be *the* ultimate spiritual moment, when a man expresses willingness to sacrifice his beloved son to demonstrate fealty to his Lord. This central text has continued to horrify generations, and in Sören Kierkegaard's words, arouses "fear and trembling."[4]

The Hebrew for a burnt offering that goes up to God is *olah*, and is used to describe Abraham's offering of his son. The Sages understand the test (from the word *nisah*) to mean a trial, one of many trials—physical and psychological incidents that retarded Abraham's adjustment in Canaan and endangered his marital status.[5] According to the midrash, fiery associations are among the many obstacles Abraham had in his journey before he got to the point of bringing his son Isaac as an *olah*. Another obstacle was the famine in the land, which caused Abraham to go down to Egypt.

The *King James Bible*, however, translates, the word, *nisah*, as "tempt," not as "test"! To tempt is to solicit to sin, to entice, to

---

NAOMI GRAETZ recently retired from thirty-five years of teaching at Ben Gurion University. She is the author of *S/He Created Them: Feminist Retellings of Biblical Stories; Silence is Deadly: Judaism Confronts Wifebeating;* and *Unlocking the Garden: A Feminist Jewish Look at the Bible, Midrash and God.*

entrap, with the purpose of bringing about the fall of a person. The *KJV* may have translated it in this way because the translators were influenced by Rashi's reading of the Talmud. If that is so, then who is the subject of the temptation?

> "SOME TIME AFTERWARDS" Some of our Rabbis say (BT Sanhedrin 89) that this line refers to after the incident with Satan who accused [God] saying "From all of the festive meals that Abraham made, he did not offer You a single bull or ram." God responded, "Everything Abraham did was for his son. Yet, if I were to tell Abraham to sacrifice him before me, he would not delay." (Rashi, 22:1)

Is it God being tempted to play with Abraham, as he did with Job?[6] Or is God testing Abraham to see if he gives into the temptation of filicide that was widespread in his time?

One might ask where God was during these trials or temptations. Why was there lack of moral guidance to Abraham? From a theological perspective, what is worse, the problem of an abusive God/father who demands sacrifices of his son/people or a God who tempts people to sin?

Looking at Abraham from a relationship perspective and in particular with his troubling relationship with God, I can understand the transition in his character from one who fights back to protect his family and the other who abandons his family to fate. There is no contradiction if we view Abraham as a person who has experienced trauma and abuse as a son, a brother, a husband, and a believer. If we regard him as a multiple victim of PTSD (post-traumatic stress disorder), then Abraham behaves consistently when he heeds God's call to sacrifice Isaac. To see how this works, we must look at the back story of Abraham's life, which is to be found in Rabbinic midrash and commentary. It is possible to argue that the midrashim we will be looking at are supplying us with the original "censored" text, especially the one having to do with Abraham's near death by Nimrod in the furnace.[7] We will start with two midrashim that explain Haran's death.

The first one depicts Terah as a manufacturer of idols. Abraham destroyed these idols. His father was furious and seized him and delivered him to Nimrod. Nimrod throws him into the fiery furnace saying, "Behold, I will cast you into it, and let your God whom you adore come and save you from it."

Now Haran was standing there undecided. If Abram is victorious, [thought he], I will say that I am of Abram's belief, while if Nimrod is victorious I will say that I am on Nimrod's side. When Abram descended into the fiery furnace and was saved, he [Nimrod] asked him, "Of whose belief are you?" "Of Abram's," he replied. Thereupon he seized and cast him into the fire; his inwards were scorched and he died in his father's presence. Hence it is written, AND HARAN DIED IN THE PRESENCE OF [*AL P'NEI*] HIS FATHER TERAH.[8]

The Rabbis translated *al p'nei* as "because of"; that is, he died because his father manufactured idols!

According to Aviva Zornberg in her book *The Murmuring Deep*, "Nachmanides treats the fiery furnace midrash as not only historically true but essential for the meaning of Abraham's narrative." There is no good reason why this narrative is omitted from the biblical text, but as Zornberg points out, "the repressed persecution story leaves us with a significant gap."[9] She states the case even more strongly:

In this stark retelling of the midrash, the essential fact is that Abraham's brother was *killed by his father,* who had originally intended Abraham's own death. By handing him over for execution, Terah is, virtually, killing him. And when he is saved, his brother's actual death is directly attributable to Terah . . . This memory of horror is not recorded in the written biblical text.[10]

The other midrash is less well known and speaks of attempted fratricide:

And Haran died "*al p'nei*" his father Terah. Until this time no son had died before the father. And this one, why did he die? Because of what happened in Ur Casdim. When Abram was shattering Terah's idols; and they were jealous of him and threw him into the fiery furnace. And Haran stood by, adding fuel to the fire and was enthusiastic about the flames. Therefore it is said that Haran died before his father Terah. In Ur Casdim. The name of the place is like the fire (*urim*), relying on a verse from Isaiah 24:15, "honor the Lord with lights." [11]

In this source Haran is among those jealous of Abraham and fanatically wishes to participate in his murder. Haran is the one, in this text, who is in charge of stoking the fire in the furnace, and he is in the process of feeding the fire when the flames shoot out and consume him. In this Midrash both the brother and father are out to kill Abraham. Haran is gleeful while making the fire as hot as possible so that killing Abraham will "make his day." Thus according to these two midrashim, Abraham has experienced abuse at the hand of Nimrod the king, his father, his brother, and indirectly by God.

Besides using the tools of Rabbinic midrash and later looking at some modern poetry to comprehend Abraham's action, I find Judith Herman's book *Trauma and Recovery* very useful for her description of PTSD:[12]

> Traumatic events are extraordinary, not because they occur rarely, but rather because they overwhelm the ordinary human adaptations to life. Unlike commonplace misfortunes, traumatic events generally involve threats to life or bodily integrity, or a close personal encounter with violence and death.[13]

This of course is what, according to the midrash, Abraham has certainly experienced. Herman writes that "the person may feel as if the event is not happening to [him]…a bad dream from which [he] will shortly awaken."[14] Herman points out that the victim who suffers from PTSD may feel

> a state of detached calm, in which terror, rage, and pain dissolve . . . Perceptions may be numbed or distorted . . . Time sense may be altered, often with a sense of slow motion.[15]

These may have been Abraham's feelings as he went up the mountain, slowly but inexorably.

When we return to Genesis 11:26–32, we find lacunae that leave much to the imagination. The text does not say why they left, nor does it say why they stayed in Charan. Was Terah alive when Abraham and Lot left? What did Abraham feel about leaving? Would he have liked to stay and comfort his father? Did his love for God get in the way of making amends with his father?

Clearly there is a need for even more "back story," which the commentators and the midrash continue to provide. According to Ibn Ezra on Genesis 12:1, Abraham's father, Terah, lived for another sixty-five years in Haran and in taking his grandson Lot away from him, he severed the family relationship and deprived Terah of his grandson Lot. When the family leaves Egypt, after strife with Lot, Abraham proposes that his nephew's herdsmen separate from his. Abraham already separated Lot from his grandfather and country and now he does so from himself.

Why is Abraham so much a master at separation from his close family? Is this a fatal flaw in him? According to Judith Herman, "The core experiences of psychological trauma are disempowerment and disconnection from others."[16] If this is so, can it account for Abraham's ease in letting Lot go, then Sarah (with the real possibility of losing her), and then Hagar and Ishmael and finally Isaac?

It would seem that the Sages picked up on this as well. For in a famous midrash the Rabbis try to change the order of the text to show that Terah died in Charan.[17] Why do they do this? To show that Terah was wicked, and like all wicked, are called dead even during their lifetime. Why do they do this? They do this so as not to detract from Abraham's greatness.

Yet in this same midrash we read that Abraham was afraid that people would say, "He left his father in his old age and departed." Therefore God reassured him by saying: "I exempt thee (*l'cha*) from the duty of honoring thy parents, though I exempt no one else from this duty." The Rabbis deduced this from the emphasis GET THEE (*LECH L'CHA*), where *lech* (go) alone would have sufficed. And this is why God recorded Terah's death before Abraham departed. So one part of the midrash implies that Terah is the old father that Abraham dishonorably leaves behind, and the other says that Terah is an evil person whom Abraham had the *right* to leave behind.

What are we to make of this contradiction? I find it strange that the Rabbis would prefer to reverse the order of the biblical text rather than acknowledge that Abraham had the right to detach himself from a possibly abusive father. In reading Kierkegaard, I am struck by how the second half of the midrash is a perfect example of the "teleological suspension of the ethical." And this first act of "suspension of the ethical" later permits him to do other unethical acts.[18] Could it be that the Rabbis sensed something murky in Abraham's past when they referred to him as a Job-like figure and vice versa and that God's test of Abraham is similar to Job's because of Satan's intervention?[19]

What are we to make of a God who submits to a challenge of Satan and plays with people like sport to the flies? Who unfairly puts his people to a test, puts temptation in their way, to see how great is their faith, their love for Him?

It is difficult to accept Kierkegaard's conclusion that God tempted Abraham to prove his faith by rejecting morality.[20] This kind of faith is seen by many as "religious" only in an extreme or fanatical way, and as such a kind of idolatry, or perversion of religion, which always factors in a moral dimension. Besides what does God gain by having an exemplar of faith act immorally? Why tempt him to do so? This is the *sine qua non* question that has plagued generations of readers, both religious and secular, when they confront the text of the *Akeidah*.

In previous work I have discussed the effects of a God who abuses his people.[21] Some of these images include executioner, mass murderer, and divine deceiver. These images are problematic because God acts unethically or immorally, uses excessive force, and sometimes doesn't offer an opportunity for repentance.[22] Most of us would prefer not to contemplate a God who is too dangerous to approach and too incomprehensible to make sense of, a God who might simply demand extreme and devastating behavior. We avoid all thought of the paradox that the very foundation of the world might also contribute to its devastation.[23]

Another troubling image of God that I will point to briefly, since I have written so much about this elsewhere, is that of God the husband/lover of Israel, who has total power over his female people. In one midrash we see Abraham depicted as a woman, a daughter whose father owns the house she lives in and is aroused by her beauty and wants to show it off to the world.

> NOW THE LORD SAID UNTO ABRAM: Go Forth from your Land etc. (12:1). R. Isaac commenced his discourse with, Listen **daughter,** and look and incline your ear; and forget your people, and your father's house (Ps. 45:11). R. Isaac said: This is a *mashal,* about someone who traveled from place to place and saw a *birah* (building, castle, capital city) burning. He wondered: Is it possible that this *birah* doesn't have a leader? The owner/master of the *birah* looked out and said, "I am the master of the birah." Similarly, since our father Abraham was constantly wondering, "Is it conceivable that the world is without a leader/guide/master/ruler?" God looked out and said to him, **"I am the *ba'al*, the**

owner of the world the Sovereign of the Universe." So let the king be aroused by your beauty, since he is your lord (Ps. 45:12): Let the king be aroused by your beauty and show it off to the world. Since he is your lord, bow to him (Ps. 45:12): hence, THE LORD SAID UNTO ABRAHAM: Go forth etc.[24]

Abraham is again depicted as a woman, this time as the unformed little sister, in another midrash on the same verse.[25] Here she offers herself up to be sacrificed in an act of *kiddush HaShem* or martyrdom. The idea that God is Abraham's lover appears also in Maimonides in the *Mishneh Torah*. Here it is Abraham who is obsessed with God and has what can only be described as lovesickness.

> Halacha 2: [Love] is an attribute of Abraham our father, who was called "his beloved" because he worshiped him out of love. And it is a quality that was commanded by Moses in that we are to "worship our God" . . .

> Halacha 3: What characterizes proper love? That a person should love God with a great excessive, very strong love, until one's soul is bound up in love of God and is obsessed by this love as if he is lovesick; and his mind is not freed from the love of that woman; and he is always obsessed by her, whether it is in his resting or rising, or whether he is eating or drinking. Moreover the love of God in the heart of those who love Him is obsessive, like the commandment to love with all your heart and soul (Deut. 6:5). This is alluded to by Solomon who stated through the Mashal, "for I am sick with love" and in fact all of the Song of Songs is a mashal/parable about this issue.[26]

Rabbinic literature is sensitive to these images of God the lover and the obsession with the beloved, but do not necessarily see them as troubling, full of potential menace, and contributing to abuse. Lovesickness, is pathological by nature—it affects decision making, it distracts one from what is moral. It further dislocates one who is already fragile.[27] Furthermore, love should not harm.[28]

When Abraham is depicted as a dependent woman, he is, like Herman's traumatized patient, primed for God:[29] "The greater the patient's emotional conviction of helplessness and abandonment, the more desperately she feels the need for an omnipotent rescuer."[30] The fact that he loves God and God loves him makes it seem natural to follow God to wherever and whatever he demands.

Despite the threats hanging over him, the Rabbis are at great pains to make it look as if Abraham is an active willing participant in what God demanded of him. A midrash says that God was with him when he willingly offered (*nadavta*) . . . to enter the fiery furnace and would have emigrated sooner to the land if he had been permitted to do so earlier.[31]

What is the nature of the God Abraham is expected to follow? The Rabbis write that this God places the righteous in doubt and suspense, and then He reveals to them the meaning of the matter. That is why it is written, "TO THE LAND THAT I WILL SHOW THEE." The Rabbis view this putting of the "righteous in doubt and suspense" as a sign of God's love.

> R. Levi said: "Get thee" is written twice, and we do not know which was more precious [in the eyes of God], whether the first or the second . . . And why did He not reveal it to him [without delay]? In order to make him even more beloved in his eyes and reward him for every word spoken, for R. Huna said in R. Eliezer's name: *The Holy One, blessed be He, first places the righteous in doubt and suspense*, and then He reveals to them the meaning of the matter. Thus it is written, TO THE LAND THAT I WILL SHOW THEE; Upon one of the mountains which I will tell thee of; And make unto it the proclamation that I bid thee (Jonah III, 2); Arise, go forth into the plain, and I will there speak with thee (Ezek. III, 22).[32]

In addition, the Rabbis are making an equation between *Lech L'cha* and the *Akeidah*. *Lech L'cha* is also a foundational text, because it encourages (perhaps in the case of going up to the Land of Israel, even enshrines) leaving loved ones behind and it encourages detachment. Perhaps if Abraham (and others who wish to leave) would think it out clearly, they might hesitate to follow the lure of *Lech L'cha*. In both cases God does not reveal his intentions to Abraham until the very end.[33]

Zornberg refers to Rashi's explication of the verse "to the land that I will show you." Rashi writes that God "did not reveal which land immediately, in order to make it precious in his eyes." Zornberg builds on this to show that "the effect of suspended naming is to achieve an intimacy . . . tantalize him and endow him with an experience of mystery." She interprets this as suspense. She describes this as follows: "He will travel without solid ground under his feet . . . [he will be] off balance . . . [it will be] a painfully tantalizing process, in which delay only increases the horror of realization."[34] Whereas she reads this positively, I read this as further abuse. Instead of giving Abraham agency, God keeps him in his power and cruelly tantalizes him until the end. Surely this is not a sign of love.

In a transaction with Abraham in Genesis 15, God appears to Abraham in a *machazeh* (a vision), telling him that he will protect him and provide for him. Following the *b'rit bein habetarim* (the covenant of the pieces of animals), Abraham falls asleep and a great dread of darkness falls upon him. He has a nightmarish vision of a smoking oven and a flaming torch, which according to Zornberg reminds him of Nimrod's fire. She writes that

> forgotten, repressed, absent from the biblical text, is the story of the fiery furnace, in which the child Abraham was thrown, to test his faith in the invisible God . . . Its total absence from the written biblical text suggest that it is an unthinkable, even an unbearable narrative, banished from Abraham's memory.[35]

It is unbearable because Abraham is being treated as a pawn by God. If he were truly a partner, God would share with him what is on his mind, so that Abraham can react appropriately, take into account all options and then make up his own mind. On the surface, this is what God seems to do in Genesis 18:17 when he says: "Am I to hide [lit. cover up, *mechaseh*] from Abraham that thing which I do."

Initially God treats him as a full partner, but since He goes on his way to do what he had planned to do all along, destroy the town and its evil inhabitants (except for Lot and all his family), what is Abraham to make of all this? Why did he not continue to protest? Did he end up being a passive bystander, or was he complicit in the destruction as the Israeli poet Meir Wieseltier (b. 1941) writes in his poem "Abraham":

> The only thing in the world that Abraham loved was God.
> He did not love the gods of other men,
> Which were made of wood or clay and of polished vermilion . . .

He did not appreciate anything in the world, only God.
He never sinned to Him; there was no difference between
them.
Not like Isaac, who loved his coarse-minded son; not like Jacob
Who slaved away for women, who limped from the blows that
God gave him at night,
Who saw angelic ladders only in dreams.
Not so Abraham, who loved God, and whom God loved,
And together they counted the righteous of the city before
they wiped it out.

Wieseltier sees a straight line from Abraham's willingness to see
Sodom wiped out and his willingness to sacrifice Isaac in the name
of love.

I would not go so far; for I see his acquiescence to what eventually happens as being the way a traumatized soul such as Abram
has reacted to what has happened in his past—and he has already
done the unthinkable by casting out his first born son.

Yet one can argue that Abraham shows great initiative in Genesis 14 when invaders took his nephew Lot from Sodom. I use Herman's words to view this is as a form of

> recovery [which] is based upon the empowerment of the survi-
> vor and the creation of new connections. Recovery can take place
> only within the context of relationships; it cannot occur in isola-
> tion. In [his] renewed connections with other people, the survi-
> vor re-creates the psychological faculties that were damaged or
> deformed by the traumatic experience.[36]

Thus, when Abram heard that his kinsman had been taken captive,
he went in pursuit as far as Dan and brought back Lot and his possessions. And when the king of Sodom said to Abram, "Give me
the persons, and take the possessions for yourself," Abram said to
the king of Sodom, "I swear to the Lord, I will not take so much
as a thread or a sandal strap of what is yours; you shall not say, 'It
is I who made Abram rich.'" So it is here that Abraham takes the
moral high ground, something he has never done before.

Unfortunately this is to prove the exception to what I am claiming is his usual way of acting and Abraham reverts to his previous behavior in Genesis 16 when the story of the interaction between Sarai and Hagar is highlighted. Without any protest, Abram

passively heeds Sarai's request to take Hagar so she can have a son through her. When Sarai blames Abram, "The wrong done me is your fault!" (*chamasi alecha*), and makes him feel guilty, Abram again passively gives in to Sarai and says, "Your maid is in your hands. Deal with her as you think right." Why this lack of concern about his potential seed? Is it fear of his wife? Is it because he knows that Sarah was also once taken and traumatized? Is this why he allows her some leeway when she lashes at those around her? It doesn't help that God condones Sarah's abusive behavior through His agent who tells Hagar to submit to this abuse from Sarah. I don't want to exonerate Abraham because of the abuse he has suffered in the past, but it seems that Herman's explanation, about the cycle of abuse passing on, is valid here. Herman writes:

> The protracted involvement with the perpetrator has altered the patient's relational style, so that [he] not only fears repeated victimization but also seems unable to protect [him]self from it, or even appears to invite it. The dynamics of dominance and submission are reenacted in all subsequent relationships.[37]

For sure the trauma that afflicted Abraham is passed on to Isaac in the form of passivity in the face of abuse—and this trait will be passed on to the biblical family. Abraham's tears, according to the midrash, blinded Isaac. As he held the knife "tears streamed from his eyes, and these tears, prompted by a father's compassion, dropped into Isaac's eyes."[38] And Isaac will, in turn, turn a blind eye to the cheating and neglect that Rebekah and Jacob inflict on Esau. Jacob, too, will be a passive parent when it comes to not seeing the family dynamics taking place with his own children. The inappropriate parenting that has taken place in Abraham's household is thus passed on to the next generation.

In addition to trauma and abuse, there is also the issue of attachment and lack of attachment. There are many types of attachment. John Bowlby was the first to use the term when he encountered trauma during World War II. He described attachment as a "lasting psychological connectedness between human beings."[39] He believed that the emotional bonds formed by children with their mothers had a continuous impact on their life choices. In this theory it is important that mothers are available to their child's needs and that the child knows that the mother can be depended on to give him a sense of security. Abraham's father is identified in the bible, but his mother is given only a name in the Talmud—Amathlai the daughter of Karnebo:

> R. Hanan b. Raba further stated in the name of Rab: [The name of] the mother of Abraham [was] Amathlai, the daughter of Karnebo [from Kar, "lamb," Nevo ("Mount of) Nebo"]; [the name of] the mother of Haman was Amathlai, the daughter of Orabti [from Oreb, "raven"] and your mnemonic [may be], "unclean [to] unclean, clean [to] clean." [Haman's grandmother was named after an unclean animal (raven, cf. Lev. 11:15; Deut. 14:14); but Abraham's grandmother bore the name of a clean animal.][40]

I am assuming Amathlai was never present for Abraham in his life. One can only speculate on her absence and her detachment from her three sons, and it is not clear what purpose the Midrash has in even assigning her a name—and more curious the connection to Haman's mother.

Perhaps the Talmudic text hints at an insecure attachment that is caused by stressful life events, such as neglect, death, abuse, and migration. In this situation you keep looking and hoping that someone or something will come about to give you back what you lost.[41] Did Abraham's lack of attachment begin in early childhood or later when he had his life spared, and his brother Haran was sacrificed in his stead? Perhaps it begins around the time of the *Akeidah*.

According to Phyllis Trible, the *Akeidah*, first and foremost, tests Abraham's willingness to detach from his son so as to be able to turn to God:

> To attach is to practice idolatry. In adoring Isaac, Abraham turns from God. The test, then, is an opportunity for understanding and healing. To relinquish attachment is to discover freedom. To give up human anxiety is to receive divine assurance. To disavow idolatry is to find God.[42]

Thus it would appear that God tempts Abraham to turn away from human attachment and choose divine attachment instead. Trible says this is to disavow idolatry, but surely Abraham's eagerness, to "over-worship" God, his excessive love of God, and his willingness to sacrifice his son to prove his love, may be considered a form of idolatry. On the one hand, Abraham wants to carry out what was a secure clear-cut command given by God, the source of all his security. Yet he is given a contradictory command not to sacrifice by the angel. Can this be another major factor contributing to his insecurity? There is

> no certainty when God's commands contradict conscience and morality. Abraham is faced with the fact that he must challenge God's commands, for they are contradictory. Both cannot be acted upon! If he totally disregards the first one, he is destroying a revelation from God, and breaching his own sense of security in God. If he totally disregards the second he is violating his own sense of justice and ethics, and also ignoring a Divine revelation.[43]

God, too, appears to be insecure about Abraham's love. Why did he doubt him and put him to the test? If, as Judith Herman maintains, "traumatized people lose their trust in themselves, in other people, and in God," it is logical that God, who knows all about the trauma Abraham has experienced, would doubt Abraham's total faith in him. This would help to explain, why with the backing of Satan (as with Job), He would be tempted to put Abraham to the test.

According to Rashi, Abraham was ambivalent about whether to choose his love of his son or his love of God. It is clear that God wins out, but the cost is that he loses his son Isaac. According to Wendy Zierler, "The outcome of the *Akeidah* is that Isaac no longer appears in the story as Abraham's loved one. Perhaps even more startling, by the end of the story God is not Abraham's loved one either."[44] In the words of the poet, T. Carmi (1925–1994) in his poem "The Actions of the Fathers": "The voice from on high disappeared . . . And the voice within him (The only one left) said: Yes, you went from your land, from your homeland, the land of your father, and now, in the end, from yourself."

Until the momentous, horrific, command of the Akeidah, Abraham has only followed orders: *lech l'cha, asher arecha, sh'ma b'kolah, kah na*, etc. What Abraham suddenly understands, in his moment of truth, is that his unavailable mother figure, Amathlai, and three past father figures, Terah, Nimrod, and God have sacrificed him to what they perceived as the greater cause. Terah, perhaps in protecting his status as an idol producer and for the love of his younger son,

Haran, offered him as a sacrifice to Nimrod. Nimrod who literally wanted to burn him up and succeeded in doing so to his brother Haran, so that nothing was left of him, and who truly was an *olah*. Finally, God, who is so fixated on getting Abraham to accept the covenant and enter the promised land that he allows and even encourages Abraham to act dishonorably in leaving his father behind, using his wife Sarah, sending off Ishmael and Hagar at Sarah's request, and, most of all, in what has been referred to as the great testing of Abraham, telling him to sacrifice his remaining son in order to prove his obedience and faith. It is not clear what exactly is God's motivation, hence all the speculation over the generations.[45]

However, Abraham's greatness is that he breaks his own cycle of abusive behavior by not following his previous role models and by not sacrificing Isaac. In Zornberg's words: "Abraham's work is to fathom the compulsions that led to filicide; to know in the present the full force of an experience of terror that lies enfolded in his past; to wake from his trance at the angel's call."[46]

God does not tell him to sacrifice the ram instead of Isaac (*tachat b'no*). It is Abraham who SEES the ram and has a "click moment."[47] The Hebrew hints at this magnificently by using the word "*achar*"—in fact the cantillations, the Torah trope emphasize it (*ah-ch-ah-ah-ar*).[48] There is another way! "*Vayisa Avraham et-einav, vayar, v'hinei, ayil ACHAR ne-echaz bas'vach b'karnav*" (Gen. 22:13).[49] Abraham makes a physical effort (*vayisa*) to raise his eyes; and then he SEES (*vayar*) an alternative (*achar*). There is another way. There is an out; he can truly see what is in front of him. Despite the hinted complication of the word (*bas'vach*, also a maze), it suddenly seems very simple. The ram (*ayil*) is for him. The "*hinei*" is representative of the two mentions of *hineini* (Here I am) in the text when he was willing to slavishly follow God's demand. Abraham is truly **here, now, in this new moment of truth,** as is the ram, the substitute for his son. He says, "I can stop the cycle of violence." Even though God has demanded proof of his love, he does not have to burn his son as a sacrifice. He has something else to offer, "*ACHAR*"; and this strange usage offers the reader closure by taking us back to the beginning of the story, *achar hadevorim ha-eleh*. It is something different, pointed to him by the Angel, something new that can lead into a more promising future—when there will be no more need to sacrifice. His greatness is that he does not have to be a repeat offender or a "serial" sacrificer.[50]

At the decisive moment when he SEES the ram he, of his own volition, chooses to sacrifice it rather than his son. Abraham has two potential models of God. One is that of an unswerving worship in Maimonidean fashion: an obsessive worship of God as a lovesick man. But God does not tell him to worship Him that way, and Abraham chooses to follow the second command, the Angel's. The Angel, is the *ACHER*, the one who gives him a way out. He is also divine, but his message is that it is okay to sacrifice the ram, and not the son. So even though it is the only action Abraham takes on his own initiative with no specific command from God, it is because he has been able to decide on his own that some of God's commands do not have to be obeyed literally and can be carried out symbolically. The ram is *tachat b'no*, in place of his son, but that is Abraham's decision.[51]

His decision is not to inflict any more abuse, to realize that he can avoid repeating the abuse (the attempted filicide and fratricide) that was done to him in the past. He can say, I have choices, and this is what I choose. This is his real test, the one where he reaches deep into himself and with great courage defies God's temptation of him to repeat the pattern of abuse. This test he passes. He has avoided the temptation. He has achieved autonomy or agency. He has, in Herman's terminology, *recovered* from his trauma. He has chosen not to use the model of Maimonides' love, but one of his own choosing.

Herman suggests several steps of recovery—and as a psychiatrist, she would probably tell Abraham to go into analysis. According to her, for successful recovery it is necessary to go through three stages:

> We need to understand the past in order to reclaim the present and the future. An understanding of psychological trauma begins with rediscovering the past. The fundamental stages of recovery are:
>
> 1. Establishing safety
> 2. Reconstructing the traumatic story
> 3. Restoring the connection between the survivor and his/her community.[52]

One can argue that the angel, by offering an alternative, has created a safe environment for Abraham to choose his own model of worship. The midrash has helped him reconstruct the traumatic primordial story of the fire and the abuse he has suffered in his past history. Now all that remains is to restore the connection between himself and the community. It would seem that the latter is the easiest, because we all know that when he sends Eliezer off to find a wife for Isaac, he is ensuring a future connection between himself and the community. Yet, we cannot forget that the trauma he has inflicted on both of his sons has resulted in neither of them communicating with him for the rest of his life.

Part of this has to do with God's place in the previous scenario of abuse. Where is God in this scenario?[53] Has he retired totally from Abraham's life in disgust? I like the idea of the abusive God saying (like some parents), "Well I acknowledge my mistakes, I am doing *t'shuvah* and yes, I may have been abusive while you were growing up, but now you are a grown-up, you are a free person and I am proud of you, in that your first act was NOT to repeat the abuse that I have raised you with. And now you must take responsibility for your own actions." Sadly, however, as a result of previous decisions, Abraham must still cope with the death of his wife (possibly his fault according to the midrash) and the disappearance of and non-communication with his son. These are not punishments, but consequences of previous abusive acts. What has been done cannot be undone, but the steps forward will hopefully teach the next generation how to behave—and note that both his sons do indeed come to bury him.

Abraham is a complicated human being, for morally speaking, he can argue with God over the fate of Sodom, yet can be morally neutral about sending Ishmael away and willing to slaughter Isaac. Once he has been willing to overstep the boundary of being a moral human, God never again addresses Abraham directly. Yet he does become more sensitive to others. He marries Keturah, has more children, provides for them during his lifetime, and sends Eliezer to arrange a marriage for Isaac and Rebekah. Thus Abraham serves as a quintessential exemplar of humanity and the cycle of stories illustrates human complexity in dealing with trauma. In this sense, there is recovery.

Wilfred Owen (1893–1918), who died in action during World War I on November 4, 1918, hints in one of his most powerful poems, "The Parable of the Old Man and the Young," that Abraham actually "slew his son." Although there are midrashic sources that hint at Isaac's slaughter at his father's hand,[54] these are not mainstream, and so it is only fair to give Abraham the last word.

In two summations of his traumatic life he says to Avimelech: "God **made** me wander from my father's house" (Gen. 20:13).

וַיְהִי כַּאֲשֶׁר הִתְעוּ אֹתִי אֱלֹהִים מִבֵּית אָבִי

and later to Eliezer: "The LORD, the God of heaven, who **took me** from my father's house and from my native land" (Gen. 24:7).

יְהוָה אֱלֹהֵי הַשָּׁמַיִם אֲשֶׁר לְקָחַנִי מִבֵּית אָבִי וּמֵאֶרֶץ מוֹלַדְתִּי

There is poignancy here, for Abraham recognizes in retrospect that he was unable to feel mourning at the time. And this is part of his recovery when he says about himself that he had been forcibly taken from his father's home and his homeland by God, forced to wander and possibly be mislead by God (*hitu*). For it was indeed God who took him from his birth land. This is the trauma from which Abraham almost never recovers. It is what is inscribed on his heart and possibly at the root of his tortuous love affair with God. This trauma, to a certain degree, is the one that we as a people, starting from Abraham through the aftermath of the Holocaust, have experienced, as one big tattoo inscribed, not only on our arms to identify ourselves, but as a trauma that, as in the prayer of the *Sh'ma*, has literally and figuratively been inscribed on our hearts and in our psyche. It is in the poet Haim Gouri's word, our "heritage," and the fact that according to him, while Abraham did not slaughter Isaac, in the end, we are "born with a knife in our hearts."[55] The continuing question is how to preserve memory of this suffering and at the same time recover from this very memory of our trauma. We need to figure out how to live lives that have meaning, nourish generations to come and help them in turn deal with the complexity of our lives and a seemingly remote and at times absent or quixotic God.

Notes

1. An earlier version of this paper was given at the Society of Biblical Literature International Meeting in the unit of Psychology and Bible in London, July 2011. A version of this article appears

on the Web Edition of *Sh'ma: A Journal of Jewish Ideas,* dated September 19, 2011 (http://www.shma.com/2011/09/trauma-and-recovery-abraham%e2%80%99s-journey-to-the-akedah/). I would like to express thanks to my three critical readers: Sidney Bloch, Michael Graetz, and Menorah Rotenberg.

2. Tikva Frymer Kensky, "*Akeda*: A View From the Bible," in *Beginning Anew: A Woman's Companion to the High Holidays,* ed. Judith Kates and Gail Twersky Reimer (New York: Touchstone, 1997), 144.

3. Wendy Zierler, "In Search of a Feminist Reading of the *Akedah,*" *NASHIM: A Journal of Jewish Women's Studies and Gender Issues* (2005): 10.

4. Sören Kierkegaard, *Fear and Trembling,* trans. Walter Lowrie (Princeton: Princeton University Press, 1941). This material was prepared for Religion Online by Ted and Winnie Brock.

5. Cf. *Pirkei Avot* 5:3.

6. Jon Levenson in *The Death and Resurrection of the Beloved Son* (New Haven: Yale University Press, 1993) discusses the *Akeidah* in conjunction with the Book of Job.

7. See Yair Zakovitch, "The Exodus from Ur of the Chaldeans: A Chapter in Literary Archaeology," in *Ki Baruch Hu, Ancient Near Eastern, Biblical, and Judaic Studies in Honor of Baruch A. Levine,* ed. R. Chazan, W. W. Hallo, and L. H. Schiffman (Winona Lake, IN: Eisenbrauns, 1999), 429–39.

8. *B'reishit Rabbah* 38:13.

9. Aviva Gottlieb Zornberg, *The Murmuring Deep: Reflections on the Biblical Unconscious* (New York: Schocken Books, 2009), 147.

10. Zornberg, *Murmuring,* 189.

11. *P'sikta Zutarta* (*Lekach Tov*) Gen. 11, 28. I thank Michael Graetz for bringing this source to my attention.

12. Judith Herman, *Trauma and Recovery* (New York: Basic Books 1992, 1997). The 4th edition of *Diagnostic and Statistical Manual of Mental Disorders* (DSM) defines trauma occurring when "the person experienced, witnessed, or was confronted with an event or events that involved actual or threatened death or serious injury, or threat to the physical integrity of self or others," and "the person's response involved intense fear, helplessness, or horror." *Diagnostic and Statistical Manual of Mental Disorders,* 4th ed. (Washington, DC: American Psychiatric Association, 1994), 427, 428.

13. Herman, *Trauma and Recovery,* 33.

14. Ibid., 42–43.

15. Ibid., 56.

16. Ibid., 133.

17. *B'reishit Rabbah* 39:7.

18. "If such be the case, then Hegel is right when in his chapter on 'The Good and the Conscience,' he characterizes man merely as the particular and regards this character as 'a moral form of the evil' which is to be annulled in the teleology of the moral, so that the individual who remains in this stage is either sinning or subjected to temptation (*Anfechtung*). On the other hand, he is wrong in talking of faith, wrong in not protesting loudly and clearly against the fact that Abraham enjoys honor and glory as the father of faith, whereas he ought to be prosecuted and convicted of murder." Kierkegaard, *Fear and Trembling*, 39.

19. BT *Sanhedrin* 89b; see also *Midrash Tanchuma* on *Lech L'cha* 10; Zornberg, *The Murmuring Deep*, 185.

20. For a discussion of this see Eugene Korn, Review Essay, "Windows on the World—Judaism Beyond Ethnicity: A Review of *Abraham's Journey* by Joseph B. Solveitchik, edited by David Shatz, Joel B. Wolowelsky and Reuven Zeigler, and *Future Tense* by Rabbi Jonathan Sacks," *Meorot* 8 (Tishrei 5771/September 2010): 1–9.

21. See Naomi Graetz, "The Haftara Tradition and the Metaphoric Battering of Hosea's Wife," *Conservative Judaism* (Fall 1992): 29–42; and Naomi Graetz, "Jerusalem the Widow," *Shofar* 17, no. 2 (Winter 1999): 16–24. Both articles are reprinted in Naomi Graetz, *Unlocking the Garden: A Feminist Jewish Look at the Bible, Midrash and God* (Piscataway, NJ: Gorgias Press, 2005).

22. Eric A. Seibert, *Disturbing Divine Behavior: Troubling Old Testament Images of God* (Minneapolis: Fortress, 2009), reviewed by John E. Anderson for *Review of Biblical Literature*, March 2, 2011, by the Society of Biblical Literature.

23. These thoughts came from a talk given by Kenneth Seeskin, "The Destructiveness of God," at the conference *Philosophical Investigation of the Hebrew Bible, Talmud and Midrash*, in Jerusalem, June 26–30, 2011, sponsored by The Shalem Center.

24. *B'reishit Rabbah* 39:1.

25. *Midrash Tanchuma Lech L'cha* 2.

26. Maimonides, *Hilchot T'shuvah*, chs. 2 and 3.

27. Aviva Gottlieb Zornberg develops this idea in her first book, *The Beginnings of Desire: Reflections on Genesis* (New York: Doubleday, 1996): 86–93. However, Zornberg does not interpret this as pathology or abuse on the part of God.

28. *Love Does No Harm: Sexual Ethics for the Rest of Us* is the title of a book by Marie M. Fortune (New York: Continuum, 1995).

29. Zornberg, *Murmuring*, 178, writes that at the moment of the *Akeidah*, "Abraham's fear and desire make him *ripe* for the sacrificial act" (emphasis mine).

30. Herman, *Trauma and Recovery*, 137.

31. *B'reishit Rabbah* 39:8.
32. *B'reishit Rabbah* 39:9.
33. I would like to thank Menorah Rotenberg for this insight, personal communication.
34. Zornberg, *Murmuring*, 137.
35. Ibid., 188.
36. Herman, *Trauma and Recovery*, 133.
37. Ibid., 138. Note, since I am talking about Abraham, I have changed the gender from female to male.
38. *B'reishit Rabbah* 56:8.
39. John Bowlby, *Attachment and Loss*, vol. 1 (London: Hogarth, 1969), 194.
40. BT *Baba Batra* 91a.
41. Perhaps Haman's lack of confidence in himself, and the need to build himself up by destroying the "other," namely Mordecai and the Jews, is blamed on his mother's absence. But the similarity ends there, since Abraham's mother is associated with *har nevo* (and a clean animal) and Haman's mother with an unclean bird.
42. Phyllis Trible, "Genesis 22: The Sacrifice of Sarah," in *Women in the Hebrew Bible*, ed. Alice Bach (New York–London: Routledge, 1999), 278.
43. Unpublished paper by Rabbi Michael Graetz, "Abraham, the First Masorti Jew," published as a weekly column called *pina masortit* on ravnet for about ten years, date unknown.
44. Zierler, "Feminist Reading of the *Akedah*," 20–21.
45. Yair Lorberbaum gave a lecture as part of the *Tikvah Center for Law and Jewish Civilization Public Lecture Series at NYU*: "'Take now thy son, thine only son Isaac, whom thou lovest': Was Isaac Truly Beloved by Abraham? By God?" (November 30, 2010). In this talk he suggested that the source of all this testing is God's insecurity and jealousy of Abraham. He simply wants Abraham for himself and puts all sorts of obstacles in his path—including keeping him childless for so many years. And now when there is a child, he tries to get Abraham to get rid of it.
46. Zornberg, *Murmuring*, 200.
47. The expression "click moment" is usually associated with feminism. However, it probably originated with photography—the moment that the photographer frames the picture in her mind, using her eyes as the guide, which is the artistic moment of truth—then s/he clicks the button and preserves this vision for the future. It has been suggested to me that one can look at the three-day time frame of the journey to Moriah as a period that Abraham put to use by reflecting, confronting his past, and

building up resilience. And so when he returns (*v'nashuvah*) to his lads, he is on his way to finding alternative behaviors to his abuse. It is true that one can argue that recovery is a process rather than a click moment, but I am not sure that Abraham has completely recovered (*nashuvah*); for his previous behavior has consequences for which he cannot totally make amends (*t'shuvah*). Furthermore the sparseness of the text and the leit-motif of "seeing" that repeats itself over and over lend themselves to the click moment associated with both feminism and photography.

48. I am fully aware that I am taking liberties with my interpretation of *Achar*; but since the vocalization is the Masoretes' choice, one could also punctuate it and therefore pronounce it as *acher*. So I am doing it both ways!

49. *The Torah: A Women's Commentary*, 103, translates this as: "Abraham lifted his eyes: he now could see a ram [just] after it was caught by its horns in a thicket." The *Etz Hayim Torah and Commentary*, 120, translates this as: "When Abraham looked up, his eye fell upon a ram, caught in the thicket by its horns." In the commentary it writes: "'a ram behind [him]' or a 'ram, later [caught].'" It points to some manuscripts that say this is "'a single ram'" (*ayil echad*), which differs by only one similar-looking letter."

50. Ruhama Weiss uses the term in Hebrew "*oked sidrati*" (a serial sacrificer) to describe Abraham. See her article in Hebrew, "Blind Sarah" on the *Kolot* Web site, http://www.kolot.info.

51. See Michael Graetz, "Abraham, the First Masorti Jew," n. 43 above in this paper.

52. This is from a nice summary of Herman's *Trauma and Recovery* on the Web site http://www.uic.edu/classes/psych/psych270/PTSD.htm.

53. See too my depiction of God (in the first person) in the *Akedah* issue of *Sh'ma* (September 2011): 8.

54. See Shalom Spiegel, *The Last Trial*, trans. Judah Goldin (Philadelphia: JPS, 1967).

55. Haim Gouri, "Heritage":

> The ram came last of all.
> And Abraham did not know
> That it came to answer the boy's question—
> First of his strength when his day was on the wane.
> The old man raised his head.
> Seeing that it was no dream
> And that the angel stood there—
> The knife slipped from his hand.
> The boy, released from his bonds,

Saw his father's back.
Isaac, as the story goes, was not sacrificed.
He lived for many years,
Saw the good, until his eyes dimmed.
But he bequeathed that hour to his descendants.
They are born
With a knife in their hearts.

Parent's Torah

Ilana B. Grinblat

The following pieces were written five years apart and represent two points in the journey of parenting. The first describes my ultrasound experience while pregnant with my daughter in 2006. The second was inspired by the first grade poetry celebration in my son's class and delivered as a sermon for Shavuot in 2011. Both pieces are part of the same project—of finding Torah in the ordinary moments of parenting. When read together, they reflect an evolution from the first glimpses of spiritual encounter in pregnancy to a fuller relationship with Torah that has grown along with my children.

The Ultrasound: A Glimpse of Humility

For the twenty-week ultrasound during my second pregnancy, I went to a specialist's office with my husband and son. We hadn't planned to bring our son, Jeremy (who was then three years old), but we requested the first appointment of the day so that my husband, Tal, could come with me before work, and later we realized that this visit was scheduled before the start of preschool. Then we figured that Jeremy might like to get a glimpse of his sibling-to-be.

Although we had told Jeremy about the baby, he didn't quite comprehend the concept. When his teacher asked what was growing in Mommy's tummy, my son confidently replied: "Elmo!" We thought that showing Jeremy a picture of the unborn child might help him understand what was inside me so he wouldn't be disappointed eventually when no Sesame Street characters emerged.

RABBI ILANA GRINBLAT (ZSRS01) teaches Midrash at the Ziegler School of Rabbinic Studies and is the author of *Blessings and Baby Steps: The Spiritual Path of Parenthood* (Behrman House, 2001). Her columns on the weekly Torah portion have been featured on the Web sites of the *Forward*, the *Jewish Journal*, and the *Washington Jewish Week*, and her blog can be found at www.parentstorah.com.

As I sat nervously in the unfamiliar waiting room, I had lots of unanswered questions. I wanted to know the gender of the baby. Since we already had a boy, I desperately longed for a girl. After complications with my first delivery, I hoped the placenta was implanted in the right part of the uterus to avoid repeating such difficulties. Above all, after an early test had indicated a higher hormone level, which can be a sign of Down syndrome, I prayed that the baby was developing properly. Yet I could do nothing to affect the answers to these questions. Nervously, I shushed Jeremy who wouldn't stop singing.

Jeremy loves to sing. Whether repeating the Hebrew and English songs he learns at school or songs from his CDs and prayers from religious services, he sings constantly. During the ultrasound exam, I noticed that he was singing *Adon Olam*. Of all the songs he could have possibly sung at that moment, there was none that could have been more fitting. The answers to my questions were in the hands of *Adon haolam* (Master of the world).

The nurse took me into the doctor's office, put a cool blue gel on my big belly, and soon we could see into the mystery of the womb. The ultrasound technician told me that the baby seemed to be developing normally, was implanted in the right area, and Jeremy was going to have a little sister! The technician measured and showed us all the parts of the baby. I marveled at the intricacy of this miniature body. I was awestruck both by God's creation and the sophistication of modern technology that allowed us to see God's work.

Throughout the lengthy ultrasound, Jeremy continued to sing *Adon Olam* loudly. He sang so much that the doctor, who turned out to be Jewish, asked Jeremy about this prayer. As the technician pointed out the measurements of the baby's heart, lungs, feet, and hands, Jeremy's singing pointed me to the sanctity of the moment. As we absorbed this information, which Jeremy couldn't understand, he seemed to intuit the meaning of the experience. (Other than during the ultrasound, I don't recall Jeremy singing this prayer either before or since, outside of services.)

The *Adon Olam* prayer begins by describing a transcendent God who is above time and has dominion over all creation, yet the prayer ends on a more personal note:

My soul I give unto God's care, asleep awake for God is near
With my soul, my body too, God is with me I shall not fear.

These words summarized exactly how I felt at the ultrasound. As never before, I perceived the majesty of the Master of the universe. At the same time, I sensed a personal connection to this power because God had answered my prayers. I took off the rest of the day from work and drove to the ocean, bought a pumpkin-flavored milkshake and a muffin, and then waddled myself across the sand to sit by the waves and celebrate. It was one of the most joyful days of my life—second only to my wedding.

Midrash Tanchuma describes what happens in heaven when a child is conceived:

> At the hour when a man comes to make love with his wife, the Holy, Blessed One intimates to the angel who is appointed over the pregnancy, and his name is night. The Holy, Blessed One tells him: "Know that this is the night that a person will be created from the seed of so-and-so. Know and protect this drop [of semen].[1]

Firstly, how wonderful to think that there is an angel appointed over each pregnancy to care for the fragile fetus as it grows!

The angel brings the seed before God who then decrees:

> What will be in the end, whether it will be male or female, whether weak or strong, whether poor or wealthy, whether short or tall, whether ugly or beautiful, whether thick or thin, haughty or humble. And likewise, God decrees on all its events.

Yet the text continues to stipulate that God does not decree "whether the person will be righteous or wicked" because:

> this matter is in the hands of the person alone, as it is written: "Behold I have placed before you today, life and goodness and death and evil . . . choose life so you and your descendents shall live."[2]

Much is in God's hands, but we have free will. The Rabbis teach: "All is in the hands of Heaven, except the fear of Heaven."[3]

A similar sentiment is found in the *Un'taneh Tokef* prayer. The prayer begins by recounting the events in a given year that are in God's hands, saying:

> On Rosh Hashanah the decree is inscribed, and on Yom Kippur it is sealed: how many shall pass away and how many shall be

born; who shall live and who shall die, who of years and who before; who shall perish by fire and who by water, who by sword and who by a wild beast; who by famine and who by thirst, who by earthquake and who by plague; who by strangling and who by stoning, who shall rest and who shall wander; who shall be serene and who disturbed, who shall be at ease and who afflicted; who shall be impoverished and who enriched, who shall be humbled and who exalted.

This rather exhaustive (and depressing) list shows how many factors in life are beyond human control, yet the next line asserts what is in our control, saying:

But repentance, prayer and righteousness cause the severity of the decree to pass.

Of all people, Rabbi Amnon (who was murdered by command of the Archbishop of Mainz) knew that death—and many aspects of life—are beyond our power to change. This prayer reminds us annually of this sad truth, but it also teaches that how we respond is within our control.

This prayer is a profound statement of humility, which is commonly misunderstood as self-deprecation. In fact, humility is an honest understanding of what is and is not in human hands. The Bible teaches that: "Moses was very humble, more than any other men who were upon the face of the earth."[4] This description of Moses is surprising. Didn't Moses know of his unique status that only he had spoken to God face to face? And if so, then how could he be so humble?[5]

Certainly, Moses was aware of his unique status and confident of his abilities. However, Moses struggled on a daily basis with an unruly people and rough conditions in the desert. He knew that much was beyond his power to control. Together with God, Moses had led the people out of slavery to freedom and imparted the Torah. Yet neither Moses nor God could prevent the people for very long from misbehaving. Through the years, Moses witnessed both God's and his own power and their limitations. This recognition was the essence of his humility. The word anavah (humility), which was used to describe Moses, is spelled nearly identically in Hebrew to einav (his eyes).[6] Humility lies in the ability to see what is within and beyond one's grasp.

Humility is also an attribute of God. In the Talmud, Rabbi Jochanan noted that: "Wherever you find [in Scripture] the power of the Holy One of Blessing, you also find God's humility mentioned" as well.[7] When we strive for humility, we are emulating this divine characteristic.

I believe that this idea is the basis of why Jewish custom mandates against buying anything for the baby during pregnancy—a tradition I strictly followed before the birth of my children. Whereas prevailing American custom involves baby showers and preparing the nursery during pregnancy, Jewish tradition bids refraining from purchases until after childbirth. Most people consider this restriction superstitious, but the underlying meaning is that the birth of a child is in God's hands. According to obstetrician Dr. Jay Masserman, despite the wonders of modern technology, "the day a woman gives birth is generally the most dangerous of her life."[8] This practice acknowledges that "who shall live and who shall be born" is in God's hands. The devastation of losing a baby (God forbid) is even worse if the parent returns home to find the empty, decorated nursery or discover that well-meaning friends have dismantled the nursery.

On a spiritual level, not getting a room or clothing ready for a baby before birth also teaches parents to acknowledge humbly that one can never truly be prepared for a child. Even if you buy every item in Babies "R" Us and decorate the nursery perfectly, you still won't be ready. One can never fully anticipate the transformation of parenthood, but somehow at each stage the parent develops the necessary skills.

Starting with the first pregnancy test, becoming a parent instills *anavah* (humility). The initial experiences of parenthood immediately show us what is beyond our power to control entirely—including the ability to conceive, the determination of gender,[9] the appearance and health of the fetus, and the mom's symptoms during pregnancy. Once the child is born, she or he continues to remind parents about the limits of their influence. Sometimes a mother or father can't stop the baby from crying and, despite their best efforts, can't figure out what is wrong. A year or two later, there is nothing more frustrating and humbling than watching a toddler's temper tantrum and failing to calm the child.

Nevertheless, parents discover that how we respond to such events is up to us. We determine whether these challenges bring us closer to our spouse or cause marital friction; we control whether they lead to a higher level of consciousness or bitterness. From the first moments of pregnancy, we are given a new vantage point with which to view the world—an outlook that is closer to God's parental perspective. These new *einaim* (eyes) can lead us to *anavah*.

As a mom, I can only hope to remember what Jeremy expressed during the ultrasound test and live in such a way that I may be of humble service to *Adon haolam*.

Torah Is Like . . .

I recently attended the first grade poetry celebration for my son's class, where the students read poems that they had written. I loved hearing all the children's adorable masterpieces. One of my favorites was a poem by Joshua Weissman entitled, "Baseball":

Players jump like
lizards
for the ball
getting outs
is like babies being
born
getting hits
is like
hitting
a leaping lizard
playing baseball
is like a party
in your stomach

This poem reminded me of the 1794 song by Robert Burns, "My Love Is Like a Red, Red Rose," which compares his beloved to a rose and a song. Like Burns, Joshua used many similes to describe his love for baseball. Like these poets, the ancient Rabbis used many images to illustrate their love of Torah. The Talmud explores many biblical metaphors that together can be understood as a love poem to Torah.

These analogies include comparing Torah to a prince, because just as a prince has power of life and death of his subjects, so too the words of Torah have the potentialities of life and death.[10] Elsewhere in the Talmud, the Torah is compared to a fig tree: "As with the fig tree, the more one searches it the more figs one finds in it, so it is with the words of the Torah; the more one studies them, the more meaning one finds in them."[11] Then Torah is related to a "hind" (a female deer) because, just "as the hind has a narrow womb and is loved by its mate at all times as at the first hour of their meeting, so it is with the words of the Torah. They are loved by those who study them at all times as at the hour when they first made their acquaintance."[12] In this passage, the Torah is further compared to a breast. "As with a breast, however often the child sucks it so often does he find milk in it, so it is with the words of the Torah. As often as one studies them so often does one find meaning in them."[13]

In another passage, the Torah is related to a thigh, since "just as the thigh is hidden, so the words of Torah are hidden."[14] A further passage explores the metaphor of fire for Torah. "Just as fire does not ignite of itself, so too the words of the Torah do not endure with one [who studies] alone."[15] The Torah is then compared to a small tree:

> Just as a small tree may set on fire a bigger tree, so too it is with scholars, the younger sharpen the minds of the older. As Rabbi Hanina said: I have learnt much from my teachers, and from my colleagues more than from my teachers, but from my disciples more than from them all.[16]

I agree wholeheartedly with Rabbi Hanina's statement with one addition. I've learned much Torah from my teachers, from my colleagues more than my teachers, from my students/congregants even more, and from my children the most.

The text continues by comparing Torah to water because "just as water flows from a higher level to a lower, so too the words of the Torah endure only with one who is humble."[17] The text further links Torah to water, wine, and milk because "just as these three liquids can only be preserved in the most inferior of vessels, so too the words of the Torah endure only with one who is humble."[18] Finally, another passage compares Torah to a "goad" (an electrically charged stick used to prod cattle). This metaphor teaches that "just as the goad directs the heifer along its furrow in order to bring forth life to the world, so the words of the Torah direct those who study them from the paths of death to the paths of life."[19]

Inspired by the first graders and the Rabbis, I wrote this poem:

Torah, you are like a prince,
You have the power to give life,
To carry us back from the valley of the shadow of death.
Thank you for bringing me back to life.

Torah, you are like a deer.
Every time is like the first time.
I always find in you something new,
A meaning that was there all along, but I never saw it before.
Thanks for never ceasing to surprise me.

Torah, you are like a breast full of milk.
You never run out.
I sometime worry that this time, just this time, I'll find you
    empty.
But you don't disappoint.
Thanks for never letting me down.

Torah you are like fire,
You leap from one person to the next to the next, linking us all
    together.
Thank you for your warmth and your light.

Torah you are like a small tree,
You are found most strongly in the tiniest of vessels, in the
    children.
Thank you for the wisdom from the mouth of babes.

Torah, you are like a thigh,
You reveal your secrets in your own sweet time
And only to those who approach you with an open heart.
Thank you for the glimpses.

Torah, you are like a goad.
Sometimes you poke and prod and it hurts,
But thanks for always nudging me in the right direction.

Notes

1. *Midrash Tanchuma P'kudei*, chapter 3.
2. The midrash quotes Deut. 30:16, to which the continuation is
   Deut. 30:19.

3. This quote is found in the version of this same story found in *Sefer Yetsirat Hav'lad*. Nahum N. Glatzer, ed., *The Judaic Tradition* (New York: Berman House, Inc., 1960), 332–35. For an exposition of this text, see Michael Rosenak, *Roads to the Palace: Jewish Texts and Teaching*, vol. 1 (Providence: Bergahn Books, 1995), 91–92.

4. Num. 12:3.

5. Aharon Yaakov Greenberg, *Iturei Torah*, vol. 5 (Tel Aviv: Yavneh Press), 67.

6. The only difference in the Hebrew is that *einav* (his eyes) has a *yod* as the second and forth letter, but *yod*s are often omitted in Hebrew. (The verse could be creatively reread: "Moses' eyes were on all the people on the face of the earth.")

7. BT *M'gillah* 31a. See also Rabbi Menachem Mendel of Kotsk in Greenberg, *Iturei Torah*, vol. 5, 68.

8. Elie Kaplan Spitz, "On the Use of Birth Surrogates," The Rabbinical Assembly, Committee on Jewish Law and Standards, *Even HaEzer* 1:3, 1997a, 545.

9. I recommend Landrum Shettles and David M. Rorvik, *How to Choose the Sex of Your Baby* (New York: Broadway Books, 1970) to help in this regard.

10. BT *Shabbat* 88b, based on Prov. 8:6.

11. BT *Eiruvin* 54a–b, based on Prov. 27:14.

12. Ibid., based on Prov. 5:19.

13. Ibid.

14. BT *Sukkah* 49b, based on Song of Songs 7:2.

15. BT *Taanit* 7a, based on Jer. 23:19.

16. Ibid., based on Prov. 3:18.

17. Ibid., based on Isa. 55:1.

18. Ibid.

19. BT *Chagigah* 3b, based on Eccles. 12:11.

Preaching Against the Text: An Argument in Favor of Restoring Leviticus 18 to Yom Kippur Afternoon

Jeffrey Brown

This article will seek to argue for the restoration of Leviticus 18 to its traditional place as the Torah reading during our Yom Kippur *minchah* services. To be sure, at first glance this will be a most unpopular idea. There is, after all, much that is strongly objectionable about the contents of this infamous chapter. This author is cognizant of, and particularly interested in, the tragic and painful history surrounding Leviticus 18:22 and its problematic and complicated impact on Western and Jewish sexuality.

It would be easy (and politically correct) for us[1] to designate Leviticus 19 (or another appropriately themed passage) as the proper reading instead. Nonetheless, I shall seek to argue that doing so would constitute a missed opportunity for our communities and their GLBTQ constituents/allies.

Introduction

Baruch Levine sums up the chapter in question by indicating that:

> Chapter 18 is the most systematic and complete collection of laws within the Torah dealing with the subject of incest and other forbidden sexual unions. It outlines in detail which unions among relatives within the ancient Israelite clan are forbidden on grounds of incest, adultery, and so on; and in so doing, it indirectly defines the limits of the immediate family.[2]

JEFFREY BROWN (C05) serves as associate rabbi of Temple Solel in Cardiff, California. He thanks his teacher, Dr. Richard Sarason, for kindly reviewing an early draft of this article prior to submission. Any errors that remain are his own.

Our halachic tradition reads the verses of this chapter as the foundation for the set of prohibitions known as גלוי עריות (uncovering of nakedness).

Our more particular concern, here, is 18:22. In the Conservative[3] and Orthodox worlds today, that verse's prohibition against gay male sex still carries the weight of law to varying degrees. Thus, Artscroll notes, in absolute terms, that:

> The chapter of [sexual] immorality ends with two forms of sexual perversion: homosexuality and bestiality. The harshness with which the Torah describes them testifies to the repugnance in which God holds those who engage in these unnatural practices ... None of the relationships given above are described with this term of disgust, because they involve normal activity, though with prohibited mates. Homosexuality, however, is unnatural and therefore abominable.[4]

It need not be stated here, in this forum, that the Reform Movement's modern understanding of sexuality and sexual orientation diverges from the traditional Jewish view. We have sought to position ourselves at/near the forefront of the gay rights movement within the wider Jewish community. As early as 1977, the UAHC resolved to support equal rights for gays and lesbians, and to work against discrimination aimed at the gay community.[5]

In that spirit, it is not surprising to find such a different reading of 18:22 in the URJ's *The Torah: A Women's Commentary*:

> In the early 21st century, this is one of the most misinterpreted, abused, and decontextualized verses in the Torah. This verse, ripped from its place in the system of levitical laws, is often mobilized to justify discriminatory legislation and behavior against homosexuals and their families. While the act of anal intercourse would present a problem to the person who organized his life according to the levitical laws, it has no place in judicial systems not governed by the total system of Leviticus—and does not cohere with contemporary sexual notions of mutual consent and sexual preference.[6]

Those of us (and our communities) who agree with this approach (and who, by extension, seek to lift up those who identify as GLBTQ) face a unique problem. How are we to navigate the annual question of whether or not to read Leviticus 18 on Yom Kippur afternoon, as Jewish tradition indicates? How do we resolve the tension between honoring the tradition that has been passed down to us, on the one hand, with our contemporary interpretation of that tradition, on the other?

Why Do We Traditionally Read Leviticus 18 on Yom Kippur Afternoon? Do Any Non-Orthodox *Machzorim* Still Follow the Custom?

The custom of reading Leviticus 18 on Yom Kippur afternoon comes to us from the *Bavli*. *M'gillah* 31a notes: "On [the morning of] the Day of Atonement we read from the section that begins with *acharei mot* . . . At *minchah* we read the *arayot*."

Why was Leviticus 18 chosen for the afternoon service? Rashi, commenting on *M'gillah* 31a, implies that Yom Kippur reminds us of all of the prohibitions that we are supposed to follow. Yet, at the same time, he highlights sexual transgressions. For Rashi, there is something unique (and threatening) about the ability of a person's "carnal desire" to "overwhelm" his ability to make good choices. This, according to Rashi, explains the Rabbis' choice of a Torah reading that is aimed at convincing people to refrain from the particular prohibitions of Leviticus 18.

Steinsaltz echoes Rashi by noting that: "These readings are meant to arouse the sinners to repentance, and to evoke feelings of remorse among those who have not yet sinned, but who may yet be carried away by the desires of their hearts."[7]

Quoting *Otzar ha-Geonim* (an early twentieth century anthology of Geonic Talmud commentary),[8] Agnon offers a similar explanation for the reading:

> The reason why the section about incest [Leviticus 18] is read during the Afternoon Prayer on Yom Kippur is because there is no atoning for sins on Yom Kippur until one has turned in Teshuvah. Hence, we read the section about incest so that if, God forbid, one of the children of Israel shall have broken the prohibition against incest, he will remember his transgression as soon as the prohibition is read before him, and will turn in Teshuvah, that he may be forgiven.[9]

Like Rashi, *Otzar ha-Geonim* privileges sexual ethics above the rest of the values that constitute Jewish morality. Both believe that if there is one subcategory of transgressions that is especially problematic—one kind of sin that Judaism should specifically convince violators to stop committing—then this is the one. And our sources imply that the best way to do that is by shining the proverbial spotlight on this sin: by reading Leviticus 18 on Yom Kippur afternoon.

There are several other, perhaps less convincing, explanations as to why the Rabbis chose Leviticus 18 as the *minchah* reading:

1. It seems that some of the Rabbis were convinced that service attendees would leave the synagogue after the conclusion of Yom Kippur and proceed directly to an illicit sexual encounter! Thus, *Mishnah Taanit* 4:8:

   > Rabban Shimon ben Gamliel used to say: The happiest days [on the Jewish calendar] for Israel were the 15th of Av and the Day of Atonement. For on those days the daughters of Jerusalem would go out dressed in white . . . . And what did they used to say? "Young man, lift up your eyes and select for yourself [a wife]."

   According to this text, Yom Kippur afternoon was a time of intense joy and celebration. For the Rabbis of the Mishnah, it was natural to celebrate the joy of the conclusion of Yom Kippur by encouraging young people to go out into the hills of Jerusalem to meet each other. Therefore *M'gillah* 31a indicates Leviticus 18 as the *minchah* Torah reading: as a reminder to those revelers about boundaries not to be transgressed.[10]

2. Bernard Zlotowitz, writing in these pages in 1975, creatively argued that Leviticus 18 and the rest of the High Holy Day scriptural readings might be understood in the context of a commentary on Christianity. Zlotowitz asserts that:

   > The rabbis included *'arayot* [and the other High Holy Day scriptural readings] primarily as an attack against Christianity. Paul had taught that once Jesus came, the Law was no longer obligatory. Such rituals as circumcision, dietary laws, and Sabbath need no longer be observed. But certain early Christians, in their zeal to overthrow the Torah, rejected the moral as well as the ceremonial law . . . Under the circumstances, what would be more natural as a Scripture lesson for Yom Kippur than *'arayot* as an anti-Christian polemic?

Proper sexual behavior was the very foundation of Jewish family survival . . . In the context of the times, this passage was certainly another natural refutation of Christianity.[11]

3. Ismar Elbogen, in a footnote buried in the back of his *Jewish Liturgy: A Comprehensive History*, explains that: "They would read Lev. 18 as a continuation of the morning pericope [Leviticus 16]."[12] Plainly, he observes that the Rabbis of BT *M'gillah* 31a designated Leviticus 18 as the Torah reading on the afternoon of Yom Kippur because they saw it as the logical "continuation" of that which had been read in the morning.[13]

Now that our survey of traditional explanations for Leviticus 18 is complete, let us survey the non-Orthodox *machzorim* of the last century to witness how those who came before us chose to navigate this question. To begin with, let us note how indebted we are to Zlotowitz[14] for his comprehensive survey of liberal liturgies through the mid-twentieth century. The following chart summarizes his findings with regards to Yom Kippur afternoon Torah readings:

Machzor Title	Year Published	Location	Torah Reading
Seder ha-Avodah[15]	1841	Hamburg	Lev. 18
Olath Tamid (Einhorn)	1858	USA	Lev. 19:1–37
Minhag America (Wise)	1866	USA	Exod. 32:11–14; 34:1–10
Avodath Israel (Szold and Jastrow)	1873	USA	Lev. 19:1–18
Seder ha-Avodah	1904	Hamburg	Lev. 19:1–18
Seder Tefillah	1908	Stuttgart	Lev. 18
Gebetuch fuer die neue Synagogue	1922	Berlin	Lev. 19:1–18
Union Prayerbook	1922	USA	Exod. 33:12–34:10
Liberal Jewish Prayerbook	1923	London	Lev. 19:1–4, 9–18
Forms of Prayer	1929	London	Deut. 30:1–20
Union Prayerbook	1945	USA	Lev. 19:1–4, 9–18, 33–37

Unfortunately, there are few sources at our disposal that indicate *why* these *machzorim* made the choices that they did. We can only speculate that the content of Leviticus 18 was not edifying[16] in some way to the nine communities who chose to indicate new Torah readings.

The inclination to ignore BT *Megillah* 31a and its advice about Leviticus 18 is a trend that has persisted in all of the following liberal *machzorim* of the last few decades:

- Our own *Gates of Repentance* (1984) offers only one choice for the reading (largely following the *Union Prayerbook* of 1945): Leviticus 19:1–4, 9–18, 32–37. Although *Gates of Repentance* does not include marginalia/commentary within the book itself, we do have access to Lawrence Hoffman's *Gates of Understanding 2* for context on how some of the key editing decisions were made. Regarding the issue before us, Hoffman writes:

  > We saw above that Reform practice prefers Torah and *Haftara* readings with themes appropriate to the spiritual expectations of modern worshippers. On Yom Kippur morning, for example, we read Deuteronomy 29–30, on human responsibility, rather than the traditional selection, Leviticus 16, which describes sacrifice. Here, too, it has been customary for us to replace the traditional reading of Leviticus 18 with selections from Leviticus 19, which is part of what Bible scholars call the Holiness Code. It details a series of ethical actions entailed in our striving for holiness.[17]

  Note that *Gates of Understanding 2* does not specify which of the many problematic elements of Leviticus 18 fail to meet the "spiritual expectations of modern worshippers" threshold.[18]
- For its Yom Kippur afternoon Torah reading, *Forms of Prayer* (Reform Synagogues of Great Britain, 1985) follows in the footsteps of its forbears by choosing Deuteronomy 30:8–20.[19]
- *On Wings of Awe* (B'nai B'rith Hillel Foundations, 1985), edited by Richard Levy, denotes Leviticus 18 as the primary reading and Leviticus 19:1–18, 32–37 as an "alternative reading."[20]
- *Kavvanat HaLev* (IMPJ, 1988–1989) offers Leviticus 19:1–18. And *Kol HaNeshemah: Prayerbook for the Days of Awe* (Reconstructionist Press, 1999) indicates the same reading, with the

caveat that: "Some communities that have not read *Nitzavim* (Deut. 29:9–30:20) in the morning may choose to substitute it here."

- *Machzor Ruach Chadashah* (Liberal Judaism [UK], 2003) suggests the same reading as *Gates of Repentance*. The editors explain their reasoning in the Notes section at the back of the prayer book: "In common with many Progressive *machzorim*, we replace the traditional reading from the Torah for YK afternoon, Lev. 18, with this selection from that section of Leviticus known as the Holiness Code, whose moral *dicta* are so appropriate to this day."[21]

Breaking the Silence

A few words must be offered here as to why this author believes that the liturgical strategy of simply offering an alternative Torah reading is inadequate on Yom Kippur afternoon. To be sure, I would generally affirm the longstanding Reform practice of choosing liturgical/lectionary selections that meet the "spiritual expectations of modern worshippers" (as Hoffman puts it). As a proud Reform clergyperson, that methodology is an important part of my rabbinate.

I would argue here, however, that Leviticus 18 (on Yom Kippur afternoon) is an extraordinary example of a reading that cannot be washed away so quickly. We are faced with a double challenge: an occasion that demands that we be even more mindful than usual of our liturgical choices; and a confrontation with the subject of homophobia, and the intolerance that it has engendered over two and a half millennia.

To read an alternate selection of Torah without explaining why the alternate reading was chosen (which is exactly what *Gates of Repentance* and all of the rest of the *machzorim* cited above does) is problematic. To do so is to argue with the Torah: in silence, and from silence. And this argument from silence, like so many others, is not convincing. It simply ignores the pain of our GLBTQ friends by pretending that Leviticus 18:22 does not exist,[22] and it does not address the problems that the text raises.

Some of my colleagues will suggest that the exact opposite is true: that choosing an alternative reading on Yom Kippur afternoon in the twenty-first century does in fact address the problem at hand. For they would argue that an alternative reading is done, *davka*, out of respect for our GLBTQ friends and their allies (so as to shield them from the pain that might be caused by having to listen to Leviticus 18). But I would humbly and respectfully disagree with this assertion. To do an alternative reading without acknowledging why—without critiquing 18:22 out loud—is to miss an opportunity to do more substantial *tikkun*: to redeem our sacred but flawed Torah and bring a small measure of healing to the members of our community that have suffered under the heterocentrism of our Jewish and secular cultures. Steven Greenberg articulates this so much more effectively, when he writes that:

> But while I do not wish to minimize the pain of the thousands before us who were tormented by these bits of ink and parchment, I believe these words to be a site of reckoning and of potential redemption. The Hebrew name of the Book of Leviticus, Vayikra, roughly meaning, "And the Lord called." So, let us imagine that we are now all called upon to stand before the open scroll, to read, and to be read.[23]

To seek "reckoning" and "potential redemption"—isn't that what Yom Kippur is all about? How does silently acquiescing to a more tasteful Torah reading bring that about? Wittgenstein postulated that "What we cannot speak about we must pass over in silence." That may be true. But we *can*, and must, speak about Leviticus 18. We must speak the truth and call the Torah what is: a holy but imperfect document.[24]

A minimalist approach to this strategy might mimic the practice of Congregation Beth Chayim Chadashim (BCC), a URJ-affiliated synagogue that seeks to sustain "a Jewish community for gay, lesbian, bisexual and transgender Jews, while welcoming all who wish to make community."[25] Lisa Edwards reports that it is BCC's practice to read Leviticus 19, but to "always" mention the traditional practice of reading Leviticus 18 on Yom Kippur afternoon.[26] Even as BCC follows *Gates of Repentance* in not reading Leviticus 18, they have broken the silence by offering a soft rebuke of it.

Plaskow, Not *P'shat*

Two recent non-Orthodox *machzorim* choose a more aggressive approach. They have both designated Leviticus 18 as the primary

Torah reading. But, to accompany those readings, these *machzorim* offer commentaries and marginal notes. Their pairing of Torah text with modern commentary asserts that it is possible to read Leviticus 18 on Yom Kippur *and* be sensitive to the needs of our GLBTQ members and their allies at the same time.

Mahzor Hadesh Yameinu (Ronald Aigen, 2001) is one such example. The *machzor* was written by the rabbi of Canada's oldest Reconstructionist synagogue (Congregation Dorshei Emet). There we find that the primary Torah reading for Yom Kippur afternoon is Leviticus 18. An alternate reading (Leviticus 19:1–18) is also offered.

Leviticus 18 might seem like a surprising choice, given the Reconstructionist Movement's long history[27] of welcome/openness to lesbian and gay congregants. Note, however, how the *machzor* seeks to offer an alternative understanding of Leviticus 18. Here is what Aigen writes for the explanatory note that accompanies 18:22:

> The term *to'eivah*, "abhorrence" is used in the Torah to describe a wide variety of objectionable practices, from forbidden eating practices (*Genesis 43:32*); to the prohibition of remarrying a divorced wife if she had subsequently married and been divorced from a second man (*Deuteronomy 24:4*); as well as the proscription against using unjust weights and measures (*Deuteronomy 25:16*). In all these cases, the term *to'eivah* refers to behaviors which are assumed to be learned and volitional. The biblical view of homosexuality did not share the contemporary understanding of sexual orientation, whether heterosexual or homosexual, as a biological given. It is on the basis of this understanding of homosexuality that contemporary liberal communities have declared that the biblical category of *to'eivah* should no longer apply in this case. Homosexual males and lesbian females ought not to be condemned for who they are, but rather fully included in the life of the community together with their partners and children.[28]

A similar strategy of printing progressive commentary on the margins of the traditional lectionary reading can be found in *Machzor Lev Shalem* (Rabbinical Assembly, 2010). In addition to appropriate historical and anthropological explanations of Leviticus 18, the *machzor* quotes a passage by Elliot Dorff on the connection between our own individual (sexual) choices and the way that those ethical choices reflect on the rest of the Jewish people: "In this, as in other areas of life, our actions should be a *kiddush hashem*, a sanctification of God's name."[29] The *machzor* then goes out of its way (like *Hadesh Yameinu*) to address 18:22 and the over-riding question of the status of lesbians and gays by offering two important pieces of commentary contributed by Judith Plaskow.

Here, we must note the significant influence that Plaskow's 1997 article "Sexuality and *Teshuvah*: Leviticus 18"[30] had on the editors of both *Hadesh Yameinu*[31] and *Machzor Lev Shalem*.

Plaskow begins that piece by situating herself:

> As someone who has long been disturbed by the content of Le-viticus 18, I had always applauded the substitution of an alter-native Torah reading—until a particular incident made me re-consider the link between sex and Yom Kippur. After a lecture I delivered in the spring of 1995 on rethinking Jewish attitudes toward sexuality, a woman approached me very distressed. She belonged to a Conservative synagogue that had abandoned the practice of reading Leviticus 18 on Yom Kippur, and as a victim of childhood sexual abuse by her grandfather, she felt betrayed by that decision. While she was not necessarily committed to the understanding of sexual holiness contained in Leviticus, she felt that in quietly changing the reading without communal discus-sion, her congregation had avoided issues of sexual responsibil-ity altogether.[32]

Plaskow goes on to argue that Yom Kippur is an occasion for Jewish communities to "connect the theme of atonement with is-sues of behavior in intimate relationships." Like Rashi, Plaskow privileges sexual acts by putting them into a category that deserves special attention on our Day of Atonement. All of this in the hope of bringing a greater sense of healing to victims, perpetrators, and our communities.

Plaskow suggests that Leviticus 18 can be a valuable teaching tool. The text, she argues, has the ability to prompt important and frank conversations. For Plaskow, the possibility of these conversa-tions is not limited to sexual abuse; rather, she reminds us that Le-viticus 18 can be a useful opening for reflections on sexuality and on sexual ethics in general. Each in their own way, *Hadesh Yameinu* and *Machzor Lev Shalem* (as well as Levy 1985, through his transla-tion of 18:22) have sought to do this. Using strategically chosen commentary (in *Lev Shalem*'s case there are two selections[33] borrowed from Plaskow's article), the editors of these *machzorim* have indicated to worshipers that the Torah text has something to offer us that goes beyond the offensive and problematic *p'shat*.

Plaskow reminds us that we have a choice. We need not avoid Leviticus 18 for fear of making our communities uncomfortable. For our tradition doesn't just give us permission to read this difficult text out loud. It also empowers us to *use* it: for our purposes and our agenda.

Plaskow suggests one possible use: coupling the reading with a conversation about sex ethics. To illustrate her vision, she appends a document to her article that summarizes her own *chavurah*'s values on this important topic. Selections from "The Su Kasha Ethic"[34] can be used as a study text in communities that might be open to that kind of creative discussion experience on Yom Kippur afternoon.

To take up Plaskow's suggestion (as *Lev Shalem* in particular has done)[35] would be a noble and worthwhile expression of *tikkun* and *t'shuvah* in and of itself. When we use Leviticus 18 for our purposes (rather than the purposes that are implicit in the *p'shat* reading of the text) we begin to redeem a broken and shameful text.

It is this author's contention, however, that *Hadesh Yameinu* and *Lev Shalem* could have gone further. The commentaries and marginal notes that they include do not adequately express the pain and hurt that a hundred generations of our gay and lesbian ancestors have suffered because of the close-mindedness of this text.

Thus, we are presented with an opportunity. As our new CCAR *machzor* is drafted, and as we come together to reimagine newly relevant, challenging, and uplifting High Holy Day worship, we don't just have the chance to follow in the worthy footsteps of *Hadesh Yameinu* and *Lev Shalem* by opening a conversation on Yom Kippur about Jewish sex ethics in general. We can also take up *Hadesh Yameinu* and *Lev Shalem*'s cause and move it one step forward: by having our new *machzor* instruct (or by worship leaders enabling) our communities to actively preach against the text.

Plaskow Redux: Preaching against the Text

Preaching against the text, by actively asserting that the Torah is (occasionally) wrong, is an approach that my Homiletics teachers advised against at the College-Institute. At the time, it never occurred to me to question their advice. But since my ordination, I have come to conclude that there are many legitimate uses for such a methodology. First among them is an awareness on my part that preaching against the text affirms my progressive identity. Divine or Mosaic authorship are notions that are outside of my own theology. To assert human authorship of the Torah (as I do) is to admit that our text is sometimes flawed, just as we are.

I know that I am not alone in these beliefs among my Reform colleagues. Many, if not most, of my friends in the Reform rabbinate take these same principles for granted. Yet, how many liberal colleagues take the "risk" of preaching against the text when it violates an obvious core belief? All too often, we choose another part of the *parashah* to preach on instead or cite a Rabbinic text[36] that tries to make something terribly problematic just disappear.[37]

There is an established discourse on these matters in liberal Christian circles. For example, consider the work of the late Peter Gomes. Citing Roland Bainton, Gomes warns against "Protestant America's bibliolatry, the worship of the text of scripture and its elevation as the sole norm of faith and practice."[38] Gomes goes on to write that:

> In addressing a moral issue with both public and personal implications on the basis of Christian principles derived from a reading of the Bible, rather than simply on the basis of biblical practice and precedent, Bainton liberates us from a simpleminded bondage to texts whose context may be unrelated and unhelpful to our own. *In other words, to be biblical may well mean to move beyond the Bible itself to the larger principles that can be derived from Christian faith of which the Bible is a part, but for which the Bible cannot possibly be a substitute. To determine with what Christian principles one reads the Bible is to undertake an enterprise that requires more rather than less engagement with the Bible and with the cultures of its interpretation. It involves a rather daunting effort to see beyond the diversions of text and context, and of precedent and practice, and into the far more complex landscape of principle and teaching by which the whole is made considerably larger than the sum of its parts.* Contrary to popular thinking, this invariably means giving more attention to the Bible, and more rather than less care to its study and interpretation.[39]

Even though Gomes is writing from a Christian perspective, his teaching can easily be applied to our own faith. Note with care how he gently reminds us that our traditions and beliefs—our ultimate values—are bigger than the words of a single verse!

We know that to be true of our own Reform Judaism. We can easily articulate the Jewish values that inform our own sense of welcoming lesbian and gay Jews: a passionate belief in *b'tzelem Elohim*, the value of hospitality, and the notion of "loving our neighbors as ourselves" (to name a few).

Gomes argues that even as we would see that "the whole is made considerably larger than the sum of its parts" that we must have more, rather than less, "engagement" with the text. I would suggest that the most effective way to engage a problematic text (like 18:22) is to critique it, or to preach against it. Doing so allows us to engage with it, and see beyond it, at the very same time.

An authentically Jewish discourse on this aspect of homiletics is virtually nonexistent. Indeed, I initially failed to turn up a single reference to a source that explores a Jewish notion of "preaching against the text." My findings were confirmed by two experts in the field.[40]

I subsequently was able to identify one article on the subject. It, too, was authored by Judith Plaskow.

Her article, adapted from the 1997 Ordination Sermon that she delivered in Cincinnati, is aptly titled "Preaching Against the Text."[41] In it, she addresses the question of why a *darshanit* might choose to speak against a problematic piece of Torah, instead of "emphasizing the positive." She writes:

> My first answer to this question is that it is intellectually dishonest to focus simply on the positive aspects of tradition. Individual religious ideas and values have contexts; they are connected to other ideas. They are parts of systems that seek to express and establish particular worldviews. Why engage with tradition if we're not prepared to look at the ways it shapes us for good *and* for evil? . . . To wrench what we like out of context and ignore the rest is to engage in a kind of pretense, to act as if we were deriving our values from tradition when what we are actually doing is seeking support for our own convictions.
>
> Such intellectual dishonesty might be excused were it to serve a spiritual purpose. But I would argue that failure to grapple with the hard parts of tradition is spiritually and socially corrosive because it leaves destructive ideas intact to shape our consciousness and affect our hearts and minds.[42]

Plaskow goes on to spell out the relationship between preaching against the text and bringing about a sense of healing:

> Remaining silent about the negative aspects of tradition not only leaves them to do their work in the world, it also deprives us of an important spiritual resource. In congregations, in Hillels, and in other places rabbis serve, many Jews are in pain. Sometimes they are in pain and feel they have been wounded directly by some aspect of Jewish tradition. More often, they have been hurt by injustices or abuse described and sometimes reinscribed by tradition, but not immediately attributable to its influence. In either case, what they frequently need and seek are not simply spiritual ideals they can counterpose to the bitterness of their experiences, but places to name and explore the contours and causes of their pain . . . Viewed in this light, acknowledging those aspects of tradition that need to be repudiated and exorcised is a necessary moment in the process of creating something new.[43]

Conclusion

Our movement is engaged, at this very moment, "in the process of creating something new." Our colleagues on the *machzor* editorial committee are doing this formally, as they toil to produce a new text for us. But the impending arrival of the new *machzor* means that we are newly empowered as well to wonder: what liturgical changes might we be moved to make on a local basis, to reflect the ultimate values of the institutions and communities that we are associated with?

Our liberal colleagues of decades and centuries past chose an alternative path for Yom Kippur afternoon by designating Torah readings from outside of Leviticus 18. Imagine how much more powerful our Yom Kippur afternoon services might be if we made a different choice: by reading Leviticus 18 (and verse 22 in particular) precisely so that we might preach against it. What might this look like, practically speaking? We might consider using the marginalia of our new *machzor* (or the creative handouts that some of us use on the Holy Days) not just to put Leviticus 18 in its proper context, but also to grant permission to our communities to do any/all of the following:

1. Read/chant Leviticus 18 (or just 18:22) *sotto voce*. There is ample precedent in our tradition for adjusting the way we chant

biblical text based on its content (and our interpretation of it). Just as we try to speed through the list of Haman's ten sons on Purim,[44] so too should we change the tone of our chanting here to reflect our objection to the words. Alternatively, we might chant the reading according to the trope of Lamentations to signify the "gloom and despair"[45] that we associate with the historical implications of 18:22's edict.

2. Arrange for an openly gay or lesbian member of the congregation/staff to chant the reading. Before or after the reading, we might give them the opportunity to say a few words about their journey and the context in which they continue to be drawn to Torah and Jewish life, even as we struggle with 18:22.

3. Empower a clergyperson or a respected lay leader to preach against the text by delivering a *d'rash* that would explicitly critique the biblical author for 18:22 and name the pain and hurt that our GLBTQ friends and relatives have suffered because of its hatefulness.

This approach will not be right for every Reform synagogue. But for those of us who are comfortable doing so, wouldn't this homiletic strategy be the one that would allow us to be most welcoming of GLBTQ Jews and their allies? Doesn't this strategy, more than the other two discussed here, enable us to clarify our values and begin to fix a text that seems inherently broken?

I conclude as Plaskow did, as she faced my colleagues who were ordained in 1997: "Confronting the hard places in tradition and in our lives is neither comfortable nor easy. But it is a necessary step in shaping a Judaism that is inclusive and life-giving, in continuity with tradition and yet responsive to the contemporary world."[46]

That confrontation is the challenge that lies before us. Let us pray that we might all, each in our own ways and communities, find the wisdom and courage to face it.

Notes

1. On a micro-level, every local *sh'liach tzibur* is empowered to decide the Torah readings for their respective communities. On a macro-level, though, we acknowledge the unique influence that our CCAR *machzor* editorial committee wields, as it makes its own decision on this matter, thereby setting a "default" tone for the rest of the movement. As of the writing of this article in the

spring of 2011, the editorial committee had not begun discussing the Yom Kippur afternoon Torah reading in earnest (e-mail from Rabbi Edwin Goldberg on May 1, 2011).

2. Baruch A. Levine, *The JPS Torah Commentary: Leviticus* (Philadelphia: Jewish Publication Society, 1989), 117.

3. See Isaac Klein, *A Guide to Religious Practice* (New York/Jerusalem: JTSA, 1992), 380–88. Note how Klein omits all reference to homosexual intimacy and/or relationships (the aspect of Leviticus 18 that this paper is primarily concerned with). Compare that with the December 2006 CJLS-approved responsum/*takanot*: Elliot Dorff, Daniel Nevins, and Avram Reisner, "Homosexuality, Human Dignity & Halakhah: A Combined Responsum for the Committee on Jewish Law and Standards"; Myron Geller, Robert Fine, and David Fine, "A New Context: The Halakhah of Same-Sex Relations"; and Gordon Tucker, "Halakhic and Metahalakhic Arguments Concerning Judaism and Homosexuality." All are posted on the "Jewish Law" section of www.rabbinicalassembly.org (viewed July 27, 2011).

4. Nosson Scherman, ed., *The Chumash: The Stone Edition* (Brooklyn: Mesorah Publications, Ltd., 1993), 653.

5. Resolution entitled "Human Rights of Homosexuals," 45th General Assembly of the Union of American Hebrew Congregations, as posted on www.urj.org (viewed April 1, 2011). See also the resolution entitled "Rights of Homosexuals," passed at the 1977 CCAR Convention, as posted on www.ccarnet.org (viewed April 1, 2011).

6. Tamara Cohn Eskenazi and Andrea L. Weiss, eds., *The Torah: A Women's Commentary* (New York: URJ Press and Women of Reform Judaism, 2008), 692.

7. Adin Steinsaltz, *A Guide to Jewish Prayer* (New York: Schocken Books, 2000), 208.

8. Nahum Rakover, *A Guide to the Sources of Jewish Law* (Jerusalem: The Library of Jewish Law, 1994), 59.

9. S.Y. Agnon, ed., *Days of Awe: A Treasury of Jewish Wisdom for Reflection, Repentance, and Renewal on the High Holy Days* (New York: Schocken Books, 1995), 262. See also Lawrence A. Hoffman, *Gates of Understanding 2: Appreciating the Days of Awe* (New York: Central Conference of American Rabbis, 1984), 145: "Why this [Leviticus 18] should have become the reading for Yom Kippur is unclear, but a traditional view, offered, for example, in 1917 by J.D. Eisenstein, is this: 'On Yom Kippur even the most profligate sinners come to synagogue, those who do not come again all year round, so that they must be warned against illicit sexual relations.'"

10. Dr. Richard Sarason cautions that we not read too much into the possible relationship between the *Taanit* mishnah and the

M'gillah gemara. The author(s) of the mishnah were recalling a pre-70 C.E. practice (of going out into the hills on Yom Kippur). According to Sarason, it would be historically inaccurate to presume that that practice was still occurring during the amoraic Period (e-mail from Dr. Richard Sarason, May 25, 2011).

11. Bernard M. Zlotowitz, "The Torah and Haftarah Readings for the High Holy Days," *CCAR Journal* 91 (Fall 1975): 102–3. Reprinted in Hara E. Person and Sara Newman, eds., *Machzor: Challenge and Change* (New York: CCAR Press, 2010), 137–49.

12. Ismar Elbogen, *Jewish Liturgy: A Comprehensive History*, trans. Raymond P. Scheindlin (Philadelphia and New York/Jerusalem: JPS and JTSA, 1993), 423 n. 72. Similarly, the 2007 edition of *Encyclopedia Judaica* (vol. 5, p. 489) notes that: "During the afternoon service three men are called to the reading of the Torah of Leviticus 18, which deals with incest prohibitions (and which is a continuation of the morning reading of the Torah according to the ancient custom which still exists in Italy)."

13. The choice of Leviticus 16 for the traditional Yom Kippur morning reading makes much more sense: Leviticus 16 contains the details of the ancient cultic observance of Yom Kippur. In my research, I did not encounter any sources to explain why (according to this explanation) Leviticus 17 would be omitted from Yom Kippur Torah readings.

14. Zlotowitz, "The Torah and Haftarah Readings," 95–98. Sarason adds to this data: "High Holy Day scriptural readings were not altered in the earliest European Reform prayerbooks (Hamburg, West London, Geiger), excepting that of the radical Berlin *Reformgemeinde*; that began in the 1850's in America. The traditional readings are also kept in most Conservative Mahzorim (although the Jules Harlow Mahzor of 1972 gives Lev. 19 as an alternative reading in the afternoon!)" (e-mail from Dr. Sarason, May 25, 2011).

15. Zlotowitz omits *machzor* title. See instead Michael A. Meyer, *Response to Modernity: A History of the Reform Movement of Judaism* (Detroit: Wayne State University Press, 1988), 422 n. 61.

16. As Hoffman points out, there are plenty of aspects of Leviticus 18 that are problematic, outside of the sphere of our GLBTQ concerns. This project, however, is devoted to addressing GLBTQ concerns in particular.

17. Hoffman, *Gates*, 145.

18. According to an e-mail conversation with Hoffman (April 12, 2011), no one on the *GOR* editorial committee ever seriously considered including Leviticus 18 as the Yom Kippur afternoon Torah reading. In his words: the issue "was moot from the start." To them, it seemed obvious that the reading shouldn't be included. Furthermore, Hoffman indicated that GLBTQ concerns were not

a factor in their decision-making process: "I do not, however, recall much (or any, for that matter) concern altogether re GLBTQ back then. This was a time when feminism was still suspect in the eyes of people senior to me. We ended up with sexist language, for goodness sake, because too many people thought God talk still had to be masculine and hierarchical. GLBTQ was an acronym no one had heard of."

19. Jonathan Magonet and Lionel Blue, eds., *Forms of Prayer for Jewish Worship: Prayers for the High Holydays* (London: the Reform Synagogues of Great Britain, 1985), 976–85. Note from the Editors' Introduction: "While this liturgy was being revised, another revision was taking place in the attitudes of the society which it serves, concerning sexual injustice in general and women's rights in particular" (pp. ix–x). To what extent did these societal "revisions" make it easier for the editorial committee of *Forms of Prayer* to ignore Leviticus 18? The *machzor* does not say.

20. Richard N. Levy, *On Wings of Awe: A Machzor for Rosh Hashanah and Yom Kippur* (Washington, DC: B'nai B'rith Hillel Foundations, 1985), 414–19. See especially p. 417 for Levy's thoughtful translation of Lev. 18:22, in which he seeks to offer both a literal *and* interpretive take: "You shall not lie with a man as with a woman; it is an abhorrence (or, an emulation of the practices of pagan religion)." This article would be incomplete without also acknowledging the recent revision (after this article was written) of Levy's *On Wings of Awe* (Jersey City, NJ: Ktav Publishing House, Inc. in association with Hillel: The Foundation for Jewish Campus Life, 2011). Interestingly, Leviticus 18 is not offered as an option in the revised edition. Instead, worshippers are are directed to read Leviticus 19:1–18, 32–37 (pp. 510–512). In a private email exchange, Levy reflected on Leviticus 18: "I included it in the original edition because the book was intended to be used by Hillel students from a variety of backgrounds, including those which customarily read that chapter in the afternoon, but in revising the book I felt that encountering Leviticus 18:22 can be taken as an insult by LGBTQ students, their friends, family, and supporters." In our exchange, Levy went on to argue that Yom Kippur is not an appropriate day to do the kind of tikkun that this author calls for here. Levy wrote: "To turn our attention from work on ourselves to critiques of others distracts us from the tikkun we need to do with our own souls. Yom Kippur is also a day when we need to re-commit ourselves to the study and practice of Torah—and to embark on a critique of Torah distracts us from the commitment as well (email from Rabbi Richard Levy on December 12, 2011).

21. *Machzor Ruach Chadashah* (London: Liberal Judaism, 2003), 499. With thanks to Sheryl Stahl of HUC's Los Angeles library for helping me to track down this text.

22. I wonder if this argument from silence does not also run the risk of unintentionally ignoring GLBTQ Jews. Yes, our alternative reading is not explicitly offensive to gays and lesbians. But it also ignores the reality of gay life in our communities.

23. Steven Greenberg, *Wrestling with God and Men: Homosexuality in the Jewish Tradition* (Madison: University of Wisconsin Press, 2004), 76.

24. See, for example, Neil Gillman, *Sacred Fragments: Recovering Theology for the Modern Jew* (Philadelphia: Jewish Publication Society, 1990), 31–32: "As for revelation, if we are serious in affirming that no myth is a fiction, then we have in the same breath affirmed both the principle and the fact of revelation . . . The thesis that Torah contains the classic Jewish mythic explanation of one community's experience of the world, is clearly still a third version of what we have called the middle option on revelation . . . In this extended sense, myth and *midrash* share many characteristics. Both are culturally conditioned, human renderings of realities that lie beyond direct human apprehension. Both exhibit startling continuities and equally surprising discontinuities as they move through history. As long as the community that shapes them remains vital, it will determine what it wishes to keep and what it prefers to discard and reshape in the light of its ongoing experience." Like so many of my Reform colleagues, I agree that 18:22 should be "discarded." I believe, admittedly paradoxically, that the best way to do that is by reading it out loud on Yom Kippur afternoon: to affirm the (whole) myth of our people, and to "discontinue" a part of that myth at the very same time (by publicly critiquing it).

25. http://www.bcc-la.org/content/about/ (viewed May 10, 2011).

26. E-mail correspondence with Rabbi Lisa Edwards (April 8, 2011).

27. See the "JRF Homosexuality Report and Inclusion of GLBTQ Persons," http://jrf.org/node/1742 (viewed April 13, 2011).

28. Ronald Aigen, *Mahzor Hadesh Yameinu: Renew Our Days—A Prayer-Circle for Days of Awe* (Hampstead, Quebec: Ronald Aigen, 2001), 666.

29. Edward Feld, ed., *Mahzor Lev Shalem* (New York: The Rabbinical Assembly, 2010), 363.

30. Judith Plaskow, "Sexuality and *Teshuvah*: Leviticus 18" in *Beginning Anew: A Woman's Companion to the High Holy Days*, ed. Gail Twersky Reimer and Judith A. Kates (New York: Touchstone, 1997), 290–302. Reprinted in Judith Plaskow, *The Coming of Lilith: Essays on Feminism, Judaism, and Sexual Ethics, 1972-2003*, ed. with Donna Berman (Boston: Beacon Press, 2005), 165–77. Citations below will reference the 2005 edition.

31. Aigen, *Hadesh Yameinu*, 656. With thanks to Rabbi Aigen for directing my attention to his introduction to the *minchah* service

(e-mail with Rabbi Ron Aigen, April 14, 2011), which invokes some of Plaskow's themes.

32. Plaskow, "Sexuality," in *The Coming of Lilith*, 166.

33. Feld, *Machzor Lev Shalem*, 363–64.

34. Plaskow, "Sexuality," in *The Coming of Lilith*, 175–77.

35. Feld, *Machzor Lev Shalem*, 364.

36. For example, Rabbi Simeon's comment (BT *Sanhedrin* 71a) regarding the wayward and rebellious son: "In truth, the rebellious and defiant son never existed and never will exist. Why, then, was the account about him written? So that you will expound the possible reasons for such misconduct and receive a reward for doing so."

37. There are exceptions to this generalization, of course. We might situate certain aspects of Jewish feminism (to name a recent example) within this phenomenon. And if we are seeking individual colleagues who embrace this methodology as a regular homiletic approach, I would name Dr. Marc Saperstein as a noteworthy example. See some of his writing on the Web site of Leo Baeck College: http://lbc.reformjudaism.org.uk/Sermons-Papers/sermons-a-papers.html, especially his 2010 and 2011 Shabbat Zachor sermons, as well as the one entitled "My Least Favourite Biblical Verse" (e-mail correspondence with Dr. Marc Saperstein, April 14, 2011) (sermons viewed on May 4, 2011).

38. Peter J. Gomes, *The Good Book: Reading the Bible with Mind and Heart* (New York: William Morrow and Company, Inc., 1996), 81. I am grateful to Professor Barbara Lundblad of Union Theological Seminary for her reference to Gomes.

39. Ibid., 82 (emphasis added).

40. E-mail correspondence with Dr. Marc Saperstein (April 14, 2011) and Rabbi Margaret Moers Wenig (April 15, 2011).

41. Judith Plaskow, "Preaching Against the Text," in *The Coming of Lilith*, 152–56.

42. Ibid., 155.

43. Ibid., 155–56.

44. Joshua R. Jacobson, *Chanting the Hebrew Bible: Student Edition* (Philadelphia: Jewish Publication Society, 2005), 165.

45. A.W. Binder, *Biblical Chant* (New York: Sacred Music Press/HUC-JIR School of Sacred Music, 1959), 100. With thanks to Cantor William Tiep for referring me to Binder.

46. Plaskow, "Preaching," in *The Coming of Lilith*, 156.

Orthodox Women (Non-)Rabbis[1]

Darren Kleinberg

"Under no circumstances should you call yourself a rabbi."
—Max Dienemann's advice to Regina Jonas

In the decades since Regina Jonas became the first ordained woman in Jewish history (1935), the Reform Movement within which she studied and worked has become accustomed to calling its female clergy by the title "rabbi." Although Jonas was permitted to study at the rabbinical seminary at *Der Hochschule fur die Wissenschaft des Judentums* in Berlin in 1924 and had, by 1930, "passed the general obligatory exams in religious history and education, the philosophy of the Talmud, and Hebrew language and Bible study,"[2] and submitted her "halachic work . . . and a biblical final paper,"[3] she did not receive formal ordination from the institution. Eduard Baneth, the man in charge of rabbinical ordinations at the time, had passed away unexpectedly and was succeeded by Chanoch Albeck, who "represented a conservative viewpoint."[4] In addition, it was Leo Baeck's wish to "avoid controversy in the general rabbinical council" and, according to Albeck's son as recorded in Elisa Klapheck's *Fraulein Rabbiner Jonas: The Story of the First Woman Rabbi*, "the Academy committee was dominated by fear of a scandal and the view that Jewry in Germany, despite being liberal, was not yet ready for a female rabbi."[5] The result was that Jonas received "only a certificate of passing the 'Academic Religion Teacher Exam' with a grade of 'overall good.'"[6]

Finally, Jonas was tested and ordained privately[7] on December 26, 1935, by Rabbi Dr. Max Dienemann. It is recalled that Dienemann's advice to Jonas was that "under no circumstances should

RABBI DARREN KLEINBERG is the director of Valley Beit Midrash, a pluralistic adult-learning institute serving the Greater Phoenix Jewish community. Ordained in 2005, he is a Ph.D. student in the religious Studies Department at Arizona State University.

you call yourself a rabbi."[8] This, despite the fact that Jonas had studied for the rabbinate, had taken the same courses and examinations as her male peers, and had written a halachic work entitled "Can Women Serve as Rabbis?" Her halachic work considered in depth the question of women rabbis from the perspective of Jewish law and concluded that there was no prohibition against women holding such an office. And yet, despite all of this, the institution she studied in, and even the rabbi that personally ordained her, felt uncomfortable with her taking the title of "rabbi."[9]

Almost forty years later, in 1972, when Sally Priesand became the first Jewish woman to be ordained formally by a rabbinical seminary, the Reform Movement overcame *Der Hochschule*'s and Dienemann's apprehensions and she entered the clergy as *Rabbi* Sally Priesand. Soon enough, following Rabbi Priesand's ordination by the HUC-JIR, the Reconstructionist Rabbinical College ordained its first woman rabbi, Sandy Eisenberg-Sasso, in 1974, and the Conservative Movement's Jewish Theological Seminary of America followed suit in 1985 when it ordained Amy Eilberg as its first woman rabbi.

More recently, the question regarding the title that women who undertake the same course of study as their male counterparts should receive has been revived, this time in the Orthodox community.[10] The question of women's ordination in the Orthodox Jewish community started to become a live issue more generally as a result of the sexual revolution of the 1960s,[11] and has grown in importance in recent decades more specifically due to the decision of the Conservative Movement in the 1980s to ordain women rabbis. Orthodox Jews see halachah as a binding force in their lives and so, because Conservative Judaism has always claimed to be a denomination guided by halachah, its rulings have often been more noteworthy in the Orthodox world than those of the Reform Movement, which does not make any such claim. Precisely at the time that the Conservative Movement's Jewish Theological Seminary of America was confronting the question of women's ordination, Orthodox leaders began to discuss the possibilities for their own community.[12]

Although a number of women have (or claim to have) received *s'michah* from Orthodox rabbis, none have yet been formally ordained as *rabbis* from an existing Orthodox rabbinical school.[13] In recent years, two women in the Orthodox community have propelled the issue of women rabbis further than ever before. In the 1990s, Haviva Krasner-Davidson (now Haviva Ner-David) applied to the Rabbi Isaac Elchanan Theological Seminary at Yeshiva University, the institutional bastion of modern Orthodoxy in America.[14] She received no response to her application to Yeshiva University, but did receive a great deal of attention from the larger Jewish community and beyond. Eventually, she moved to Israel and studied privately with Rabbi Aryeh Strikovsky[15] from whom she received private ordination. Interestingly, and in a manner that was reminiscent of Max Dienemann's advice to Regina Jonas decades earlier in Germany, it was reported that "Aryeh Strikovsky, the Orthodox rabbi who ordained her, doesn't want her to use the title ["rabbi"] in places where it might arouse controversy. 'He told me, "the Orthodox community is not ready for it, and they'll just laugh at you.""'[16] In the end, Ner-David's ordination has become a moot point with respect to the Orthodox community as she has since disassociated herself from the movement. As her bio on the Web site of the organization she directs states, "Rabbi Dr. Ner-David . . . considers herself a post-denominational rabbi."[17]

The most recent case of an Orthodox woman following the same course of study as men training for ordination as rabbis is that of Sara Hurwitz. On March 22, 2009, a conferral ceremony was held for Hurwitz at the Hebrew Institute of Riverdale, New York, under the auspices of Rabbi Avi Weiss. At this ceremony, and in similar fashion to the experience of Regina Jonas, despite studying and being examined on the self-same curriculum and materials as men studying for the rabbinate (incidentally, Rabbi Weiss is also the founder of Yeshivat Chovevei Torah rabbinical school),[18] Hurwitz was *not* ordained—in fact, the word "ordination" was never used to describe the ceremony—as a *rabbi*. For her conferral ceremony the neologism MaHaRa"T[19] was coined.

At the conferral ceremony of MaHaRa"T Hurwitz, copies of a document entitled "Responsa Regarding Women's Roles in Religious Leadership" was distributed.[20] The document includes, among other things, a copy of the relatively brief remarks offered at the ceremony by Rabbi Avraham (Avi) Weiss. It is in the context of Weiss's remarks as the conferring rabbi that the ceremony, the document, and the title "MaHaRa"T" are so noteworthy. The title and role that is being conferred upon Hurwitz is central to his remarks specifically and to the document in general. In addition to Weiss's remarks, three legal responsa are also included in the document. Crucially, the leadership role(s) for women that the authors of the responsa are considering in their legal arguments are inconsistent with Weiss's characterization of what is being conferred. Furthermore, as we shall see, the very title "MaHaRa"T" belies Weiss's central claim in his remarks. These documents and the legal arguments therein offer some insight as to how at least these four men (rabbis) appear to understand the place of women in relation to the Orthodox rabbinate. As we will see, the withholding of the title "rabbi" from women and the invention of a new title along with the curtailing of the role of women in positions of religious leadership is not simply a case of "separate and unequal" but rather it is an exertion of oppressive power on the part of Orthodox Jewish men over Orthodox Jewish women.

Rabbi Avi Weiss is the senior rabbi of the Hebrew Institute of Riverdale, a modern Orthodox synagogue in the Riverdale area of the Bronx.[21] Weiss has been the senior rabbi of this congregation for over thirty years and has often been an advocate for greater equality between the sexes with respect to religious concerns confronting Orthodox women.[22] As reported in the pages of the *New York Times*, in 1997 Weiss hired Sharona Margolin Halickman as the first female congregational intern at his synagogue. This event came only days after Julie Stern Joseph became the first woman to take on such a role in the Orthodox community when she was hired by the Lincoln Square Synagogue in Manhattan.[23] Halickman went on to become the synagogue's first *Madrichah Ruchanit* (spiritual guide), described on the Hebrew Institute of Riverdale Web site as "a member of the professional religious leadership team of the Congregation."[24] After describing the function and role of the *Madrichah Ruchanit*, the Web site makes it clear that she "is not a Poseket Halakha, nor can she perform ritual actions in the Synagogue, or at weddings and other Semachot, which Halakha limits to males."[25] It is unclear exactly how to understand the end of this sentence ("which Halakha limits to males"), i.e., whether it is a contravention of halachah for Halickman to act as a "Poseket Halakha" (decisor of Jewish law) *and* to perform ritual actions of various kinds, or whether the breach of Jewish law occurs only in the performance of ritual actions (or maybe even that it occurs only with regard to the rituals occurring at "weddings and other Semachot"). In the last two readings, it would seem that the other roles would be prohibited for nonlegal (extra-halachic) reasons.

Leaving this question aside, what *is* clear however is that, even though the description of her role is never explicitly distinguished from that of a male rabbi,[26] the role of *Madrichah Ruchanit* is unquestionably being delimited in that way. While it certainly would be unnecessary to state that the *Madrichah Ruchanit* is not a rabbi—after all, the creation of a new title for a woman taking a leadership role in an Orthodox synagogue makes that quite clear—it was still apparently necessary for the Hebrew Institute to make it explicit that the woman filling this position would not be taking on the *roles and responsibilities* traditionally associated with a (male) rabbi. To be clear, it was precisely the roles of "Posek Halakha" and performer of "ritual actions in the synagogue, or at weddings or other Semachot"—roles traditionally associated with the (male) rabbi—that were indicated as *not* being within the orbit of a woman's leadership role at Weiss's synagogue. The implicit meaning being thus: a woman serving in the role of *Madrichah Ruchanit* in Weiss's synagogue was not, and could not, be a rabbi because certain roles central to the office of a rabbi cannot be fulfilled by a woman.

In 2004, Sara Hurwitz became the *Madrichah Ruchanit* at the Hebrew Institute of Riverdale following "three years of learning at Manhattan's Drisha Institute." During her tenure in that position, she "repeated the course work under Weiss' supervision,"[27] which led to her formal conferral as MaHaRa"T Sara Hurwitz on March 22, 2009. Hurwitz's conferral as a MaHaRa"T communicated that Hurwitz was filling some new office, both distinct from that of her previous role as *Madrichah Ruchanit* and, crucially, from that of a (male) rabbi.

Presumably with the intention of both celebrating the occasion and, at the same time, defending against the appearance of a radical break from tradition, the program for the morning leading up to the conferral ceremony included study sessions on issues related to women in Jewish communal leadership roles.[28] The actual "Tribute and Conferral Ceremony" included speeches from leaders in the modern Orthodox Jewish community as well as a speech from one of the authors of the legal responsa distributed on the day.[29] The program reached its crescendo with Weiss's remarks and the formal conferral of Hurwitz as MaHaRa"T, followed by Hurwitz offering her own prepared remarks in the form of a talk entitled "Women in Ritual Leadership: Past, Present, and Future."

In addition to the study sessions and speeches, the document "Responsa Regarding Women's Roles in Religious Leadership" was also distributed at the ceremony. Halachic responsa play the critical role of demonstrating in traditional Orthodox literary form that a given custom, practice, or interpretation of Jewish law is defensible from the Bible, Talmud, and Codes of Jewish Law.[30] The document includes three responsa from three different rabbis: two in Hebrew with accompanying English translations from rabbis living in Israel and a third in English from an American rabbi. In addition, the document includes a copy of the (unsigned) "Writ of Authorization and Title" in Hebrew and English, and, as noted above, a copy of the text of the conferral speech offered by Weiss[31] at the ceremony.[32]

In Weiss's remarks the emphasis is placed on the new title that Hurwitz will receive and the nature of her role once she has been conferred. The speech begins by declaring that "Today, we confer on Sara Hurwitz, the title מהרת—תורנית רוחנית הלכתית מנהיגה,[33] as she becomes a religious leader in Israel.[34] This title reflects everything that religious leadership is about and welcomes Sara as a *full*[35] member of the clergy." Over the course of his short speech, Weiss refers to the scope ("full") of Hurwitz's role as a religious leader four more times: "מהרת—תורנית רוחנית הלכתית מנהיגה,[36] a halakhic, spiritual and Torah leader. A *full* communal, congregational, religious leader, a *full* member of the clergy, leading with the unique voice of a woman"; "Sara's step of becoming שרה מהרת [MaHaRa"T Sara]—a *full* communal, congregational, and religious leader"; and "Sara, under the tutelage of halakhic experts, has studied the established traditional texts that are required to become a religious leader, and based on her mastery of these texts, is assuming a *full* religious leadership position in a synagogue." Although the word "rabbi" is never used in Weiss's speech, it is clear from the repeated reference to the "full"ness of Hurwitz's position that it is the role of the male rabbi that Hurwitz's new position as MaHaRa"T is being compared to.

When Weiss refers to the fact that Hurwitz "has studied the established traditional texts that are required to become a religious leader," the "established traditional texts" refer to the curriculum of male rabbinical programs, and the "religious leader[s]" he mentions refer to male rabbis. Put differently, and taking Weiss's own synagogue as an example, what it means to be a person assuming "full religious leadership" is to serve in all of the varied roles assumed by male rabbis. These roles include, but are not limited to (and in no particular order), teaching classes and giving sermons, answering questions related to Jewish law, offering pastoral care, leading synagogue services, presiding over life-cycle rituals from birth to death, acting as a member of a religious court for conversions to Judaism, serving as a witness to various life-cycle rituals (weddings and funerals being the most prominent), and, more generally, being a role model of Jewish living for the congregation.[37] "Full religious leadership" for a (male) rabbi in an Orthodox synagogue undoubtedly includes much more than this, but certainly no less. And, of course, part of assuming a position of "full religious leadership" for a male rabbi includes taking on the title of "rabbi."[38]

At the same time that Weiss presses the point that Hurwitz is "a full member of the clergy" he undermines it by explaining the meaning of Hurwitz's new title and the scope of her role as a "full" member of the religious leadership of Israel. In his speech, Weiss explains that "Sara is a מנהיגה הלכתית [*Manhigah Halachtit*], a halakhic leader with the authority to answer questions of Jewish law asked by her congregants and others" and that "Sara is a מנהיגה רוחנית [*Manhigah Ruchanit*], a spiritual leader with the qualifications to offer pastoral care and spiritual guidance, and the right to lead life-cycle ceremonies within the framework of halakha." And, finally, that "Sara is a מנהיגה תורנית [*Manhigah Toranit*], with the knowledge to teach Torah, the written as well as the oral law in every aspect of Jewish learning." In this description we see that the roles that Hurwitz will fill as MaHaRa"T Hurwitz are limited to responding to questions of Jewish law, pastoral care and spiritual guidance, limited involvement in life-cycle rites, and teaching. Certainly, this distinguishes the role of MaHaRa"T from that of *Madrichah Ruchanit*, for whom halakhic decision making was clearly proscribed.[39] At the same time, however, the responsibilities outlined in Weiss's speech fall far short of describing a "full member of clergy" when measured up against a male rabbi. Weiss's speech is contradictory in that it claims one thing while describing another. As such, it is an apparent attempt to obfuscate the very real differences between the role of a MaHaRa"T and that of a (male) rabbi.

The distance between the role of a MaHaRa"T and that of a male rabbi is further underlined in the responsa from the same document. The rabbis whose responsa are collected in the document are, in the order they are presented, Harav Yoel Bin-nun,[40] Rabbi Dr. Daniel Sperber,[41] and Rabbi Joshua Maroof.[42] The responsa do not address the question of whether or not Orthodox women can become "rabbis." Interestingly, they each provide their own formulation of the question they are responding to. In addition to the clear distinction between the role being considered in the responsa and that of a male rabbi, it is also important to note how each of the authors diminishes what might otherwise be considered a monumental step forward for the role of women in the Orthodox community. Rather than heralding a new age of female not-yet-rabbis who are advancing the improved place of Orthodox women in religious leadership, the authors each offer one or more reasons why this should not be considered the case. In all, three arguments are presented to "contextualize" the justification of this apparently not so new, or so special, role for women in Orthodoxy. I refer to these three arguments as (1) the argument from history, (2) the argument from capacity, and (3) the argument from redundancy. Each argument offers, in its own way, an undermining of what might otherwise be considered the importance of the moment. The tension between Weiss's heralding of a new role of "full religious leadership" for women in Orthodoxy (even as he describes a role that is anything but that) and the respondents' diminishing of the importance of the moment is unmistakable. Not only is the role of MaHaRa"T far less than that of a "full member of the clergy" but, as the respondents further argue, the conferral ceremony offered nothing new to the landscape for women in Orthodox Jewish life. Put differently, while Weiss overstates the nature of the role and responsibilities of the MaHaRa"T, the authors of the responsa understate, and effectively undermine, the importance of the moment for Hurwitz and other Orthodox women who might wish to follow in her footsteps. What is left is a role for women that is, apparently, neither "full" nor all that noteworthy.

As mentioned above, each of the three authors of the responsa offers their own formulation of the question that they are answering. For Bin-nun, his responsa offers an answer to the question "regarding the possibility of appointing a woman, who has learned Torah, and especially the *halakhot* of *Orah Hayyim*[43] and *Yoreh Deah*[44] from outstanding Torah scholars, and who according to her skills, knowledge, *middot*[45] and lifestyle is worthy of serving in Rabbinic roles, fulfilling a [sic] Rabbinic responsibilities in the community, and to be called *Morateinu* [Our Teacher], or *Hakhama* [wise one]."[46] In this responsa, the question being answered is whether or not a woman, assuming she has fulfilled all the necessary prerequisites related to her education and character ("*middot* and lifestyle"), can "serve in Rabbinic roles," fulfill "Rabbinic responsibilities," and take a title appropriate to those roles and responsibilities. What is clearly implied by "serving in Rabbinic roles" and fulfilling "Rabbinic responsibilities" is that the roles and responsibilities are part of, but do not amount to the sum of, the role of a male rabbi. As such, the title "rabbi" would be out of place, hence the consideration of alternative titles. Here there are no claims that a woman in this role will be a "full member of the clergy." Instead of "rabbi"— and, interestingly, instead even of "MaHaRa"T"—the titles "Our Teacher" and "wise one" are offered as possibilities.

Bin-nun goes on to explain the meaning of the specific roles and responsibilities that this woman would take on in this capacity. He writes that "this question touches upon the questions of offering Torah instruction and teaching Halakha in the community, giving *psak*,[47] women in authoritative positions (שררה), and the boundaries of modesty (*tzniut*) in an [sic] congregation that consists mainly, or entirely, or men." This elaboration of the question at hand clarifies why the title "rabbi" is not under consideration: conspicuously absent from the description of rabbinic roles and responsibilities are the additional and, in the contemporary Orthodox congregational rabbinate, critical rabbinic roles of prayer leader, life-cycle officiant, and witness to legal-halachic transactions such as marriages and divorces, as well as the central role played by rabbis in conversions to Judaism.

In the responsa of Rabbi Dr. Daniel Sperber, the question at hand is much narrower: "Can a woman answer halachic questions, that is to say be a halachic decisor?" Here, in contrast to Bin-nun, there is no mention of "Torah instruction and teaching Halakha in the community" nor of "women in authoritative positions." For Sperber, the question at hand is that of *p'sak halachah* (ruling on questions of Jewish law). It is therefore clear why there is no mention in Sperber's responsa of the question of whether it is permissible in the Orthodox community for women to become rabbis; according to Sperber, all that is at question is the permissibility of a woman to answer questions of Jewish law. This, of course, falls far short of even approximating the responsibilities that come with being a "full member of the clergy."

In the last of the three responsa, Rabbi Joshua Maroof frames the question in a similar vein to Sperber. As Maroof writes, "I was asked to respond to the question of whether a woman who is knowledgeable in Torah Law may issue rulings on matters of halakha." Here again, as with Sperber, the question is narrowly focused on the ability to decide questions of Jewish law with other concerns left by the wayside. And here again, the question of whether or not women can become rabbis in the Orthodox community is not raised because the role of a rabbi includes so much more than simply that of halachic decisor.

Not surprisingly, given the fact that these responsa were distributed at the conferral ceremony, each of the three respondents answers their stated question in the affirmative. However, in the course of confirming that Jewish law permits women to serve in the limited roles outlined in their questions, the authors manage to further marginalize and minimize the place of women in leadership roles in the Orthodox community. They achieve this by employing one or more of three arguments to support their ruling. As mentioned above, I refer to these three arguments as (1) the argument from history, (2) the argument from capacity, and (3) the argument from redundancy.

The argument from history is found in both the responsa of Bin-nun and Sperber. As Bin-nun puts it, "This is not a new question and there is nothing in it that is revolutionary, or 'modern.'" Of course, Bin-nun is only at pains to make this clear at the outset (this quote is from the beginning of the third paragraph of a three-and-a-half-page typed responsa) because something new and revolutionary does, in fact, *appear* to be happening. Bin-nun goes on and writes that "the appointment of an exceptional and unique woman to a *tafkid torani* (religious office), even the premier position in its generation, is an act that has been performed from time immemorial" after which he lists the names of women who held such positions throughout Jewish history: Sarah, Miriam, Devorah, Hannah, the wife of Manoah, the Shunamite, Queen Shlomtzion, *Marat* Beila, *Marat* Osnat, and *Marat* Hava Bachrach. Sperber offers a similar argument from history, declaring that "from the time of our ancestral mothers, Sarah, Deborah the Prophetess, Beruriah the wife of R. Meir, there were learned women who dealt in hal-achah, and gave halachic rulings." Both authors appeal to Jewish history to downplay what they see as the possibility that one could mistakenly conclude that the conferral of MaHaRa"T Hurwitz is a new development for women.

Here again we encounter the tension of the moment: Bin-nun and Sperber declare that nothing new is happening in the very responsa written for distribution at the conferral ceremony of a woman taking on a new title and role in the Orthodox community. Furthermore, while they claim that nothing new or revolutionary is taking place, Weiss claims (mistakenly, as I have shown) that Hurwitz is taking on the role of a "full member of the clergy," which is certainly nothing short of a new development. Finally, it is curious that both authors can claim that these roles have "been performed from time immemo-rial" and "from the time of our ancestral mothers" and yet are able to name most of the women known to us from Jewish history who have taken on such roles. These women have unquestionably been the exception in Jewish history, not indicators for the way things have always been. The very fact that we have the names of these few women (some of whom are themselves fictional) does not suggest that nothing new is happening in the conferral of a MaHaRa"T, but rather that Hurwitz is another rare exception to the rule. And yet, by employing the argument from history, these authors undermine the possibility of Hurwitz being seen as a groundbreaking force for greater equality for women in religious leadership in the Orthodox community. Instead, according to this argument, she is just another woman doing something that Jewish women have always done.

The second argument, the argument from capacity, can also be found in the responsa of Yoel Bin-nun. In this responsa, the au-thor states that "a community can accept upon themselves an *Isha Hakhama*[48] as their teacher (*Morah*) in Torah, in all of the regular roles of a community and synagogue rabbi." As quoted above, for Bin-nun the "regular roles of a community and synagogue rabbi" are defined as "offering Torah instruction and teaching Halakha in the community, [and] giving *psak*." In this formulation of the argument from capacity, Bin-nun states that a woman can certainly serve as a rabbi while at the same time limiting the definition of what it means to be a rabbi. Better yet, by implying that the rab-binic roles not available to women are other than the "regular roles" of the rabbi, women are not excluded from being "rabbis" as such, but only from performing "special" additional functions only available to men. By downgrading what it means to be a rabbi, Bin-nun is able to allow women into the role. The tension here between extending and retracting is palpable.

The third argument, the argument from redundancy can be found in the responsa of Rabbi Joshua Maroof. Maroof's responsa considers the larger question of what it means to be a rabbi. Maroof distinguishes between "the original form of *semikha* [ordination]" and "ruling on matters of halakha." According to Maroof, "the original form of *semikha* . . . was conferred from Rabbi to student from the days of Moshe Rabbenu until persecution led to its discontinuation during the Talmudic period."[49] In effect, this form of ("real") *s'michah* was replaced by what Maroof calls "ruling on matters of halakha." Referring to the second, lesser, form of *s'michah*, Maroof write that "the core of any given act of הוראה[50] is the process of Torah study upon which it is based and from which it emerges, and that this process is equally accessible to competent men and to competent women." As opposed to the earlier form of *s'michah*, which was handed down from (male) teacher to (male) student, this latter form is, at least in theory, available to anyone (male or female) who studies the material and is successfully examined on it. Furthermore, the earlier form of *s'michah*, is of an entirely different nature to the latter form in that, according to Maroof, "[t]he quality of being a מוסמך[51] or a בעל המסורה[52] inheres in the recipient, endowing his person with unique legal authority (שררה) and his decisions with legitimacy and binding force." While it is hard to know what it is that Maroof means when he refers to certain qualities "inhering" in people who receive this earlier form of *s'michah*, what *is* clear is that it is of a higher caliber than the form of *s'michah* that eventually replaced it. Not only was the original form of *s'michah* believed to have been handed down in an unbroken chain from Moses, but that it also reflected or invested some new and different quality in the recipient; whereas the latter form of *s'michah* is simply an indicator of a given person's level of knowledge. It is also noteworthy that Maroof does not suggest that, as in the case of "rulings on matters of Halakha," the recipient of the original form of *s'michah* could just as well be female as male. Apparently, the special quality inherent in (male) recipients of the original form of *s'michah* was not present in, or available to, women.

What Maroof seems to be saying is that, first, what it means to be a rabbi today is to answer questions of Jewish law. We have already seen in the argument from capacity that this is a severe downgrading of the role of the contemporary Orthodox rabbi. Secondly, he states clearly that women can be qualified to rule on questions of Jewish Law, that is to receive our diminished form of s'michah because, after all, our form of s'michah is not the "real" s'michah and so it is available to anyone. Here Maroof makes the role of halachic decisor available to women by devaluing it. Third, and finally, Maroof implies that, *if we did have "real" s'michah*, it would be reserved for men only because it is related to certain inherent qualities that, evidently based on the record, are only found in men. Taking these three arguments together, we can understand the argument from redundancy: in effect it states that women can certainly take on this role because, after all, *anyone* can take it on.[53] Again, as with the argument from history and the argument from capacity, the argument from redundancy leaves us with the conclusion that the conferral of MaHaRa"T Hurwitz is not noteworthy. In fact, according to these responsa, her conferral only highlights the meaninglessness of what she has achieved: according to these authors her conferral is neither new nor revolutionary; it is limited in its scope; and it is available to her only because it is available to all.

The chasm between Weiss's overstatement that MaHaRa"T Hurwitz is a full member of the clergy and the understatement of the authors of the responsa that, at least when it comes to women in religious leadership, there is nothing new under the sun, is clear and, no doubt, the reality is somewhere between these two poles. Put simply, the fact is that MaHaRa"T Hurwitz has more responsibility than in her previous role as *Madrichah Ruchanit* but less than that of a male rabbi in the Orthodox community. Both Weiss and the authors of the responsa have misrepresented the meaning of this new role and the title that accompanied it. But what of Hurwitz herself?

In her speech at the conferral ceremony, Hurwitz restates many of the themes already discussed above. Echoing the argument from history, she shares her belief that "in every generation there have been 'nashim chachamot' who have felt a spiritual calling and dedicated themselves to the service of their communities" and goes on to list some of the names of women who, rather than crop up in every generation, stand out as rare exceptions. Hurwitz also embraces the argument from capacity when she, the only person bold enough to explicitly identify her role with that of a male rabbi, states that "A rabbi is an authority on halakha . . . A rabbi is a pastoral counselor . . . a rabbi is a public leader." By limiting the role of the rabbi, Hurwitz is able to identify with that role, all the while knowing that a rabbi is so much more in practice. She makes this case most strongly when she declares that

> when one focuses on the day-to-day practical aspects of the rabbinic job, we find that there is a very short list of rabbinic functions that women cannot halakhically perform. As of now, Orthodox women do not lead services and women are barred from acting as edim—witnesses—for marriage, divorce, and conversion. Beyond these few halakhic constraints, women, with the appropriate training **can** perform the other 95% of the tasks performed by Orthodox rabbis. [emphasis in original]

The claim that leading prayer services—which take place thrice-daily in the Orthodox community, not to mention the Sabbath and holiday services—and officiating at critical moments in the life cycle as well as conversions to Judaism account for only 5 percent of the contemporary rabbinate is impossible to defend.[54] It is especially ironic that Hurwitz would make this claim while working at Weiss's synagogue, which has placed prayer and ritual at the very heart of that community's identity.[55] Here one is hard-pressed to avoid the conclusion that Hurwitz is either knowingly obfuscating reality (presumably for political ends) or that she is subject to a state of false consciousness[56] and is in denial about the reality of her situation.

Of all the teachers, speakers, and documents that were a part of the conferral ceremony on March 22, 2009, the only clear understanding of the meaning of what was taking place was heard in the words of Blu Greenberg.[57] In Greenberg's remarks, following her praise for Hurwitz's achievements, she states that

> even as our hearts are full of praise and joy today . . . I would be less than candid were I not to acknowledge that even this joyous day has its moments of qualification, that I and many others, and I suspect Sara [Hurwitz] and Rabbi Weiss as well—had hoped that the new credential this day would have been 'rabbi', as Sara has shown herself to be qualified both in her learning and her leadership in that she has met the test for 5 years of dedicated

and loving service to this congregation, and has passed the same *bechinot* that entitle men to semicha and the title of rabbi. I would be less than honest not to wonder aloud whether this is an interim title or one that will stick and become for all time the full fledged female counterpart title for rabbinic leadership.

Greenberg's sage insight and ability to see the conferral ceremony for what it really was—a step, but not the completion of the journey—was a lone voice.[58] It is her appreciation that titles matter that separated her from the other speakers and writers from that day. The difference in title is a reflection of the difference in role and that, even if Hurwitz were correct that her role amounts to 95 percent of that of a male rabbi, as long as there is even 5 percent of difference between them, women will not be "full" members of the clergy alongside male rabbis.

Even in the modern branches of the Orthodox community, men who claim that women are equal while withholding equality from them (in this case, Weiss) and men who offer women equality, but at a cheaper price (Bin-nun, Sperber, and Maroof) serve only to maintain power over women. While these men may not be self-aware of their role, and the women themselves may be subject to false consciousness (as I am suggesting Hurwitz might be), it is nevertheless the case that men in the Orthodox community maintain a paternal grip over women and get to decide *on behalf of women* what they can and cannot be, what titles they can and cannot claim, and what roles they can and cannot take on. The conferral ceremony of MaHaRa"T Hurwitz is a clear example of this imbalance of power at work in the Orthodox community.

If Sara Hurwitz is the Regina Jonas of the American modern Orthodox Jewish community, then there is hope that at some point in the next thirty-seven years (the time between Jonas's private ordination and the public ordination of Rabbi Sally Priesand) there will be women rabbis in the Orthodox community. But it will take an honest appraisal of how far women have *and have not* come before that step can be taken.

Notes

1. In this paper, I offer an analysis of the documents distributed at the conferral ceremony of MaHaRa"T Sara Hurwitz. As has been well documented in general and Jewish media outlets, there

have been subsequent developments in this story and much controversy within the Orthodox community. These latter developments will not be considered in this paper.

2. Elisa Klapheck, *Fräulein Rabbiner Jonas: The Story of the First Woman Rabbi* (San Francisco: Jossey-Bass, 2004), 34.

3. Ibid.

4. Ibid.

5. Ibid.

6. Ibid.

7. Private ordination refers to students being tested in areas of Jewish law by rabbis outside of the context of a rabbinical seminary or similar institution. For more on the history of rabbinic ordination, see Julius Newman, *Semikhah [Ordination]: A Study of its Origin, History, and Function in Rabbinic Literature* (Manchester: Manchester University Press, 1950).

8. Klapheck, *Fräulein Rabbiner Jonas*, 443.

9. Ibid., 38–93, for a lengthy discussion of the extent to which Jonas was referred to as "rabbi" (*rabbiner/rabbinerin*) following the completion of her studies and up until her final years at Theresienstadt.

10. It is overly simplistic to refer to the Orthodox Jewish community as a singular entity; in truth, there is a spectrum of affiliations within Orthodoxy. Groups commonly identified as part of the Orthodox community include: modern Orthodoxy, centrist Orthodoxy, *Yeshivish*, *Litvak*, Chasidic, Chareidi, etc. For more on Orthodox Judaism in America, see Jeffrey S. Gurock, *Orthodox Jews in America* (Bloomington and Indianapolis: Indiana University Press, 2009).

11. For one of the early influential essays to take a progressive view on the subject of woman and Orthodox Judaism, see Saul Berman, "The Status of Women in Halakhic Judaism," *Tradition* 14, no. 2 (1972): 5–28.

12. For the best example of this, see the symposium entitled "Women as Rabbis: A Many-Sided Examination of all Aspects, Halakhic—Ethical—Pragmatic," *Judaism* 33, no.1 (1984): 6–90. Noteworthy contributors to the symposium from the Orthodox community are Blu Greenberg, Emanuel Rackman, and Chaim Seidler-Feller.

13. The two best known examples are Mimi Feigelson and Evelyn Goodman-Thau. For more, see Mimi Feigelson, "The Matmida" (no citation available). Also see http://www.jweekly.com/article/full/17388/outed-as-a-rabbi-orthodox-woman-to-speak-here/ and http://www.haaretz.com/rabbi-thau-versus-rabbi-thau-1.136206.

14. Haviva Ner-David, *Life on the Fringes: A Feminist Journey Toward Traditional Rabbinic Ordination* (Needham, MA: JFL Books, 2000).

15. Aryeh Strikovsky is the most senior teacher at the Pardes Institute of Jewish Studies in Jerusalem.

16. http://www.jwi.org/Page.aspx?pid=841.

17. http://www.reutcenter.org/eng/.

18. For more about Weiss's rabbinical school see www.yctorah.org.

19. MaHaRa"T is an acronym made up from the sounds of the first letters of four Hebrew words: _Manhigah Halachtit, Ruchanit, Toranit_, which translates as Legal, Spiritual, and Torah Guide.

20. The full document can be accessed at http://www.jofa.org/pdf/ Responsa%20on%20Ordination%20of%20Women.pdf.

21. For a sympathetic description of the synagogue community led by Weiss, see Rabbi Sidney Schwartz, _Finding a Spiritual Home: How a New Generation of Jews Can Transform the American Synagogue_ (Woodstock, VT: Jewish Lights, 2003), 95–134.

22. Weiss was one of the early supporters of separate women's prayer groups in Orthodox synagogues. For his case on this subject, see Avraham Weiss, _Women at Prayer: A Halakhic Analysis of Women's Prayer Groups—Expanded Edition_ (Hoboken, NJ: KTAV, 2001/1990). Additional examples of Weiss's progressive views on women and Orthodoxy can be found in Avraham Weiss, "Women and the Reading of the Megilah," _The Torah U-Madda Journal_ 8 (1998–1999): 295–317; and Jeffrey S. Gurock, _Orthodox Jews in America_ (Bloomington: Indiana University Press, 2009), especially chapters 9 and 10.

23. http://www.nytimes.com/1998/02/06/nyregion/unusual-but-not-unorthodox-causing-stir-2-synagogues-hire-women-assist-rabbis.html?pagewanted=all (accessed July 20, 2011). A defunct page on the HIR Web site contradicts the order of events and states that Margolin Halickman became the congregational intern in 1997, thereby predating Lincoln Square Synagogue and making her the first female congregational intern. See http:// www.hir.org/torah/sharona/sharona.html. Rabbi Adam Mintz was the senior rabbi of Lincoln Square Synagogue at the time.

24. http://www.hir.org/madricha_ruchanit.html (accessed January 6, 2011).

25. Ibid.

26. For the purposes of this paper, I will consider the specific role of the synagogue rabbi. While it is true that there are rabbis who are teachers in day schools, chaplains, and university-based educators, etc., these roles are not being considered per se in this essay.

27. Abigail Pogrebin, "The Rabbi and the Rabba," _New York Magazine_, http://nymag.com/news/features/67145/.

28. The three study sessions were: "Honoring Women Torah Scholars: A Sephardic Perspective" presented by Lynn Kaye;

"Maintaining Personal Boundaries as a Leader: Biblical and Talmudic Models" presented by Rachel Kohl Finegold and Dr. Carol Fuchs; and "Women's Leadership Avenues in Orthodoxy: History, Challenges, and Triumphs" presented by Dina Najman.

29. The speakers were: Devorah Zlochower, Rabbi Joshua Maroof (responsa author), Rabbi David Silber, and Blu Greenberg.

30. "Codes of Jewish Law" refers to those legal works, beginning with the *Mishneh Torah* of Maimonides (1135–1204), that codify Jewish law systematically based on different categories.

31. The text can be compared to a video recording of Weiss's speech—they are essentially identical. http://www.youtube.com/watch?v=CguoGS9Mc0s.

32. There is also a copy of a letter of congratulations from one of the authors.

33. See note 19, above.

34. Here, Israel refers to the Jewish people and not the country.

35. Emphasis added here and on each successive use of the word "full."

36. See note 19, above.

37. While some may make the case that a rabbi, from the perspective of Orthodoxy, is halachically defined as no more than someone who has studied Jewish law and passed exams to demonstrate proficiency, such a definition, while possibly technically accurate, is immaterial when measured up against the myriad responsibilities undertaken by the contemporary congregational rabbi.

38. Or another equivalent title, such as "rav," "rebbe," etc.

39. It is worthwhile to ask what has changed—was it merely the lack of training that prevented the *Madrichah Ruchanit* from deciding questions of Jewish law, or is this a clear example of the sociological tides shifting within the modern Orthodox camp?

40. Rabbi Yoel Bin-Nun is an Israeli educator and Rosh Yeshivah who has spearheaded the revolution in *Tanach* study in Israel, primarily at Yeshivat Har Etzion and the Herzog Teachers' College in Alon Shevut. He has written numerous articles and books on *Tanach*, Jewish history, Jewish thought, and halachah. Bio taken from http://www.yctorah.org/component/option,com_docman/task,doc_view/gid,703/ (accessed July 21, 2011).

41. Rabbi Dr. Daniel Sperber is a professor of Talmud at Bar-Ilan University in Israel, and an expert in classical philology, history of Jewish customs, Jewish art history, Jewish education, and Talmudic studies. Bio taken from http://www.torahinmotion.org/spkrs_crnr/faculty/bioDanielSperber.htm (accessed July 21, 2011).

42. Rabbi Joshua Maroof is the rabbi of Magen David Sephardic Congregation-Bet Eliahu Synagogue in Rockville, Maryland.

He received his baccalaureate degree with honors from the State University of New York at Stony Brook, and his masters degree in Educational Psychology from the City University of New York (CUNY). He received *s'michah* (ordination) from Rabbi Yisrael Chait, Rosh Yeshivah of Yeshiva B'nai Torah in Far Rockaway, New York. Bio taken from http://www.mdscbe.org/OurRabbi.html (accessed July 21, 2011).

43. One of the four sections of the *Shulchan Aruch*, dealing with the laws of daily life.

44. Another one of the four sections of the Shulchan Aruch, dealing with, among other things, dietary laws.

45. Character traits.

46. An English translation of Bin-nun's responsa is included in the document. The translation is by Mishael Zion.

47. Answering questions of Jewish law.

48. A wise woman.

49. See note 7, above.

50. *Hora-ah* (legal ruling).

51. *Musmach* (ordinee).

52. *Baal HaMesorah* (master of the tradition).

53. This formulation is reminiscent of the statement of Rabbi Herschel Schachter, Rosh Yeshivah of Yeshiva University who, in reference to the question of whether a woman is permitted to read the marriage document under the wedding canopy at an Orthodox wedding, wrote that, "Yes, even if a parrot or a monkey would read the *kesuba*, the marriage would be one hundred percent valid." Interestingly, there is an editor's note at the beginning of the essay that reads in part: "The statement about monkeys or parrots reading the *kesuba* was clearly intended to dramatize the *halachic* insignificance of the reading of the *kesuba* from the standpoint of the *siddur kiddushin* (marriage ceremony). It was not intended to imply or insinuate anything else." http://www.torahweb.org/torah/2004/parsha/rsch_dvorim2.html (accessed July 21, 2011).

54. It is true that in the Orthodox rabbinate there is no requirement for rabbis to lead prayer services. Many Orthodox synagogues, in fact, employ cantors or can rely on (male) members of the laity to lead services. The extent to which Orthodox rabbis lead prayer services is different from congregation to congregation. There is no doubt, however, that the ability to do so, especially on special occasions, adds to the charismatic authority of the rabbi in his given community.

55. See note 21, above.

56. For an argument against the claims of false consciousness, see Tova Hartman, *Feminism Encounters Traditional Judaism: Resistance*

and Accommodation (Waltham, MA: Brandeis University Press, 2007). For another argument against the conclusion of false consciousness in the Muslim world, see Saba Mahmood, *Politics of Piety: The Islamic Revival and the Feminist Subject* (Princeton, NJ: Princeton University Press, 2005).

57. Greenberg is the matriarch of the Orthodox Feminist community.

58. Maroof comes close to Greenberg's observation, although does not go so far as to lament the fact that Hurwitz was not given the title of "rabbi," or that she would not fill the role of a (male) rabbi. For Maroof's speech at the conferral ceremony, see http://www.youtube.com/watch?v=wNZLnXdwi2Q.

Shabbat Weddings Revisited: The Pro Side for a Change

Reeve Robert Brenner

It is not that there are no reasons to avoid or refuse to officiate at Saturday evening weddings before sundown. It is that these reasons are so flimsy and lame and these reasons, discussed in this article, are outweighed by far in my mind by several firmer reasons to agree to officiate on Shabbat (with pleasure). We should welcome the custom of late Shabbat day weddings already entrenched and established as a *minhag* and see it as an opportunity to connect with many lives—most especially with a young couple. And, if the professional dynamics are well played out, it will serve to connect a few lives to the experience of Shabbat's special sacredness.

Here are some of my reasons. I acknowledge that when you provide a number of reasons, it's likely because there is no one good reason or there are no particularly good reasons. This applies to the traditional *machmir* reasons offered as well as the *meikal* reasons offered by the permissive side. Let the reader judge the reasons provided by both sides. But first, as in all good legal questions, a case study is the proper place to begin.

> Jean converted to Judaism and will wed Jonathan. She has a large number of elderly guests coming to the wedding. Among whom are her Christian grandparents, one in a wheelchair. She wants to accommodate their needs, which calls for a wedding as early as possible in the evening so that they do not have to choose between staying up late or missing a part of the event. For various

RABBI DR. REEVE ROBERT BRENNER (NY64) serves Bet Chesed Congregation, Bethesda, Maryland, and is the retired Sr. Staff Chaplain of the National Institutes of Health. Among his books are *The Faith and Doubt of Holocaust Survivors; Jewish, Christian, Chewish, or Eschewish? Interfaith Marriage Pathways for the New Millennium*; and *While the Skies Were Falling: The Exodus and the Cosmos*, soon to be published; *The Jewish Bible Quarterly* has published several articles including "Ramah: Upswept, Uplifted, Upraised" (April-June 2011) from the book.

good reasons including work and vacation time, a summertime wedding is clearly advisable. Having the ceremony after the party is aesthetically a turn-off, and none of her friends who have been married recently were required to have their wedding ceremonies later, after the party and dinner. To this family, such an arrangement would be preposterous. In their minds celebrating the *simchah* event before the wedding event would turn everything planned upside down. Many guests might be somewhat inebriated and perhaps unseemly boisterous as well during the ceremony. The Jewish side of the family would spend the evening being apologetic and rather embarrassed. And Jews and Judaism would, in their words, look bad inconveniencing so many over a dubious ruling.

The wedding had to be on a Saturday night for the out-of-towners, and in that case, Sunday would be an additional opportunity to interact with loved ones who come from afar. Everyone looked upon this arrangement as a good deed for a number of specific individuals they could name and not merely as an abstraction. Sunday is a day off requiring no rush to work. Besides, all her friends, mostly Jewish, had their weddings on Saturday before sunset—every wedding at about 6 P.M. That is the custom, the *minhag*. The family feels strongly that the ceremony precede the party celebration that is intended to celebrate the marriage, and because all friends on both sides have had Saturday weddings, toward evening, they wished the same. Also important is that sleeping over after the celebration, without going to work the next day, along with travel arrangements—for some a long drive of many hours—require a Saturday night/Sunday free event, giving the family an entire weekend. Any other time would keep some family members from a distant location from coming altogether. In this matter, there was nothing frivolous or convenient or expedient; it was rather an expression of common courtesy, decency, and consideration. And love for family.

One of the reasons against Shabbat weddings is that "it's just not done." It is a habit or a *minhag* based largely if not legally on the notion that unlike other life-cycle events, a wedding, as reflected in the *ketubah*, was once a business arrangement. The *ketubah* reflected dowries of goods and cash and other financial considerations. That is not the text of the *ketubah* today. Today for Reform Judaism the language is of love, sacred bonds, covenant, relationship, commitments, and responsibilities—without reference to finances.

We learn from the *Shulchan Aruch*[1] that at one time weddings were to be conducted only on a full moon and that, we are told, was the *minhag* then. Obviously that *minhag* is no longer our *minhag* today. Red ribbons are no longer hung in a room where a woman is giving birth. Yemenite Jews living in Muslim lands still practiced polygamy into the mid-twentieth century but have given it up and not because of trouble with multiple mothers-in-law. Also ignored are other *minhagim* and rulings such as that a wedding ring must not be bejeweled. A linguist at Columbia University, John McWhorter, refers to the notion that "something that seems normal or inevitable today began with a choice that made sense at a particular time in the past, but survived despite the eclipse of the justification for that choice."[2] *Minhagim* change, often with good reason.

Moreover, it can no longer be argued that weddings on Shabbat just is not done, seeing that in the community where the couple lives, and many other communities, the custom of not conducting weddings on Shabbat does not exist; the prohibition is a thing of the past like full moon weddings. Rather, granting consent for late Shabbat weddings follows an established *minhag* with good reason, including concern for the elderly and for others who would otherwise not attend (and be separated from the community). These provide far better reasons to follow the *minhag*, the custom of late Saturday afternoon (usually 6:00 P.M.) weddings. If custom carries weight and it does according to the Talmud (we are instructed to observe and conform to the customs of the community), the *minhag* of prohibition has turned into a *minhag* of observance. And there is no question that the sanctity of Shabbat could be enhanced just as a bar and bat mitzvah and *b'rit* (and baby-naming) provide opportunity to sanctify Shabbat. A wedding on Shabbat can *become* a moment of Shabbat sanctity with a little effort and imagination. It may include conducting a creative Shabbat afternoon *Minchah* service before the wedding, should that occasion arise.

In the mainstream Reform halachic texts I consulted there is cited invariably the case of the woman who was involved in an exceptional wedding. The exception was that the rabbi, Polish Talmudist Moses Isserles, agreed to officiate late Friday night, after Shabbat began, out of economical considerations and sensitivity to the bride. This sensitivity translated itself into the working out of financial matters on her behalf. Most important, the *ketubah* was in that day and age clearly a business arrangement (among other things, to be sure) as the rabbi explained (unlike the *ketubah* in non-Orthodox use today).

Sensitivity to the feelings and needs of the bride was the justification for the leniency that allowed Rabbi Isserles to officiate on Shabbat. The rabbi did not wish to shame the girl and he therefore performed the marriage on Shabbat. The rabbi could have said, "You should have worked this out long before you came to me today. I will not officiate. Besides it is Shabbat and this is a business arrangement." He did not invoke such reasoning and wisely made things happen by way of a radical departure from tradition. His departure from tradition is notable precisely because of money matters on Shabbat. And he married the couple anyway. *Kal v'chomer*, no such consideration need deter a non-Orthodox wedding officiant inasmuch as business and finances are not reflected in the couple's *ketubah*.

All *poskim* admit that the prohibitions are not biblically based but were issued by the Rabbis. All admit, as Walter Jacob notes, that "rabbinic arguments against a marriage on Shabbat rests on weak foundations. They fall in the category which includes swimming on Shabbat as a prohibition. The rabbinic prohibition was made only to keep individuals from writing the ketubah on Shabbat or the acquisition of property."[3] There also was no question that any wedding conducted on Shabbat was to be considered valid in every sense. The *ketubot* today in Reform congregations are not business arrangements but love and marriage covenants. There are no last minute financial negotiations for a modern day Isserles to resolve.

Walter Jacob also points out that "the traditional prohibition against weddings on Shabbat in the *Shulchan Aruch* rests on foundations in the Talmudic tradition which we, as Reform Jews, no longer observe." The prohibition, Rabbi Jacob continues, rests on "weak foundations" and "technically such a marriage may reflect only a minor infringement of Shabbat."[4]

Nevertheless, Rabbi Jacob considers this "infringement of Shabbat" a "major matter." A "minor infringement" may in certain circumstances develop into a major matter, apparently. Not a few minor matters, however, continue to decline in weightiness, standing, and relevance for *K'lal Yisrael*. (One might think of the use of the *kippah* at worship and in public among Reform Jews.) Is that not the very essence of progressive Judaism?

Economic reasons also dictate consideration of Saturday weddings because if all Jewish weddings were postponed for the following day, Sunday, the impact financially would be great upon caterers, their employees, and other staff people, all of whom would find their revenues more than halved and many forced out of business including several Jewish caterers, photographers, and musicians for whom a Shabbat evening prohibition would be disastrous. It is plausibly argued that a Shabbat wedding requires work on Shabbat. It does. Rabbis also work on Shabbat. One might suggest however that this is an individual choice concerning Shabbat and *parnasah*. And we must not make decisions for others that may be causing hardship on other people's lives by compelling Shabbat observance on businesspeople and workers for whom the prohibition would impact seriously on their lives. This consideration invariably is ignored and often denounced.

Walter Jacob would prefer discouraging weddings being held even on Saturday evening for they involve preparations on Shabbat. Perhaps there is justification that such weddings be discouraged but should that influence or prevent our participation and officiation if the discouragement is outweighed by more substantial considerations, among them many valid reasons already named, especially Jewish attitudes concerning respect and regard for the needs of *nechim* and *k'shishim?* I think not.

Another reason given to discourage if not prohibit Reform rabbis from officiating at weddings before sundown is because other rabbinical bodies will look askance at our anti-traditionalism. They do so anyway. Do we not officiate at cremations? And at gatherings where nonkosher food is served? Automobiles and electricity? Disregard for the clock at other events and religious occasions? Patrilineal descent? And a large number of other Reform adjustments to reality as reflected in progressive Reform halachic traditions have become well documented by the most gifted *poskim* of our time, including Solomon Freehof, Walter Jacob, and Mark Washofsky, to whom we owe our gratitude. Moshe Zemer's book on *sh'eilot* and *t'shuvot* is, after all, entitled <u>Evolving Halakhah</u>.[5] The conclusion is inescapable that consent or capitulation to the *chidush*-become-*minhag* in the matter of twilight Shabbat weddings, considering so many other weightier *shinuyim* with which Progressive Judaism is associated, will not change the attitude of *K'lal Yisrael* on the right despite our desire, in Walter

Jacob's elegant words of *tikvah*, "to advance the unity of the Jewish people."

It has been said that when a number of reasons are provided for a ruling, it is often a sign that there is no valid reason or that reasons have to be conjured up with little justification for their existence. Such is the case in connection with weddings on Shabbat or Yom Tov.[6] The reasons are *talui al blima* (hanging on no support).

Of the five reasons Walter Jacob and the Responsa committee provide, economic considerations get the most space. Moses Isserles chose to proceed with a Shabbat Friday night *chatunah* precisely for economic considerations. On Shabbat. Also, as has been said, most importantly, Isserles agreed to officiate at a Shabbat wedding for reasons of sensitivity toward the feelings of the bride—as in the above case for the bride, Jean—saving her discomfort and embarrassment. But in truth today financial matters are not dealt with at the time of the wedding. The wedding is pure celebration, a life-cycle event like a bar/bat mitzvah. One can also argue that a bar mitzvah has financial considerations (envelopes of cash and checks) as does almost every life-cycle event. The weddings I have conducted have never been financial except to pay the bills for the wedding party—after Shabbat.

Over the some thirty years serving as rabbi in the greater Washington, D.C., community, I have come to know a number of professional Jewish wedding planners who routinely organize and run Saturday twilight (before sunset) Jewish weddings. They invariably report not an occasional wedding of Jews at twilight time but that "nearly every Shabbat is booked through the summer before sunset." The half dozen hotels and country clubs I know of must be secured as much as a year or more in advance much like a bar/bat mitzvah date at a number of large Washington synagogues. Moreover, certain Reform rabbis in the area report that they routinely officiate at such weddings. The statistics anecdotally or systematically gathered may be seen as an additional verification that while "a *minhag brecht* a *din*," many *minhagim* break down and *dinim* change as every Reform Jew knows.

It is difficult to identify a more ambiguous concept in Judaism than *minhag*. Custom, as a serious concept, suggests that there is great folk wisdom in flexibility, growth, change, and adjusting to new conditions. Jewish *minhag*, like Jewish law, does not twist with the wind or spring like a bungee cord (witness Napoleonic Jewry grappling with the emperor's requirements) but knows to bend that it not break. *Minhagim* are not written in stone. Often dissonant and divergent, they are nevertheless hardly irrelevant.

In a popular book on the teachings and practices of Judaism, entitled *A Basic Jewish Encyclopedia*, the section on "custom" by Rabbi Harry A. Cohen (under the *hechsher* of Professor Louis Finkelstein), there is this conclusion: "the *minhag*, our sages tell us, should not be lightly abolished, for it aides in preserving tradition and it strengthens solidarity. On the other hand, the *minhag* often stands in the way of necessary change and causes harmful division. Furthermore, many *minhagim* are plain superstitions. One of the greatest Jewish authorities of all time, Rabbi Jacob Tam, grandson of Rashi, opposed many *minhagim*, pointing out that the word *minhag* (mnhg), when inverted, spells *Gehinnom* (ghnm), 'hell,' and declared that 'if fools are accustomed to do certain things, it does not follow that the sensible should do likewise.'"[7]

In perhaps one of the greatest passages in all of English literature, Herman Melville in *Moby-Dick* reflects on the carcass of a whale to dilate upon entrenched but baseless *minhagim*:

Nor is this the end. Desecrated as the body is, a vengeful ghost survives and hovers over it to scare. Espied by some timid man-of-war or blundering discovery-vessel from afar, when the distance obscuring the swarming fowls, nevertheless still shows the white mast blowing in the sun, and the light spray heaving high against it; straightaway the whale's unharming corpse, with trembling fingers is set down in the log—*shoals, rocks, and breakers hereabouts: beware*! And for years afterwards, perhaps, ships shun the place; leaping over it as silly sheep leap over a vacuum, because their leader originally leaped there when a stick was held. There's your law of precedents; there's your utility of traditions; there's the story of your obstinate survival of old beliefs never bottomed on the earth, and now not even hovering in the air! There's orthodoxy! . . . Are you a believer in ghosts, my friend?

Minhagim are complicated, and determining what is and what is not a *minhag* has occasioned some of the finest rifts of Jewish humor and amusing self-derision. With good reason. It is axiomatic that—as a recent bat mitzvah youngster simplified— "Christianity tells you what to think. Judaism tells you what to do." What we do is based on both law and custom. Arriving to live in a new Jewish community, one does not say, let's find out what the community thinks and I will adjust my own thinking accordingly. Rather, we're advised to follow the local *minhagim* to know what to do. Wisely, the tradition teaches, "separate not yourself from the community." Needless to add, if a community is following a false messiah—not at all a thing of the past—or breaking Toraitic laws—the whole town including the Jews breakfast on bacon—every *posek* would undoubtedly say keep away from the place or leave at once.

As has been noted, Walter Jacob lists five reasons for Shabbat weddings prohibitions.[8] Moshe Zemer offers one.[9] Notably not included among them is the Talmudic teaching, "*ein m'arvin simcha b'simcha*"[10]—not an outright prohibition—that we not amalgamate or incorporate the observance of two mitzvot/*s'machot* and observe them simultaneously thereby diminishing the importance of each. We separate our *s'machot*. One mitzvah needs no intrusion by another. They stand alone and no *hasagat g'vul* is to be permitted without good reason.

However, no mention was made of this well-known aphorism. It is surprising that this teaching was not cited. Philosophically it ought to have been raised in the matter of Shabbat weddings, but the sources, Orthodox and Reform mentioned in this paper, do not reflect that concern. Isserles, no less or more than our Reform *poskim*, ignores the teaching in officiating at a wedding on Shabbat. The absence of evidence is a kind of evidence. Of course, we don't know how Isserles would have answered the question of overlapping mitzvot when he officiated as *m'sader kiddushin* at a Shabbat wedding. I wish he were to say, perhaps tongue in cheek, that the mitzvah of *p'ru ur'vu* precedes *sh'mor et haShabbat* in the Torah; indeed it is commanded even before the creation of Shabbat. Surely he would have said, in the not so arbitrary ranking of mitzvot, often one supersedes another. That is precisely the point being made in this article.

Furthermore, invoking that teaching and making of it a prohibition assumes doubtfully that there may be even a single guest who would otherwise be celebrating a *simchah*, performing a different mitzvah, perhaps davening *Minchah* and *Maariv* with a *minyan* or concerned with the requirements of *Motzi* Shabbat and *Havdalah*. (We therefore must also leave aside the teaching that *osek b'mitzvah patur m'mitzvah* and similar teachings.) There are no potentially conflicting mitzvah opportunities from which one would have to choose but there is, by far, the rich opportunity for a rabbi of investing the lives of scores of people with whatever forms of *kiruv* the rabbi alone knows may be best invoked given the Shabbat occasion of *simchah*.

If *minhag* is highly ambiguous, *m'arvin* is as much. In truth, the concern over *m'arvin* came to mind at once and undoubtedly crossed other minds as well, and it prompted a search for a reference by progressive *poskim* concerning the prohibition of intermingling joyous occasions among their commentaries on Shabbat weddings, but none could be found. It may also be noted that we do not expect a bar or bat mitzvah celebrant to be called to the Torah midweek on Monday or Thursday rather than Shabbat to avoid intermingling *s'machot*.

Rabbi John Sherwood points out that "It is an interesting but little known aspect of Jewish ritual history that weddings were often held on Friday afternoons in order to allow the wedding *s'udah* to take place and simultaneously be the family Shabbat dinner. This was never seen as a violation of *ein ma-arbin simchah b'simchah*."[11]

It is instructive that there were a number of occasions (Rabbeinu Tam more than once) in Jewish history that rabbinic authorities were willing to "violate" Shabbat (a Toraitic prohibition) to conduct a wedding (a rabbinic injunction). The defining term then was "violate," which does not necessarily mean that the wedding—the *nissuim* piece of the *chatunah*—brought about the "violation." Rather the *ketubah* signing and the acquisition of property constituted Shabbat violation. Today these considerations are not relevant and do not cause a violation in Reform Jewish communities. Nor do we see ourselves bound by the earlier requirements of separating the betrothal from the marriage, the *nissuim* from the *kiddushin*. Judaism always adjusts to new realities.

The relevance of the citations by Rabbi Walter Jacob concerning the High Priest who had become a widower may be seen in that he is "required" to take a wife. Even on Yom Kippur before he officiates in the Jerusalem Temple! But that priestly requirement is as questionably relevant for Jews today as is driving to a Shabbat wedding in non-Orthodox communities. The reference to the *Kohein Gadol* is important in another sense: it strongly supports the theological significance of marriage—as distinct from Catholicism's clergy for example—and undeniably the *p'ru ur'vu* mitzvah is profoundly a weighty imperative in virtually every one of these and similar considerations of weddings and marriage.

In short, it can be argued that Shabbat twilight weddings have attained the status of *minhag* (normal standard of conduct). They are no longer mere convenience. They bring families together and do not overlook the needs of the elderly and infirm and indeed other needs of the family including the heartfelt wishes of a couple to spend more time with loved ones. And this is not even bringing up the subject of determining the many different ways and procedures connected with how a Shabbat/holiday wedding may in fact be conducted to enhance rather than detract from a sacred Jewish Shabbat and festival day. For many it will be their only exposure to anything Jewish that day or any day. What else might be built upon that reality?

Should it ever occur that a couple asks a rabbi to officiate or participate in a Shabbat *morning* wedding (which has never happened in my fifty years of experience), the rabbi is obviously busy at Shabbat services but, under certain circumstances, might consider officiating during Shabbat services or directly afterwards at shul. Or if asked for a Shabbat afternoon, the rabbi might say yes or decline as have I the one time I was asked, because after services I need Shabbat rest having been on my feet if not on my toes all morning. But after *Minchah*, before sunset, after a long summer Shabbat day of rest and family and study? I'll be there for the late Shabbat *simchah*. I'll even stay awhile and do some rabbinical mingling and maybe meet someone for *kiruv*. Has happened.

Notes

1. *Yoreh Dei-ah* 179:2.
2. Quoted in David Brooks, "Tools for Thinking," *New York Times*, March 29, 2011.
3. Walter Jacob, ed., *American Reform Responsa: Jewish Questions, Rabbinic Answers* (New York: Central Conference of American Rabbis, 1983), 412–15.
4. Ibid.
5. Moshe Zemer, *Evolving Halakhah: A Progressive Approach to Traditional Jewish Law* (Woodstock, VT: Jewish Lights Publishing, 2003).
6. Jacob, *American Reform Responsa*, 412–15.
7. Rabbi Jacob Tam: Irving Agus, ed., *Teshuvot Baalay Hatosafot*, 58; *Teshuvot Maharam Mintz*, 66. Referenced in Harry A. Cohen, *A*

Basic Jewish Encyclopedia (Bridgeport, CT: Hartmore House, 1965), 113.

8. Jacob, *American Reform Responsa*, 412–15.
9. Moshe Zemer, *Evolving Halakhah*, 9–12.
10. *Mo-eid Katan* 8b.
11. Internet posting, Rav Kav, March 24, 2011.

An Eye for an Eye—Indeed!

Stephen Passamaneck

In order to be perfectly clear about what this essay is about, a preliminary word is in order. I offer my purposes and my procedure.

First, the purposes; this is not an academic exercise, bursting with footnotes and learned citations. It is rather an examination of Talmudic text, BT *Bava Kama* 83b, Mishnah and Gemara that painstakingly argues that the biblical verses, Exodus 21:22–25, the famous "eye for an eye" passage, really means pecuniary compensation rather than retaliation in kind. My purpose therefore is to demonstrate the reasoning that dismissed *lex talionis*. The Rabbis reached for what they held to be the genuine—and eternal—meaning of the text. They did not employ their interpretive skills nor their battery of hermeneutics to rewrite Scripture but rather to determine what had to be its real meaning. Whether or not we agree with their conclusions is beside the point. These ancient sages were well aware of the simple meaning of the uninterpreted biblical text, but that clear and simple meaning was not acceptable to them either as a matter of theory or a matter of practice in their real world, where they very probably did have to preside over cases of battery with injury and mayhem.

There is a second purpose as well. The second purpose is to suggest my own view of the reason why the Rabbis could not accept retaliation as the proper punishment in such cases. My argument will be from the point of view of enforcement of such a law, since a law that could not be enforced would not be much of a law. The Rabbis were not really averse to severe physical punishments as such. Over the centuries, rabbis have prescribed severe floggings, mutilations, and even death when and where they believed the circumstances required such punishments, and when and where

RABBI DR. STEPHEN PASSAMANECK (C60) is professor emeritus of Rabbinic Literature, HUC-JIR/LA.

they had the authority to impose them.[1] They were not uncomfortable with such penalties, despite modern contentions that Jewish tradition eschewed them. My suggestion or argument rests on the actual feasibility of retaliation as an option in the "real world," and the Rabbis did live in a real world when they considered cases of battery and injury. So much for my purposes.

My procedure is simply to render the Talmudic text as it unfolds and remark upon its cohesion. This will serve the first purpose. An examination of the biblical basis of "an eye for an eye" and remarks on the Rabbinic text that expresses the classic Jewish understanding of "an eye for an eye" will meet the second purpose.

Obviously "an eye for an eye" is retaliatory punishment; it is not just revenge. The punishment is the result of some sort of judicial process. Let us look at the biblical origin of the matter, Exodus 21:22–25. This passage envisions a fight between two men, in the course of which a pregnant woman is injured and shortly thereafter gives birth. If the child is born alive and well, the man who injured her shall pay a fine set by the woman's husband, and pay as the judges determine. If however, "harm" is a consequence of the injury, then the punishment is "life for life, eye for eye. . . ." Since an eye for an eye is a lawful punishment, which means there had to be some sort of judicial process to determine its applicability, we get into deeper waters.

A judicial process requires witnesses and evidence. Deuteronomy 19:15 specifies that a matter is established in court by two—or three—witnesses. The Rabbis, reviewing the biblical passage, doubtless would have assumed that proper testimony had been presented in this matter; the punishment is after all both severe and irreversible. The unsupported word of the aggrieved party would surely not have been sufficient to call for retaliatory punishment, so who were the witnesses? That is the problem.

There are various possibilities. Clearly, the encounter occurred in the presence of the others. It is hardly likely that the pregnant victim was the only witness to the fight. We should keep in mind that the family or the clan was doubtless the basic social unit of the period. Any given individual was first and foremost a member of his family and his family was a unit of his clan. The first possibility assumes that the combatants were members of the same extended family. In this situation, there is the distinct possibility that any witnesses might be related to each other in such degree that they would be ineligible to testify against their fellow family or clan member. Close relatives were excluded as witnesses in Rabbinic law. A second possibility assumes that the combatants were members of rival families or clans. In this case it is reasonable that the clan of the defendant may protect him, hide him, or facilitate his escape. Alternatively, the witnesses for both sides may be excluded because of their close relationships to the combatants. A third possibility is that members of some other family or clan witnessed that combat. In this situation there is the distinct possibility of witness intimidation. Witnesses who were also members of other families and clans might well not care to incur the enmity of the accused's family. There may be other combinations of fact that would stand in the way of securing credible witnesses, but these are sufficient to demonstrate the difficulty of eliciting testimony to condemn a person to violent and irrevocable punishment.

If the combatants were members of the same family or clan, one wonders why their fellow family members did not separate them before the injury occurred.

But let us assume that there was proper testimony available in court, the accused was not spirited away by his brethren, and the case was duly adjudicated. The accused was thus condemned to lose an eye—or tooth, hand, etc., as the case may be. In order to carry out the sentence of the court, there had to be some entity charged with the infliction of the retaliatory wound. It would hardly do to allow the wounded victim to exact the punishment. Such an agent for punishment could hardly have gone unnoticed in biblical literature, not to mention Rabbinic literature. But no such group or officer appears anywhere in any guise.

The actual enforcement of retaliatory punishment appears beset with problems. If a law cannot be enforced, it cannot serve its purpose. The notion of retaliatory punishment may appear to provide a sure and simple redress in cases of severe bodily injury, but its enforcement in its literal sense may well have not been practical.

If one simply stops to consider the difficulties in retaliatory punishment—finding the culprit, separating him or her from family and clan, the credibility of witnesses, the possibility of flight, the mode of inflicting the retaliatory injury, and the exacerbation of interfamily or interclan strife—*lex talionis* (retaliation) appears a thoroughly inefficient method of redressing wrongs.

Simply put, it just doesn't work unless there is a mechanism to make it work. It has to be enforceable, and enforceability appears to have been a difficult if not impossible task.

Finally, whether or not the infliction of retaliatory punishment would have been in the hands of a "public" or "private" authority, these punishments would have had negative social consequences. In time there would have been a more or less permanent underclass of crippled and blinded persons composed of victims, which would have been bad enough, but also of the perpetrators. Each such case would have doubled the number of persons who could no longer be fully productive. Such a system is hardly designed to right wrongs and strengthen the body politic. Retaliatory punishment does obviously provide redress, but it is negative redress. The aggressor's family or clan is weakened to the same extent that the victim's family or clan was weakened. This redress is hardly calculated to resolve antagonisms among groups.

It will not do, of course, to dismiss "an eye for an eye" as simply theoretical. The Rabbis clearly did not. People did get into fights, and those fights doubtless resulted in serious bodily injury from time to time. The legal system perforce had to deal with these situations. Thus the problem of enforcing a rule of retaliation appears to be sufficient basis for the Rabbinic jurists to assert and insist that punishment by means of inflicting crippling wounds simply never could have formed a satisfactory resolution for cases of battery with injury. An eye for an eye had to mean compensation—and never anything else.

We turn now to the text of the Mishnah and Gemara itself to see how this conclusion is argued when the biblical rule seems so clearly to the contrary. The Rabbis present argument after argument, challenging and testing each one of them. The vigor and thoroughness evident in their discussion attest to the seriousness with which the Rabbis approached the subject. After all, an "eye for an eye" seems so simple, clear, and direct; but nevertheless it had to mean compensation from its inception on Sinai.

The *Mishnah Bava Kama* 8:1 (BT *Bava Kama* 83b) asserts the rule clearly and anonymously:

> A person who severely wounds another person is liable for five things [payments]: For injury; for pain; for medical expenses; for time spent idle; for embarrassment.

Depending on the circumstances, and no doubt the findings of the court, an offender may be liable for all five payments or some lesser number of them. We contemplate serious injury, not a black eye or a bloody nose. The Mishnah now describes the particulars of each category:

1. Injury: how is this? One has blinded the eye of another, or cut off his hand; or broken his leg: We view (the victim) as if he were a slave for sale in the market. We estimate how much he had been worth and how much he is presently worth.
2. Pain: he burned (his victim) with a metal spit or a (metal) nail, even (if only) on a finger nail, a place where no (permanent) wound (is caused thereby). We estimate how much a person of equal standing would be willing to accept to suffer such a wound.
3. Medical expenses: If one injured another, the injurer is liable for medical expenses (incurred by his victim). If the victim developed ulcerations because of the wound the injurer is (also) liable for the medical expense (to heal them), if they occurred for some other reason, he is not liable. If the wound partially healed, broke down, partially healed, and broke down again, the injurer is still liable for all those medical expenses. If the wound healed completely and then broke down, there is no (further) liability for medical expenses.
4. Time spent idle. We view the victim as if he were a watchman of a cucumber field. (He is reimbursed for his idleness on that basis.) He has already given him the value of his hand or his leg.
5. Embarrassment. This is assessed according to the status of the person causing the embarrassment and the person embarrassed.

Rashi ad loc comments on the matter of embarrassment that a man of inferior standing who "embarrasses" a person of higher station causes a greater embarrassment since the person of higher rank suffers more from such a public insult. No one actually describes what such an embarrassing wound might be. It seems to me however that it is reasonable to suggest that it involved a permanent scar or disfigurement that would always be visible. This would include a facial scar that involved a blinded eye, or stumps of fingers, and the like. The *M'chilta* (ed. Lauterbach, *Neziqin*) to this passage mentions that Scripture contemplates a wound that is visible, exposed to view, a constant and unpleasant reminder of the encounter; a scar on an area of skin that would not ordinarily be visible would carry far less public embarrassment.

We now move on to the Gemara. The intricate reasoning that carried the day for payment rather than retaliation involves more than one line of reasoning. I have amplified the terseness of the original text in order to achieve clarity and accuracy in modern English.

Gemara: Why should the Mishnah demand payments? Does not the Bible speak of retaliation—"an eye for an eye?" I should say the rule requires an actual eye! Do not let this enter your mind! A *baraita* has asserted: one may possibly think that if "A" has blinded "B's" eye, "A's" eye should be blinded; if "A" has cut off "B's" hand, "A's" hand should be amputated; if "A" has broken "B's" leg, "A's" leg is to be broken! Scripture however teaches, "one strikes an animal . . . one strikes a man" (Leviticus 24) just as in the former case the penalty is pecuniary compensation, so, too, in the latter case, pecuniary compensation is called for rather than retaliation.

Precisely which verse in Leviticus 24 is in point will come up in the course of the argument. The Gemara now opens a second line of argument. Both arguments will eventually be assessed and each will be found flawed in some respect. The arguments in combination will be more compelling. The Gemara states: If you wish you may say as follows: the Bible says (Num. 35:31), "you shall take no ransom money for the life of a murder who is condemned to capital punishment." The implication therefore is that you take no ransom for the life of a murderer, but you *do* take such ransom as punishment for injury to the principal limbs that do not regenerate. Thus we have payment and not retaliation for bodily injury.

The implication drawn here may or may not be altogether sound. To argue that since you may not do X, does not necessarily mean you may do Y. No matter, it sufficed for the Rabbis: one does not ransom a murderer—implying one may exact "ransom" for bodily injury.

The Gemara now reverts to the matter of Leviticus 24. (It may be useful to have a Bible at one's elbow at this point!) The word *makeh* (smites) occurs several times in Leviticus 24; which occurrence is in point in this matter? One might suggest Leviticus 24:21, "one who *smites* an animal with deadly force shall make it good; one who *smites* a person with deadly force shall be put to death." This suggestion is rejected; the smiting here refers to a murderer not a wounder. Rather, it is next suggested, the verse in point is Leviticus 24:18 in combination with Leviticus 24:19: "One who *smites* and kills an animal shall make it good—life for life," which is immediately followed by, "If a man shall *give* serious *injury* to his fellow, as he did, so shall it be done to him." The fact that the retaliation noted in verse 20 is the clear sense of Scripture does not weigh at all with the Rabbis. They are intent on demonstrating an air-tight case for payment. But they do have a problem with this latter verse—the word *smite* does not appear in it, and *smite* was the crucial term in Leviticus 24:18. The matter does not delay them for long. The word in verse 19 is *mum* (a serious injury, a crippling deformity). Such is the *result* of a smiting. Therefore there is sufficient identity of meaning so that as the *smiting* with reference to the animal is a matter of payment, so too, the *mum*, the obvious result of "*smiting*," may properly be understood as a matter of payment, not retaliation.

There is yet another biblical hurdle for the Rabbis to leap in their argument against retaliation and for payment in cases of injury. There is Leviticus 24:17: "The man who shall *smite* any human being (and cause death!) shall be put to death." Since this verse is followed by verse 18 (with the interruption of the part of verse 18 concerning an animal), the Rabbis conclude that verse 17 does not treat of murder. That is covered in verse 21. Therefore it must concern severe injury, something less than murder, and the "death" mentioned would refer to the body part destroyed as a retaliation! The Gemara brusquely declares that this apparent reference to retaliation is an incorrect understanding: injury is redressed by money! This assertion is not immediately accepted: Why say money? Why not actual retaliation? The answer follows immediately: Do not think that way! For one thing, injury to a person is compared to an injury to an animal, which is redressed by pecuniary compensation; and further, immediately afterwards (i.e., verses 18, 19, and 20) " as he would give serious injury to a person so shall it be given to him." The element of "it be given" appears at the end of 24:20. One understands the language of "give" to mean pecuniary compensation—and nothing else.

The Gemara then raises another question. If this interpretation of Scripture just concluded is a sound basis for rejecting retaliation, what then is the necessity for the second line of argument based on Numbers 35:31? The answer follows in short order. The reason is that the tannaitic authority had the following problem: Why should a matter involving human beings not be derived from a case (murder) similarly involving human beings, where retaliation would be required? The immediate answer is that cases involving damages should be derived from other cases involving damages and not from a capital matter. The argument is then turned around—on the contrary, asserts an anonymous voice, one should derive matters involving human beings from other matters involving human beings—not animals!

Both points are well taken. One may argue that it is better to examine a case of damage in the light of other cases of damage. Or one may argue that laws involving human beings are of a different level from laws involving animals, and the debate should be defined by the rules concerning human activity. The former path leads to compensation; the latter, to retaliation. Therefore the second argument based on Numbers 35:31, which deals only with persons, became necessary in order to cure the fault in the "man–animal" line of reasoning.

The Gemara now closely examines this Numbers 35:31 argument. If you wish you may say as follows: "You shall take no ransom for the life of a murderer who is condemned to capital punishment, but he shall surely die." You shall take no ransom for the life of a murderer, but you do take ransom for injury to principal limbs that do not regenerate. A further question is raised. Was this provision about no ransom for a murderer asserted to rule out retaliation for principal limbs; or is its point rather to rule out a double punishment: the exaction of a pecuniary penalty as well as death? It cannot bear both meanings. (There is much historical precedent for the estate of a person put to death by the authorities to revert to the state, or the ruler.) The Gemara responds that this latter provision—no double punishment—is derived from a part of Deuteronomy 25:2, "according to his wickedness." The person receives only one punishment commensurate with the crime and not a double punishment of any sort. Then someone raises another challenge to the interpretation of it as compensation for limbs: Perhaps the verse is to eliminate the possibility that the murderer might pay a ransom and regain his freedom! The answer is framed in classic style: If that were the point of the verse, it should have read, "You shall not take ransom for one who is to suffer capital punishment;" but there is an additional phrase in the verse and what then is the point of the additional "for the life of the murderer?" The point of this phrase is understood to underscore the rule against ransom for a murderer only, thus allowing the positing of a pecuniary payment for the loss of a principal limb.

The Gemara now understands this second argument to be well founded and on point. If, then, this argument from Numbers is good, what need was there for the argument based on the smiting of the animal and the smiting of a person? This challenge is answered by the proposition that on the basis of non-ransom for the murderer but ransom for principal limbs, one might argue that a person had a choice: he could part with his physical eye or tooth or tender the value of that eye or tooth, but the argument based on the smiting of the animal leaves no such leeway. The punishment is pecuniary, and the offender must pay. The two principal arguments against physical retaliation have now been presented and tested. As far as the Rabbis are concerned, they are both sound and both necessary. One loose end, however, will be tied up in the course of the arguments that now follow.

The Gemara next presents a series of alternate arguments against physical retaliation. Most of them are refuted or dismissed. They all are, however, secondary to the main argument we have reviewed. One senses that there was a powerful impulse to argue away even the thought of physical retaliation.

The first alternate argument is a *baraita* in the name of R. Dostai b. Judah.[2] His argument is that an "eye for an eye" must mean pecuniary compensation because eyes may be of different sizes! If so, it would be improper to take an eye of one size for an eye of a different size. If in such a case however the law would allow the substitution of pecuniary compensation for retaliation, we have to reckon with the principle that Scripture requires *one single law to govern all such cases*. We cannot allow one type of punishment, payment, to obtain in one case of blinding an eye and yet allow a retaliation in another case of blinding an eye. This argument is rejected. One should obviously argue that eyesight must be taken in recompense; not the eye, but eyesight was taken—that is the point! The size of the organ is irrelevant—eyesight is what matters. This objection is supported by reference to a case in which a person of small physical stature kills a person of large physical stature and becomes liable for a capital penalty. That penalty applies irrespective of the sizes of the assailant and the victim—the law has to apply equally to all persons. Therefore if a life is taken, a life becomes forfeit—so, too, in the case of eyesight. Thus, this attempt fails to provide any basis for compensation over retaliation.

The Gemara cites another *baraita,* this time in the name of R. Simeon b. Yohai.[3] The *baraita* proposes the case of a blind man who blinded another man, or a man with one hand who severed the arm of another man, or a crippled man who cut off the leg of another man. In this sort of situation how would retaliation occur? We must abide by the rule that one law, one punishment, must apply in all such cases: an eye for an eye. Pecuniary compensation thus appears the better course. This attempted argument is also rejected. The counterargument runs that where it is possible to apply physical retaliation, it is applied; but where it is impossible, as in the cases adduced, it is not applied and the assailant goes free! This counterargument is supported by reference to the *treifah* (a person who is dying from some fatal disease). The Talmud asserts (BT *Sanhedrin* 78a) that if such a person commits murder, he is not to be executed for that crime—he is already as it were under a death sentence. So we see that where it is possible to inflict a retaliation, it may be inflicted; but where it is not, the offender goes free. There is thus no valid argument here to support compensation over retaliation.

There follows next another argument to support pecuniary compensation. This argument appears somewhat more substantial. The school of R. Ishmael[4] taught that the element "thus shall it be given to him" (Lev. 24:20) indicates pecuniary compensation for injury. But, it is immediately responded, what of the element in the first part of that verse, "as he would *give* an injury"—certainly this use of the verb *ntn* (give) need not refer only to payment? Surely we have retaliation! This apparent contradiction is resolved by claiming that the school of R. Ishmael expounded an apparently "superfluous" element in the biblical text.

One of the elements in Rabbinic interpretation of Scripture is that no word or letter of biblical text is in fact superfluous. Any material that appears to be so is actually present to bear a particular interpretation. In this case Leviticus 24:19 appears to cover the matter of severe bodily injury entirely and indicate retaliation; what then is the purpose of the end of 24:20? That appears to be an unnecessary element, and therefore available for the interpretation of pecuniary compensation rather than retaliation. The presence of both clauses has finally been justified: Since it was necessary to assert the apparently superfluous element, Scripture has also stated the previous clause (24:19) that mentions the injury. This reasoning may appear artificial, but it is wholly consonant with Rabbinic canons of biblical interpretation.[5] The Rabbis had their own rules for deciding what texts meant, and they were quite scrupulous in adhering to them. For the Rabbis, this argument was valid for the proposition that pecuniary compensation was the proper punishment for bodily injury.

The school of R. Hiyya[6] advances yet another argument in favor of compensation. The school of R. Hiyya expounded the words "hand in hand" in Deuteronomy 19:21 as indicating pecuniary compensation: something given from hand into hand, which is, of course, payment. The response to this suggestion is immediate: what then is the purpose of "foot for foot" which follows "hand for (in) hand?" Surely money does not pass by foot, and so does not one have to fall back on the explanation of retaliation rather than compensation? This objection is also met with assertion of an apparently "superfluous" biblical term that is available for the necessary interpretation of compensation rather than retaliation. The argument runs like this: The Bible is here addressing the matter of the "scheming witness" (Deut. 19:19–22) who lied in his testimony, thus scheming to have the accused held guilty. If, so the argument goes, actual retaliation is the correct punishment for injury, why then does Scripture continue and state "hand for hand, foot for foot," etc.? Does the text not already state he is to receive the punishment he "schemed" to inflict on the accused? The element "hand for hand" that appears shortly after in Deuteronomy is thus superfluous and available for the interpretation of compensation! A final query is posed: Why then do we also have the element "foot for foot"? The argument disposes of this point by characterizing "foot for foot" as only a stylistic element; since Scripture states "hand for hand," it also added "foot for foot." The argument therefore remains substantially sound. Another support for compensation is registered.

The *Amora* Abaye[7] presents the argument of the tannaitic school of Hezekiah. The biblical text requires an eye for an eye, but not an eye and a life for an eye. It may well happen that in the course of physically destroying his eye, the culprit would die of the injury! Compensation is a far better option. This argument is rejected rather brutally. The guilty party should be physically examined just as those subject to floggings are physically examined, as specified in the third chapter of *Mishnah Makot*. If the person is judged strong enough to endure a retaliatory injury, it should be inflicted; and if not, the injury should not be inflicted. If the culprit is deemed hardy enough to endure the physical punishment, and he nonetheless dies of it, well, then, he dies! We have learned in *Mishnah Makot* 3:14 that if a person judged strong enough for a flogging nevertheless dies of it, the court officer wielding the lash is not liable for any offense. Let the miscreant die, if that should be his fate—retaliation is the proper punishment for his offense. We have before us a clear, if rather rare, case of indifference to severe suffering. We may not be pleased with its tone and intent, but it is the Rabbinic view of the matter. The forces for compensation do not, of course, yield to this line of reasoning.

The text next reviews two rather indirect arguments in favor of some compensation and rejects both of them. In the first R. Zebid[8] in the name of Rabbah proposes that the Bible (Exod. 21:25) states "wound for wound" to establish that an additional payment is given for the pain caused by the injury. This is clearly put in the Mishnah that initiated this entire exposition. The argument proceeds with the observation that if actual retaliation is required, then both parties are in pain. One is justified then to believe that there need be no separate payment for pain. The theory behind the suggestion here however is that people differ in their sensitivity to pain; some hurt more than others from the same sort of wound. This is the concept behind the payment for pain. The Mishnah has already indicated as much in its description of how the pain payment is calculated. Since there is this disparity, a pain payment may be assessed even in the case of actual retaliation. The amount of payment represents the difference between what "A" would take for suffering such a wound and what "B" would accept for the pain of the same injury. The presumption is, of course, that the amounts are unequal. The injured party would receive the difference between the amounts as payment for pain. Retaliation is thus no bar to a pain payment, and no case for payment over retaliation is established. There is no mention of how the amounts might be kept within reasonable bounds. "A" might demand a large amount to suffer such pain; "B" might demand even more!

R. Papa[9] in the name of Rova advances the same sort of argument for payment of medical bills in the case of retaliation. The argument is rejected just as the pain payment argument was. Since people heal at different rates, and presumably have doctor bills in differing amounts, the theory is that even if retaliation is the mode of punishment the difference between the medical bills should be payable to the victim. There is therefore no credible argument from either the pain payment or the medical payment to rule out retaliation.

The last argument, however, finally and fully upholds the Mishnaic rule of compensation rather than retaliation. R. Ashi[10] presents the case: The term *tahat* (understood as meaning "for") is the basis of the interpretation. The word *tahat* appears with reference to the injured animal (Exod. 21:36); and we also have it in Exodus 21:24 "an eye for, *tahat*, an eye." Therefore the context of money payment may legitimately be transferred from the case of the ox to the case of the eye, a simple *g'zerah shavah*. The objection is then raised that there is no real basis for deriving the meaning from the case of the ox when Exodus 21:23, in the immediate context of the "eye for an eye," speaks of a "life for a life" so that actual retaliation is as sound an interpretation as compensation. This challenge is met with an argument previously raised: Cases of injury should be interpreted on the basis of other cases of injury, not on the basis of homicide, which is a whole different category. The answer to this point is also the same one we have already seen: On the contrary, one should interpret cases involving human beings on the basis of other cases involving human beings, which in this instance supports retaliation. The arguments are of equal validity. R. Ashi cuts the Gordian knot. He cites the case of the rape of the unmarried virgin (Deut. 22:29). The rapist is to pay the victim's father forty silver shekels *tahat* (for) "he has raped her." We thus have a case of *tahat* in the context of both an injury to a human being and in the context of money payment. The "eye *tahat* the eye" may then justifiably be understood as payment on the basis of the *gerzah shavah* comparison, with the money *tahat* the rape. Compensation has finally carried the day. There are no further attempts to offer alternate explanations or justifications of compensation rather than retaliation. The point has been made.

The Gemara concludes this extensive discussion with the resolution of one final troublesome matter. The *Tanna* R. Eliezer[11] appears to favor retaliation rather than compensation. He says an eye *tahat* an eye, actually! The Gemara is thunderstruck: Does he then stand against all his fellows? Rabbah (or perhaps Rova) says that R. Eliezer means that the estimation of the person's limb to determine the amount of compensation is not made as though he were a slave, which seems to contradict the Mishnah. Abaye counters with the question, how then should the estimation (for compensation, of course) be conducted? By the valuation of the limbs of a free man?! A free human being is not subject to valuation! R. Ashi again resolves the difficulty. The valuation is made of the eye of the culprit, not of the injured person. That is, an *actual* eye is valued, the existing eye of the offending party, in order to determine the amount of compensation due. R. Eliezer does not disagree with the others. He only specifies the method of assessment in a rather cryptic and confusing fashion.

The Rabbis argued long and hard over a period of centuries to establish the principle that the scriptural demand of an eye for an eye really meant compensation not retaliation. We cannot know why these Rabbis expended so much time and energy on the matter. It is hardly likely that they were indulging in mere intellectual games. The proper interpretation of Scripture was a task they look quite seriously. Further, whether or not these discussions reflect any actual experience with bodily injury and compensation cannot be ascertained. Surely the Rabbis did have to decide cases in which "A" injured "B." The propositions that one person is more sensitive to pain than another and one person heals more rapidly than another may be vague hints of cases actually decided.

What seems to be really at stake here is an enduring effort to combat a natural human desire for retaliation. After all, the expression "an eye for an eye" is a simple, direct, easily comprehended formula for dealing with offenders. It has an undeniable appeal for the wounded party. All that notwithstanding, such a formula undermines civil society. It is moreover incredibly difficult to administer in any but a brutal and repressive society. I have already adverted to these difficulties and to the fact that there appears to be no officer under Jewish law who was ever charged with performing mutilations. The court's flogger of *Mishnah Makot* chapter 3 discharged his duties under strict rules; and flogging, as brutal as it is, does not rise to the level of brutality inherent in the phrase "an eye for an eye." The Rabbis ever and again insisted that Scripture ever and always meant compensation rather than retaliation. This insistence appears to be a testament to their grasp of just what civilized society demands of it members, to their humanity, and to their devoted efforts to render the penal provisions of Scripture workable in their world.

Notes

1. See Stephen Passamaneck, *Modalities in Medieval Jewish Law for Public Order and Safety* (Cincinnati: Hebrew Union College Supplements, no. 6, 2009.)
2. R. Dostai b. Jehudah, a contemporary of Judah Hanasi. He transmitted traditions of R. Simeon b. Yohai.
3. R. Simeon b. Yohai, latter second century C.E.
4. R. Ishmael, roughly 120–160. His school argued against the rulings of R. Akiba.
5. Moses Meilziner, *Introduction to the Talmud*, 4th rev. ed. (New York: Bloch Publishing Co., 1967). This classic is still an excellent primer on the techniques and terminology of Rabbinical argumentation.
6. R. Hiyya, a Babylonian scholar who moved to Israel. He was a friend of Judah Hanasi.
7. Abaye, a Babylonian *Amora*, third to fourth century; he was a nephew of Rabbah b. Nahmani.
8. R. Zebid, fourth century Babylonian *Amora*.
9. R. Papa, Babylonian *Amora*, died ca. 375. He was a pupil of both Abaye and Rava.
10. R. Ashi, Babylonian *Amora*, d. 427. He headed the academy at Sura for fifty-two years and is traditionally associated with the compilation of the Babylonian Talmud.
11. R. Eliezer (b. Hyrcanus), a contemporary of R. Akiba, with whom he debated; second century, Israel.

Eric Bram: A Portrait of a Rabbi as an Educational Visionary

Samuel K. Joseph and Jeffrey Schein

In the literature on Jewish educational change, the role of the rabbi is generally assumed to be critical, yet the exact nature of that role is arguable. Some view strong rabbinic leadership as the sine qua non of meaningful educational change.[1] Others view the rabbi as a likely but not the only possible source of an idea champion that will provide the senior leadership for an educational change project.[2] In this view, strong lay leaders and educational directors may serve that role as well.

The authors of this article will leave it to Elijah of blessed memory to resolve the *kushiot* (the conceptual and valuational clashes) between these two points of view. We more modestly have been presented with an opportunity to etch a portrait of a friend and colleague, Rabbi Eric Bram, *zichrono livrachah.*

Eric died in August 2010 after a yearlong battle with brain cancer. Each of the authors had an opportunity to work with Eric deeply on educational change and transformation at Suburban Temple–Kol Ami (ST-KA), where Eric served as rabbi from 2002–2010. Yet, we are not the only voices present in the article, as we have interviewed the professional staff and congregants of ST-KA as well as community educational professionals in Cleveland.

We have titled this article "a portrait" of rabbinic leadership. In keeping with the spirit of portraiture as a genre of educational research, we have tried to provide some of the details and the texture of Eric's work. While comfortable drawing from the literature on congregational and educational change, ultimately what we

SAMUEL K. JOSEPH (C76) is professor of Jewish Education and Leadership Development, HUC-JIR, Cincinnati.

JEFFREY SCHEIN is professor and director of the program in Jewish Education at Siegal College in Cleveland.

have tried to accomplish is as much an act of channeling from our personal affection for Eric our appreciation for his ability to touch Jewish human beings in such a profound way.

Even our own channeling is selective. We have thought it wise to provide multiple perspectives on Eric's work as an educational and congregational leader. We first describe the authors' connections as consultants to two linked projects of educational change and transformation spearheaded by Eric. The projects and Eric's critical role within them are presented chronologically, first the work of educational visioning of 2004–2006 in which Jeffrey Schein was the principal consultant and then the work of Sam Joseph with Eric on a Legacy Heritage Grant from 2006–2008. We also locate these achievements within the literature on congregational and educational change.

We then turn to the voices and perspectives of congregants who were the intimate partners and/or beneficiaries of these changes. Finally, we embrace the wisdom of Rabbi Tarfon: It was not Eric's responsibility to complete all of his work (even with the gift of better health and a longer tenure at ST-KA). We ask ourselves, given the powerful beginning to this work, what remains to be done to complete the transformational journey.

Eric Bram and Educational Visioning at Suburban Temple—Kol Ami

(Jeffrey Schein)

In June 2004, following the publication of *Visions of Jewish Education*,[3] I was invited by the Mandel Foundation to be part of a small group of professors of Jewish education who shared a common interest in exploring the importance of vision for the philosophy of contemporary Jewish education. Of the various professors I was given the unofficial "honor" of being the liaison to synagogue education. At first blush, the implications of the vision book for academics and policy makers was clearer than for synagogue education.

Shortly thereafter, I was fortunate enough to find a willing partner in this attempt to move from vision to congregational education in Rabbi Eric Bram of ST-KA, who had arrived at the congregation only two years prior and was interested in working on this process with me. Suburban Temple–Kol Ami, a classical Reform congregation, was already undergoing many changes in its historical commitment to the classical mode of Reform Judaism. Eric himself was a harbinger of more profound change.

Eric saw in my invitation to launch a congregational visioning project at ST-KA an opportunity to move forward his own agenda of becoming a congregation of learners. I believe he also saw the visioning process as a lever for changes well beyond the narrower purview of the congregation's education program. The ultimate fruit of this effort was congregational leadership and governance as well as education.

Eric convened a diverse group of twenty congregational professionals, teachers, and lay leaders to explore the visioning process. Sixteen of the participants committed to a six-session, twelve-hour seminar to craft the educational vision. This committee included the education chairperson, the vice president for Jewish education, teachers, youth leaders, several past presidents, the synagogue administrator, as well as the congregation's rabbi, principal, and family educator. The vision was completed during the first six months of 2005 and was approved by the board of directors of the synagogue in fall 2005. It was critical to test the vision by translating it into educational practice, which in turn resulted in innovations that provided deeper understanding of the vision itself, an iterative process that extended over several years and in some real ways is still ongoing.

By 2007, sophisticated professional development in relationship to Israel and teen education had taken place in collaboration with the Jewish Education Center of Cleveland. A faculty trip to Israel designed to galvanize the focus on Israel connection as a major educational goal had taken place. In retrospect, the trip to Israel was one barometer of how much change Eric and others had succeeded in introducing, as the synagogue itself had been organized seventy years before, in part as a protest to the overemphasis on Zionism of a larger Reform congregation (led by Abba Hillel Silver).

As the community consultant and vision coach for this process, I came to appreciate three particular aspects of Eric's leadership. Firstly, during the six sessions of study that informed the vision, Eric did remarkable *tzimtzum* (contraction) of the authority he might have otherwise exercised. He was a quiet but very present participant in the study. I believe this reflected two phenomena. In general, it was another manifestation of his style of empowerment of congregants that runs throughout this article. In several other congregations where I led a visioning process, the rabbi insisted on having the last word on the vision itself. Eric did not.

I think this posture also reflected Eric's political astuteness. Why not let an outsider (me!) absorb the brunt of any strong reaction to radical ideas that might be introduced? I could play the role of educational prophet. Eric was shrewd enough to know that his best role here was one of educational priest, overseeing the advocacy for and management of the vision.

I was also struck by how deeply and seriously Eric treated challenging ideas from the study. The group spent several sessions studying an article by Michael Meyer on the educated Reform Jew from *Visions of Jewish Education*.[4] One phrase seemed to penetrate Eric's educational core. Meyer argued that the much-vaunted value of earlier generations of Reform Judaism of "autonomy" was improperly placed at the beginning of the educational process. In fact, it was a later function of exercising critical judgment once one had moved inside the "circle of Jewish living and learning."

For Eric this meant something as abstract as a more contemporary way of thinking about Jewish identity formation and something as concrete as standing at the doorway of the synagogue on Sunday morning to greet parents and children so that they might know quite explicitly that they were being initiated into a sacred circle of learning and community.

Finally, I believe Eric's greatest gift as an educational visionary was his absolute willingness to measure the real life of the congregation by the vision. I will always remember one of our meetings at Starbucks in 2006. Eric and Debbie (the educational director and Eric's wife) were meeting with me to discuss next steps in the implementation of the vision. They both were pleased with the efforts over the past several months to make the educational vision visible through attractive copies of the vision placed in each classroom. Near the temple office hung a blown-up version of the vision inviting congregants to sign the document as if it were a *ketubah* pledging covenantal loyalty to one another.

There was only one problem Eric confessed at the meeting. There was no Hebrew in the *ketubah* even though knowledge of the Hebrew language was one of the prominent educational goals in the vision. With a characteristic mixture of self-effacing humor and serious reflection Eric reminded himself (Debbie and myself as well) of how far ST-KA had to journey before the vision was half as real as we would like.

Building Community at Suburban Temple–Kol Ami
(Sam Joseph)

My connection to Eric and ST-KA became official in summer 2006. Suburban Temple–Kol Ami received a legacy grant and hired me to be the educational process person helping them implement the project portion of the grant. The project—empowering ST-KA families to "do" Jewish things and live out their Judaism without needing professionals to do this for them—came directly out of the vision crafted by the congregants of ST-KA. To understand the vision behind the project (and in a certain sense the vision behind the vision) one needs a deeper appreciation of the nature of transformational leadership

Steven Covey once wrote, "The goal of transformational leadership is to 'transform' people and organizations in a literal sense—to change them in mind and heart; enlarge vision, insight, and understanding; clarify purposes; make behavior congruent with beliefs, principles, or values; and bring about changes that are permanent, self-perpetuating, and momentum building."[5]

Transformational leadership is a concept that is becoming so overused in Jewish circles that it is losing its meaning. Every leader of a synagogue, professional or lay, claims to be transformational in his or her practice. This causes us to believe that the institutions they lead are transformed. This is probably not so by a long shot.

It was James McGregor Burns, in the 1970s, who made the contrast between transactional leadership, which is leadership power over followers who are motivated by rewards and punishments, and transformational leadership, which can be characterized as a process where leader and followers work together in a way that changes or transforms the organization, the followers, and the leader.

The heart of transformational leadership is the leader's desire and ability to raise the consciousness of others by appealing to powerful moral values and ideals. The leader is able to transform followers beyond the dishonorable emotions of jealousy, greed, and fear to higher principles of liberty, justice, and humanitarianism.

As Burns would say, the followers are raised from their "everyday selves" to become "better selves." Transformational leaders influence followers by serving as a teacher, mentor, and coach. They seek to elevate and empower others to a higher level. Transformational leaders can be found within any organization and at any level in the organization. This is a leader that can influence superiors, peers, or subordinates.[6]

In the synagogue world, transformational leaders are trying to transform synagogues, so transforming synagogues is itself a hot topic and has been on the front burner for synagogue leaders for over twenty years. It is driven by a desire for the synagogue, especially in the non-Orthodox world, to be fully engaging in the midst of a pervasive popular culture that is so secular and overwhelmingly individualistic.

How do synagogues transform themselves from "limited liability institutions to sacred communities; from shuls with schools to congregations of learners; from having clergy who make hospital visits to having congregants who visit one another; from having a small and somewhat beleaguered social action committee (or no social action committee at all) to joining a city-wide social justice coalition that engages a broad range of congregants"?[7]

The role of the rabbi is vital towards transforming a synagogue, so the rabbi must be, by definition, a transformational leader. And the goal of the rabbi, working in full partnership with lay leadership, is a transformed synagogue.

In the stereotypical synagogue, the rabbi has much-ascribed authority. Congregants assume that the rabbi's words are powerful. Congregants assume that the rabbi is the chief leader, the boss of the congregation. It is assumed that the rabbi, possibly along with the president of the congregation, sets the priorities of the synagogue. Nothing of consequence may occur inside the congregation without the rabbi's full agreement.

In the transformed synagogue, the rabbi is not the sole carrier of the values, vision, and program of the congregation. As a transformational leader, the rabbi with his or her congregational leader partners promotes values and vision. The empowered congregants carry the program.

Ultimately, to use the typology of the authors of *Sacred Strategies*, it means not what may be called a functional congregation, but creating and sustaining a visionary congregation.[8]

Functional congregations are just that, functional. They are not necessarily places of tension, anxiety, deficit budgets, and rotating staff. Yet they are especially passive, with professional staff determining direction and doing all the work, resistant to change, and have leaders who are more interested in program than purpose or vision.

The visionary congregation is extremely participatory on all levels and is characterized by leadership, professional and lay, who are highly reflective. The rabbi and the leadership carefully consider details, alternatives, relationships, and a planful approach to change. Purpose and vision are very highly prized.

Suburban Temple–Kol Ami was clearly a functional synagogue. In 2002 Rabbi Eric Bram arrived, following a long-serving rabbi. Tom Galvin, search committee member and soon to be president of the congregation, reports, "Eric came with a vision for ST-KA in mind. Transforming the congregation to an engaging, vibrant, participatory congregation was core to that vision. Eric felt it was important and necessary. The timing could not have been better because we were ready."

Interestingly, what does Galvin mean when he says ST-KA was ready for a rabbi with a vision? Tom says, "We were a perfect match. As a congregation, we had a history of educational outreach, but there was little enthusiasm within the congregation. Eric believed that congregants should own their congregation. He did not believe that the rabbi owned it. So Eric created an open process where all congregants contributed to the emerging vision. He made the process simple. He led from behind and cheered us on."

Within this framework of transformational leadership one can then see the intentions of the work I began to do with Eric through the Legacy Heritage Grant.

"Neighborhoods" became the ST-KA way to create empowered congregants. Congregants were encouraged to organize themselves into groups of five or more families. The organizing principle was based on a number of variables such as geographic proximity to one another or a common situation in life such as the *b'nei mitzvah* year, empty nester, family with young children, or retired. Then each of these family groupings would be called an ST-KA Neighborhood.

It may be instructive to view the text of the ST-KA invitation to congregants to learn about the Neighborhoods. It was authored by Rabbi Bram and the educator, Debbie Bram, his wife:

Are you: An empty-nester? Intermarried? A single parent? A family celebrating a Bat/Bar Mitzvah this coming year? Gay or Lesbian? Living on the West side of Cleveland? A family with young and/or adopted children? Retired? A newly married couple without children?

Do you enjoy: Discussing current events? Studying Torah? Volunteering to help those in need? Making matzah ball soup? Reading Jewish books? Jewish Travel?

Would you like: The opportunity to meet new Temple friends? In-home get-togethers to share, celebrate, learn, and grow with other Suburban Temple–Kol Ami families?

We are looking to create new neighborhoods of Suburban Temple–Kol Ami families who have similar family situations and/or interests. Are you curious?

We will offer these options and more, depending upon your interests—please feel free to attend and bring your own organizing ideas!

Suburban Temple–Kol Ami invites you to your Neighborhood Open House

Notice the thrust of the language: diversity, empowerment, freedom, decentralization, and not lead by the rabbi. All are characteristics of a visionary synagogue. The language and the sentiment represent a thrust toward a transformation of the way ST-KA functioned heretofore. Visionary learning was the keystone to Rabbi Bram's vision for a transformed ST-KA. The congregation could not be a place of pediatric Judaism if it was to be a force in people's lives, cradle to grave. ST-KA needed to be a community of empowered adult members who owned their Jewish lives and would not cede them to professionals. ST-KA needed to be a congregation of learning for its own sake, connecting Torah to members' lives, weaving learning into all activities.[9]

In an early step towards realizing the vision, Eric created a Torah study group and an adult *b'nei mitzvah* program. He knew that the congregation seriously needed cadres of learned and learning Jews if members were to own their Judaism in order to "do Jewish." Members had to become the force in the congregation driving all levels of learning.

Fairly rapidly the Torah study group became popular. The huge library table was filled body close to body. With the table seating filled, people took seats on the periphery. It was a crowded room. With bibles spread open, Eric would bring people to the passage being studied and then the discussions and debates began. The time flew by each week. People loved the study and the interaction. According to Tom Galvin, "Eric taught us that Jewish learning was not a mountain to climb but a flat land to traverse."

Grass Roots Perspectives: Interviews with Cleveland Jewish Educators and Suburban Temple– Kol Ami Staff and Lay Leaders

(Jeffrey Schein)

In fall 2010, I conducted three different interviews with people who had worked closely with Eric on one or more of these educational projects:

> Group 1: Amnon Ophir, Judith Schiller, and Nachama Moskowitz of the Jewish Education Center of Cleveland;
> Group 2: Debbie Bram, education director of ST-KA and Lisa Kollins, family educator;
> Group 3: Barbara Feldman, Eileen Kollins, and Laura Berick, lay leaders from ST-KA who were also active participants in the Shabbat morning Torah study Eric had initiated.

I also received a written reflection from Kathy Klein, a member of the study group. Kathy is an early childhood educator who is pursuing her master's degree in Jewish education at Siegal College. Not Jewish by birth, she had studied with Eric to become a Jew.

What follows is a composite picture derived from these interviews. I begin and end with anecdotes from the interviews. In the middle, I try to insert my own sense of the totality of the interviews into perspectives about adult learning and growth.

Perhaps my strongest overall impression is summarized by a Talmudic quotation offered by one of the interviewees. From *B'rachot* 27b–28a: "Any student whose inside is not like his outside should enter the house of study." In the end, everyone seems to agree that Eric's deep humanity was the most essential building block of his style of educational leadership. To quote another Talmudic insight: "if a sage speaks one way and acts another it is better if he had not been born into the world"; a lack of congruence between the "talk" of a leader and his or her "walk" minimizes the positive potential of the leader to impact the Jewish growth of his students and congregants. Eric seemed to have suffered no such limitation.

Probing a bit deeper, it is clear to me that a sophisticated psychology of human growth and philosophy of Jewish living reinforced the sine qua non of Eric's personal integrity. I understand many of the comments I heard through the lens of the theories of adult development of Laurence Dalouz. He suggests that one can understand the mentoring possibilities as divided into four quadrants: low support–low challenge, high challenge–low support, low challenge–high support, high challenge–high support.

One can easily translate these categories into the interaction of a rabbi with teachers, students, and congregants. A rabbi offering low support–low challenge might very well have his or her mind on other matters. (Scholarship? Congregational business? His or her next vacation? The list of possibilities is endless.) A low support–high challenge rabbinic leadership style might signal a rabbi who takes seriously the challenges of Jewish life but has not figured out the human side of helping support the mentees as they reengage with Judaism. A high support–low challenge scenario might reflect the failure to generate a congregational culture that can sustain creative work. It may also indicate an "enabling" style that dwells on the warm dependence the congregant might feel towards his or her rabbinic mentor who never quite fully galvanizes the internal resources of the learner.

This last insight mirrors an analysis once offered by West Coast educator Vicky Kelman. In one of the foundational articles for the field of Jewish family education that was beginning to emerge in the mid 1980s, "Scaffolds or Life-Supports: A Philosophy of Jewish Family Education," Vicky reminded readers of the complexity of synagogue life and the sometimes "confused" nature of contemporary Jewish identity.[10] Drawing from the writings of the Russian Jewish psychologist Lev Vygotsky she observed that "scaffolds" were the key to all human growth. A scaffold—whether in the form of language, a thought structure, or a support group—extends the range of an individual's growth (technically known in Vygotskian thought as "the zone of proximal development"), so he or she can experience the thrill of a good stretch. It keeps the individual from breaking as they stretch. Yet, once this new skill or muscle is well-exercised the scaffold is removed much as a painter or construction worker can remove a physical scaffold once a task is completed.

Often enough in synagogue life, instead of creating scaffolds we create "life-support systems." A subtle message is communicated to congregants, students, and families. Without me (the Jewish professional) or the institution (the synagogue), we know you don't have the skills to live Jewishly in a meaningful way. We're glad to be your life support system. We feel good about it and in the end we save you from a "Jewish death."

My distinct impression from my interviews was that Eric would have none of this subtle enabling. He offered challenges and support in equal measure. The greatest and most subtle scaffold he offered those who came to love and respect him was the high support–high challenge confidence he had in their capacities.

Along with a healthy psychology of human growth, these interviewees seemed to be the beneficiaries of a philosophy of adult Jewish living and learning attributed to Franz Rosenzweig, the German Jewish philosopher of the early twentieth century. Like Rosenzweig, Eric understood the power of the journey metaphor of Jewish life. Rosenzweig famously observed that in "modern" Jewish life we often moved from the periphery of secular to the center of Jewish life and thought. The periphery had its own glory that never needed to be sacrificed or bracketed in favor of a more "authentically Jewish" perspective. For Rosenzweig, German culture and politics initially engaged these Jewish learners in a more fundamental way than Jewish values. In the end, Rosenzweig could only assert as a matter of faith rather than empirical fact that we all had a Jewish soul and center to which we could return.

Eric's deep love of popular American culture and his constant willingness to simultaneously grant musical and cultural icons a value *lishma* (for their own sake) and at the same time see them through Jewish eyes was noted in several interviews. The seamlessness of American Jewish living as embodied in Eric's own person was an educative force for Eric in his relationships with those he mentored.

Two stories from my interviewees move this section of the article towards a conclusion. I learned in one interview that Eric would sometimes wear a tallit to Shabbat services and sometimes not. I was told that this was by design. It was Eric's way of saying that your own Jewish journey might or might not involve at this point in time taking on new Jewish ritual behaviors. To have always worn or never worn a tallit would have projected the wrong meta-message.

I was also told that during the *Oneg Shabbat* celebration on Friday nights Eric was often found back in his office. On the surface this seems a bit "oxymoronic" for a person as social as Eric, who placed such an emphasis on building community. A number of interviewees thought this was by design. While available (you could always stroll back to chat and receive a warm *Shabbat Shalom*), Eric seemed to have found a powerfully symbolic way of physically enacting the value of *tzimtzum* (contraction for the sake of others). A popular rabbi could easily dominate the social scene of the *Oneg Shabbat*. This would have been contrary to Eric's intent of building community.

Finally, a closing observation of my own: The Dutch theologian Jans Huzinga once objected to the characterization of human beings as *Homo sapiens* (the wise species). Of course human beings were capable of such wisdom, but the most fundamental distinguishing feature of human beings was, according to Huzinga, that they were *Homo ludens* (the playful creature).

Perhaps in the person and work of Rabbi Eric Bram we see the resolution of this *mahloket* in the direction of *eilu v'eilu*, both these and these are valid positions. I know of few other rabbinic colleagues who combined playfulness, skill, and wisdom in the same way Eric did.

Unfinished Work

(Sam Joseph)

Eric's tragic, untimely death left unfinished work. The experts in transformational change teach that it takes at least four to five years to get any good idea embedded into the culture. Eric had barely seven years (he fell ill during High Holy Days 2009 and died a year later) to learn the congregation and for the congregation to become comfortable with him; to stabilize facets of the congregation that appeared shaky; and along with Debbie Bram, the education director, and Lisa Kollins, the family educator, to revitalize the religious school. The crafting of an educational vision; revisioning the high school program with Project Curriculum Renewal, which became Kolaynu; the creation of adult learning programs; and the

Neighborhood initiative of the Legacy Heritage Grant all occurred within a relatively short six-year period.

Certainly a key issue for transforming a congregation from functional to visionary has to be the question of who becomes a lay leader of a congregation, what do they do, and how is the lay leadership structured? This was on Eric's "to do" list. The members of the board of trustees of ST-KA mainly represented and reflected the functional synagogue. They focused on congregational programs and institutional arrangements. Overall, their concern was about congregational resources, mainly financial. Very little of the board's agenda dealt with the purpose of the congregation and a vision for it.

There were notable members of the board who were moving toward this kind of thinking about the board's role, that is, purpose and vision. Some board members were regulars at the Torah study group and some were in the first cohorts of the adult *b'nei mitzvah* program. One of these people, Tom Galvin, became president of the congregation. "I considered leaving Suburban Temple–Kol Ami. The next thing I know I am president," he reported. Tom's experience, along with that of Barbara Feldman, another study group and adult *b'nei mitzvah* participant (who also became temple president), shows the power of learning in a safe, accepting, welcoming community. With knowledge and support people become invested in the community, and that vesting brings a desire to help the community better itself. Tom called this "a subtle process of accountability."

In early 2008, Eric and I created a plan directed toward a different way of thinking about ST-KA leadership. An excerpt from a draft of that plan:

> A goal . . . The Strategic Plan, dated March, 2005, page 8, states, "Helping congregants feel a connection to the work of the Board of Trustees" and "Addressing current leadership patterns" as Strategic Issues. The Goals are to "open channels of communication" and to "create and cultivate engaged and effective leaders." The message was to recruit, train and retain leaders who would be directed toward purpose and vision, not solely focused on the financial resources, or lack thereof, of the congregation.

Eric wanted a redesign of leadership at ST-KA; he knew this would require a complete leadership development process.

At the very practical point where the rubber of congregational vision meets the road of the real life of the congregation, Eric wanted to analyze the Temple's nominating process and work with the nominating committee. He, quite rightly, knew that leadership development began at least from the nomination committee's deliberation on the qualifications of a future ST-KA leader. Eric suggested we train the nominating committee about these kinds of issues. He wanted the nominating committee itself to be peopled with visionaries. Here is another excerpt from the draft 2008 plan:

> Leadership development begins long before one is nominated to a position of leadership. The process of nomination to leadership requires examination and suggestions for future practices that will lead toward fulfilling its mandate with effective leaders. We will closely look at the current manner in which such work is done. We will suggest more effective practices where needed. We will help develop guidelines and criteria for the nominating committee.

Here are some of the qualifications that emerged in the 2008 planning for nomination committee training:

- How is this nominating process different from all other processes? Coordinating the board and officers' nominating committees so that maximal continuity can be achieved for this critical process
- Three Ws (Work, Wisdom, Wealth) are not good enough qualifications
- Intellect: really sharp, strategic thinkers who are open to building community and hearing the voices of others
- Low premium on "worker bees"
- Appropriate for being part of a strategic think tank with responsibilities
- Strong interpersonal skills
- The ability and commitment to attend
- Other qualities/requirements
- The current openings (number, an open chair is better than a poorly filled chair, good enough is not enough)

But there was not time for Eric to put his full attention and energies to leadership development. He did work with the congregation's nominating committee in order to try to teach them to think in a different way about the people being recommended for leadership. But more is left to the future than has been accomplished to date. Many more cycles of nominations and training and retention of leadership are still ahead for ST-KA, if the vision is to be realized.

Without leaders who are firmly committed to visionary learning, the value of Jewish learning cannot become part of the congregation's values, culture, and ethos. Eric and I even discussed that "is currently an active participant in adult Jewish learning" be a criterion for nomination to leadership at ST-KA.

The challenges facing ST-KA loom large, but are certainly far from insurmountable. The work Eric began can move forward, but real change takes a long time to stick. Cultures seem to want homeostasis, so introducing anything that is different from what is considered normative thinking and behavior may be treated by the culture as a foreign body to be attacked and defeated. The leadership and the new rabbi will have to make it a top priority to continue the work they all did together when Eric was alive.

First, ST-KA must keep focused on the vision it articulated, adopted, and began to implement. This vision of lifelong learning must suffuse all facets of congregational life. The religious education of children must be integrated into an overall picture of adult learning, family learning, worship, and community.

Second, leadership development and having the resources to do so is a key to advancing the vision. Active, passionate, learning congregants have to populate the governance structures of ST-KA.

Third, *meaningful* engagement in congregational life must be the goal. The congregants of ST-KA can move the vision forward. Congregants do not need to be dependent on a rabbi, or any other professional, to do this for them. Hopefully, the new ST-KA rabbi will believe in strong partnered leadership with congregants. Top down leadership will not bring about the change that Eric and his lay leaders imagined.

Conclusion

One way to envision a different type of congregation is to rename it a *k'hilah* (a community of learners and doers). A *k'hilah* demands conscious attempts to create community, in the programs of the congregation and in the very words the congregation chooses to describe itself. The *k'hilah* values participation; it is deliberate and transparent in its governance and is committed to social action.[11] Though Suburban Temple–Kol Ami may still have a long road ahead to realize fully its best aspirations, one can hardly doubt that it has already embarked on the journey towards becoming a *k'hilah*.

Notes

1. Joseph Riemer, *Succeeding at Jewish Education* (Philadelphia: Jewish Publication Society, 1997), chs. 1 and 2.

2. Isa Aron, *Becoming a Congregation of Jewish Learners* (Woodstock, VT: Jewish Lights, 2000), ch. 6 ("Leading the Initiative: The Task Force and the Leadership Team").

3. Seymour Fox, Israel Scheffler, and Daniel Marom, eds., *Visions of Jewish Education* (Cambridge, UK: Cambridge University Press, 2003).

4. Ibid., 149.

5. Stephen Covey, *Principled Centered Leadership* (New York: Free Press), 287.

6. http://www.hillconsultinggroup.org/assets/pdfs/articles/transformational-leadership.pdf.

7. Isa Aron, Steven M. Cohen, Lawrence A. Hoffman, and Ari Y. Kelman, *Scared Strategies, Transforming Synagogues from Functional to Visionary* (Herdon, VA: Alban Institute, 2010), 235.

8. Ibid., 25, 43.

9. Ibid., 100–114.

10. Vicki Kelman, *The Family Room* (Los Angeles: Whizin Insitute for Jewish Life, 1995), 1–18.

11. Ibid., 210.

Why Jews Wear Costumes
on Purim

Farhad Arbab (فرهاد ارباب) *and Daniel M. Berry* (דניאל ברי)

1. Introduction

The purpose of this article is to propose an answer to the question "Why do Jews wear costumes on Purim?" hereinafter called "the question." In the rest of this article, section 2 reviews the Jewish tradition of the story of Purim, as described in *M'gillat Esther*, and section 3 reports three problems with this Jewish tradition. Section 4 lists various theories from Jewish tradition of why Jews wear costumes on Purim and when they began to do so, while observing that none of them is totally satisfying. Section 5 presents a Persian version of the story of Purim with a key difference from the Jewish tradition of the story, and section 6 attempts to resolve the differences between the two stories. Section 7 shows how the resolved version of the story of Purim answers the question and addresses the problems. Section 8 explains the source of the Persian version of the story of Purim. Section 9 compares the way Purim is celebrated by modern Iranian Jews with the way it is celebrated by Jews elsewhere. Section 10 concludes the article with a summary and some discussion about the article itself. For more details than are possible in this limited space, please consult the full report on which this article is based.[1]

2. Jewish Tradition of Purim

The Jewish tradition for Purim is described in *M'gillat Esther*[2] and its commentaries.[3] This book of the Bible tells the story of how a

FARHAD ARBAB is professor of Computer Science and chair of Software Composition, Leiden University, Leiden, The Netherlands, and senior researcher in Foundations of Software Engineering Centrum Wiskunde and Informatica (CWI), Amsterdam, The Netherlands, farhad@cwi.nl.

DANIEL BERRY is professor of Computer Science and Software Engineering, University of Waterloo, Waterloo, Ontario, Canada, dberry@uwaterloo.ca.

Jewish Queen of ancient Persia, named Esther, saved her people from being killed, pursuant to a decree to kill all Jews issued by her husband, King Ahasuerus, in response to a request by Prime Minister Haman to have all Jews in Persia killed. Haman was "enraged"[4] at all Jews because one Jew, Mordecai, who happened to be Esther's uncle and adoptive father, "would not kneel or bow low" (Esther 3:2) to Haman, and "Mordecai did not rise or even stir on his [Haman's] account" (Esther 5:9). Mordecai refused to bow down to Haman, because Mordecai "had explained to them that he was a Jew" (Esther 3:4). "He was a Jew and he would never bow down to any human being wearing the image of a pagan idol on his chest."[5]

The king's decree ordered to "all the king's provinces to destroy, massacre, and exterminate all the Jews, young and old, children and women, on a single day, on the thirteenth day of . . . Adar . . . and to plunder their possessions" (Esther 3:13). According to *M'gillat Esther*, this date was selected by drawing lots, leading hence to the name for the holiday, "Purim," which is Persian for "lots." A peculiarity of the Persian Empire was that once issued, a decree by the king could not be revoked, not even by the king. The authors of this article believe that a king's decree was not revocable, so that one could obey a king's decree without worrying about legal liability for failure to follow a possible missed or not-yet-arrived nullifying decree. A possible contributing factor was that there was no way, with the extremely slow, low reliability, horse-back-driven, posted-decree, and-word-of-mouth means to distribute royal decrees of those days, to be sure that all recipients of a first decree had received any corresponding subsequent cancellation decree. For either reason, the only way to prevent the *effects* of one decree was to issue another decree whose effect would be to mitigate or avoid the effects of the first decree.

According to *M'gillat Esther*, the way that King Ahasuerus tried to avoid having all Jews in Persia, including his Queen and her uncle, killed was to issue a second decree that "permitted the Jews of every city to assemble and fight for their lives; if any people or province attacks them, they may destroy, massacre, and exterminate its armed force together with women and children, and plunder their possessions—on a single day in all the provinces of King Ahasuerus, namely on the thirteenth day of . . . Adar" (Esther 7:11–12). *M'gillat Esther* reports that the Jews were victorious in the ensuing battles on the thirteenth and fourteenth of Adar and possibly shortly afterwards, killing 75,810 men in self-defense. In honor of this miraculous, crushing turn of fortune, Jews celebrate the holiday of Purim on the fourteenth of Adar, whose eve is at the end of the thirteenth of Adar.

3. Problems with Jewish Tradition

The Jewish tradition is problematic on three counts:

1. There is nothing in *M'gillat Esther* that explains why the celebration of Purim includes wearing a costume.
2. *M'gillat Esther* says that the Jews lived in peace among the Persians after the events commemorated by Purim. However, if in fact the Jews had avoided being killed by decisively defeating and killing 75,810 Persian men in battle, it is hard to see how there could have been peace between the Jews and Persians. Such battles and defeats would likely have prompted a long-lasting blood feud with revenge and counter-revenge, as we see in the Middle East to this very day.

   Several observers[6] have expressed concern and moral revulsion over the large number of Persians reported killed in chapter 9 of *M'gillat Esther*, 75,810 altogether, including the 800 *men* killed over two days in the city of Shushan, the 10 hanged *sons* of Haman, and the 75,000 *foes* killed in the other provinces. Some of these observers have attempted to justify the killing or mitigate the severity of the apparent overkill by pointing out that the Jews were acting in self-defense. Moreover, the Jews did not plunder as they had been *permitted* to do so by the Jewish tradition second decree, which had been carefully crafted to be a direct mirror of what was *ordered* in the first decree to be done to the Jews. In fact, if "foes" means only fighting men, then the Jews had not killed women, children, and old men as the Jewish tradition second decree had permitted them to do, again, as a direct mirror of what was ordered in the first decree to be done to the Jews. Some of these observers have explained that the 75,000 figure is clearly an exaggeration, citing the general tendency in those days to exaggerate sizes of palaces, numbers of people attending celebrations, sizes of fortunes, sizes of armies, etc.

3. *M'gillat Esther* says that the date chosen by lots was the thirteenth of Adar. It is highly unlikely that a decree by a Persian king would specify a Hebrew date such as the thirteenth of Adar. The decree would probably give a date in the Persian calendar. Perhaps, in the year in which the events took place, the specified date just happened to be the same day as the thirteenth of Adar.

4. Currently Understood Theories of Why and Since When Jews Wear Costumes on Purim

While *M'gillat Esther* does not address the issue of why Jews wear costumes, other elements of Jewish tradition have attempted to answer that question:

1. For many, Purim is the holiday of opposites.[7] What actually happened is the opposite of what Haman had planned to happen. Thus, all sorts of opposites are encouraged to celebrate Purim. One such opposite is for the normally sober Jews to drink wine until they cannot distinguish between "cursed Haman" and "blessed Mordecai." Another is to dress as the opposite of normal (e.g., a man as a woman and vice versa, pupils as teachers and vice versa, and Jews as non-Jews). Perhaps, this tradition of dressing as one's opposite gradually mutated into wearing costumes in general. Also, the general partying would encourage a carnival-like atmosphere that would in turn encourage dressing up in costumes. The difficulty with this explanation is that it could apply to most other event-commemorating holidays. In each of these events, with God's help, what happened was the opposite of what some villain carefully planned to happen.

2. Since none of the words for God appear in *M'gillat Esther*, God was hidden in *M'gillat Esther*.[8] One way to hide oneself is to wear a costume.

3. "And many people of the land professed to be Jews, for the fear of the Jews had fallen upon them" (Esther 8:17). Some say that after the Jewish victory described in *M'gillat Esther*, Persians dressed as Jews because they feared Jews.[9]

4. Eliyahu Kitov suggests that the custom to wear a disguise on Purim and to appear as a non-Jew arises from Jacob's wearing

Esau's clothing to trick his father Isaac into giving Jacob the blessings and inheritance that were due to Esau.[10] Kitov suggests that the disguising custom arises also from a verse of the Torah, "ואנכי הסתר אסתיר פני ביום ההוא" ("I shall surely hide My face on that day") (Deut. 31:18) and the fact that the verb אסתיר (I will hide) shares four letters with the name אסתר (Esther). Thus it is proper to hide one's face on the day of Esther, the day of Purim.

Eliezer Segal reminds us of the passage *Chulin* 139b in the Babylonian Talmud in which this very Torah verse was used, by far-fetched logic, to demonstrate that Esther was mentioned in the Torah: Esther had refused to reveal her Jewish origin to King Ahasuerus.[11]

Other elements of Jewish tradition have attempted to identify *when* costume-wearing was introduced to Purim celebrations. Much of this tradition cites a costume-wearing tradition that may have began in a place other than Persia and long after the events of *M'gillat Esther*:

1. Wearing costumes is not mentioned in the Babylonian Talmud, part of whose content was determined in Persia after the Persian conquest of Babylonia. Wearing costumes is mentioned only later on, for example, by Kalonymos ben Kalonymos, who in his *Touchstones*, written in 1322, addresses the celebrations in honor of Mordecai and Esther on the fourteenth of Adar. He says, "The youth of Israel, for honor and glory, will rave and be rowdy, because by going crazy and being rowdy, they remember wondrous doings and they make miracles known. They shall cover themselves with magnificent ankle-long overcoats, in honor of Mordecai and Esther . . . Men will wear the dress of a woman, with pendants around their necks. They will act as the vacuous ones, with drum and dance, joy and triangles, they with them, men with women, on the occasion of the Purim eve meal."[12] He adds, "On that night, one is not to say 'water is water.' He who drinks live wine is a light shining on the sky . . . One must drink live wine with a big and full cup . . . until he does not know . . . 'blessed Mordecai' from 'cursed Haman' . . . until he does not know his left from his right."[13] Ben Kalonymos's description of

Purim celebrations implies that there *was already* a tradition, prior to the early fourteenth century, of wearing costumes, at least of cross-dressing, in the context of wild celebrations involving sanctioned, heavy wine drinking. Nevertheless, we have no idea how much before the early fourteenth century this tradition began.

2. Citing M. Steinschneider,[14] who is probably repeating the *Touchstones* information, the 1905 *Jewish Encyclopedia*'s article on Purim observes that "One of the strangest species of merrymaking was the custom of masquerading, which was first introduced among the Italian Jews about the close of the fifteenth century under the influence of the Roman carnival. From Italy this custom spread over all countries where Jews lived, except perhaps the Orient."[15] Again, while we know that wearing costumes was part of the Purim celebration in Italy from the close of the fifteenth century, we do not know if the custom was already present in the fifteenth century, and if so, for how long the custom had been present. The possibility exists that the custom was present from the very first Purim celebrations.

3. In *The Jewish Festivals* by Hayyim Schauss, published in 1938 originally in Yiddish and translated to English by Samuel Jaffe,[16] in paragraphs on page 251, referred to by the index entry "Purim . . . a nature festival, 250, 251," one reads:

> What kind of festival was Purim before it became the popular festival of Jewish salvation?
>
> Many theories and hypotheses were advanced in answer to the above question. But none of them is well founded or entirely satisfactory, and not worthy of thorough examination here. From all the conjectures we may accept the following:

> > Purim originally appeared amongst the Jews of Persia, and was adopted by them from their non-Jewish neighbors. Persian Jews observed, in common with their neighbors, a festival which was celebrated yearly in the middle of the last winter month . . . It also seems that Purim, from the beginning, had the characteristic of a spring masquerade, and was a festival of play and frolic, of merriment and mischief, of abandon and wine-drinking.[17]

Schauss's text gives no indication of the origins of this characterization of Purim as being derived from a nature festival. Since the book is for educating those not in the know, such as children, it appears to these authors that Schauss is reporting something that he thought was generally known by those in the know.

None of these explanations of why or when gets right to the heart of the issue of why *Jews wear costumes or dress as non-Jews on Purim*. That is, none of these explanations of why Jews wear costumes to celebrate Purim are as strongly related to the story of Purim as, for example, the explanation of why Jews light candles for the eight days of Chanukah is to the story of Chanukah or the explanation of why Jews eat matzah to celebrate Passover is to the story of Passover. In the cases of Chanukah and Passover, a ritual of the celebration in question serves as a direct reminder of a specific, central event in the story of the holiday being celebrated. As shown in section 5, a Persian version of the story of Purim provides both

1. a disguising, costume-wearing event that can be commemorated by celebratory costume wearing, and
2. an origin that is compatible with the account of Schauss in item 3 above.

Adding to the mystery, at least one source describing in detail how to celebrate Purim, by Mindel,[18] fails to even mention costume wearing. The section on the Purim celebration in *Gateway to Judaism* by Albert Shulman[19] does not mention wearing costumes as an aspect of the celebration. In fact, its only reference to masquerading is in its brief list of laws concerning Purim, "Masquerading in male or female attire permitted only on the Purim holiday." The overall impression of the section is that masquerading is not a required part of the celebration; however, if you wish to cross-dress, it's acceptable, but only because it's Purim!

5. A Persian Version of the Story of Purim

There is a Persian version of the story of Purim known by some, but not all, present day Iranians. Because knowledge of this version of the story is not universal, even among Iranian Jews, at most, the version can be called "a Persian version of the story of Purim." Nevertheless, to simplify identifying this Persian version of the story in the remainder of this article, this Persian version is henceforth called simply "the Persian version." See section 8 for details about how common is knowledge about the Persian version.

The Persian version of the story is similar to the Jewish tradition in many ways. Also the Persian version tells:

1. that a decree was issued to kill all Jews in the entire Persian Empire on the thirteenth day of a month;
2. that the King Xerxes (خشایارشا [khashayarsha])[20] had no intention of harming the Jews; instead, the king was tricked by Haman (هامان [haman]), a man that the king trusted highly enough that the king gave to Haman the king's signet ring in order that Haman could stamp a decree that Haman had issued in the king's name, a decree whose exact effect Haman had misrepresented to the king;[21]
3. that Xerxes is surprised when his queen Esther (استر [ester]) reveals to him that a decree has been issued in his name to exterminate her people and asks, "Who is the man who dared to do such a thing?"
4. that once issued, a decree cannot be canceled;
5. that all that can be done about a decree issued in error was to issue another decree whose effect avoids or mitigates the effect of the first decree;
6. Xerxes seeks the advice of Esther and Mordecai (مردخای [mordekhai]), who devise a plan to circumvent the implementation of the first decree; and
7. Xerxes proves that he never intended that Jews be killed and indicates his trust of Mordecai by giving to Mordecai his signet ring so that Mordecai can issue the second decree in the king's name.

However, from here, the Persian version of the story begins to differ from the Jewish tradition in significant ways that avoid the problems mentioned in section 3.

First, the date on which the killing decree was to be carried out was not the thirteenth of Adar, a Hebrew date, but the thirteenth of Farvardin (فروردین [farvardin]), a Persian date. As is shown in section 7, these two dates can never coincide.

The date of the extermination of the Jews was set in the first de-cree on the thirteenth of Farvardin, which is the thirteenth day *after* the Persian New Year (نوروز [noruz]), which is on the day of the Spring Equinox. The thirteenth day of the new year is the Persian holiday Sizdeh Bedar (سیزده بدر [sizdeh bedar]), which has been celebrated throughout its history even until today.[22] One possible significance of the day is to avoid the bad luck of the number thir-teen.[23] The name of the holiday literally means "thirteen get-outta-here!" Another possible significance of the day comes from another understanding of "بدر [bedar]" as short for "رفتن به درودشت [raftan-e beh dar-o dasht]," which means "going outdoors to the country-side." Regardless, on Sizdeh Bedar, Persians were to dress up in their finest clothes, go out of the house, and spend the day on a picnic in nature, on grass and near a river, celebrating with wine.[24] For Zoro-astrians, Sizdeh Bedar was a religiously mandated joyous celebration of nature. Persians would return from the picnic only at the end of the day, leaving the bad luck of the thirteenth day behind for the whole year, in the case of the first significance. In those days, a per-son's station in life was announced by his clothes, so one could tell by looking at any person's clothing if he or she were upper class, lower class, Persian, Jewish, etc. Thus, the finest clothes worn by a person on the thirteenth of Farvardin announce his or her station in life.

The major difference between the two stories was the contents of the second decree issued to help avoid or mitigate the first decree. The second decree, which Mordecai thought of and issued in the king's name, specified that on the next thirteenth of Farvardin, the date on which the first decree was to be carried out, *all* Jews were to dress as Persians and to go out to the countryside and celebrate Sizdeh Bedar on a picnic. So, on the day that the mass killing of Jews was to happen according the first decree, the Jews obeyed the second decree and dressed as Persians. As a result, when the agents of Haman came to kill Jews, there were simply no Jews to be found. All the would-be killers found were Persians dressed in their finest and celebrating Sizdeh Bedar, and the Jews were saved!

6. Resolution of the Traditions

The shared Persian and Jewish tradition of the peaceful coexistence of Persians and Jews following the implementation of the second decree seems more likely with the second decree according to the

Persian tradition than with the second decree according to the Jewish tradition. Probably the truth is some mixture of the two traditions.

6.1. Dates

There seems to be more to the date of the thirteenth day of the month Farvardin, which Haman supposedly picked by casting lots. *M'gillat Esther* reports that this event happened in the twelfth year of the reign of Xerxes. This year means 474 B.C.E. According to *Calendrical Calculations*,[25] the Persian New Year or the first of Farvardin in this year was a Monday. Therefore, the picnic festivities of expelling the bad omen on the thirteenth day of the new year would have been on Saturday. For Haman's purposes, this configuration of days presented a golden opportunity that would not occur for another seven years: While all the Jews in the realm would be at home observing Sabbath, all Persians would be out on Sizdeh Bedar picnics. The extermination of the Jews could be carried out swiftly and cleanly by his operatives, because they would easily find all Jews in their homes and they could kill these Jews without stirring up sympathetic feelings of the Jews' Persian neighbors, who were out of their homes for a day in nature, and running the risk of the mess that could arise if the Jews' Persian neighbors were around.

6.2. The First Decree

The Jewish tradition describes the contents of the first decree as specifying that all provinces were ordered to exterminate the Jews. Who was to do the actual extermination? It makes no sense to assume that the general population was expected to do the killing. No one in a position of power in the court who was really intent on exterminating the Jews would resort to relying on the general population of a vast empire to carry out this mission. It would be unreliable and messy and would likely lead to chaos and civil war, with unpredictable results. It would be much more effective, and more rational, to use some reliable trained troops to swiftly carry out the royal decree in a disciplined and orderly fashion.

6.3. The Second Decree

The content of the second decree according to the Jewish tradition raises questions of its own. It ordered the Jews to arm and defend themselves. Such actions make sense as a Plan B, to reassure the would-be victims. However, without a Plan A to avert the brunt of the upcoming attack, arming a militarily untrained 20 percent of the population of a large empire and ordering them to defend themselves against the professional operatives acting in the name of the king is not only foolhardy, but is also a sure-fire recipe for a civil war and a disaster whose outcome no one could have controlled, much less predicted. If the Jews were ordered by the king and their own leaders to simply dress up as Persians and to join the Persians in their ceremonial outing on the date of the first decree, they would have avoided most of the attack and subverted the extermination plan without bloodshed.

Perhaps the true second decree combined the contents of the second decrees according to both Jewish and Persian traditions. As a real solution, it told the Jews to dress as Persians and join the holiday celebration, and as a reassuring gesture, it allowed the Jews to arm and defend themselves if attacked. The active ingredient in this recipe would be Jews disguising themselves as Persians, successfully avoiding the massacre, and preventing the need for an armed conflict altogether. It is understandable, then, how subsequently the Jewish tradition could have focused on one part of the decree, whereas the Persian version simply ignored that part because it played no substantial role in the actual course of events that transpired.

6.4. The Fateful Day

To understand fully why the actual second decree is probably a mixture of the two second decrees, it is useful to explore how the first decree and the two second decrees would be received and acted upon by various actors in the events of the fateful day of Sizdeh Bedar.

M'gillat Esther says that Haman was hanged on the same tall gallows that he had erected for the hanging of Mordecai. It is useful to examine Haman's hanging in the Persian sociopolitical context, both in the king's court and among the general population throughout the empire.

The exact date of Haman's execution is not known, but his fate was certainly sealed by the time the first and second decrees were to be carried out. By that date, Haman would have certainly been removed from office and would have been at least in custody if not already executed. Haman was a trusted minister of the king who had abused the king's trust and had misrepresented to the king the contents of the first decree, on which Haman had put the king's royal seal. Recall from item 2 of the Persian version of the story of Purim in section 5 that the king had no intention of harming the Jews. Thus from the king's viewpoint, Haman had betrayed the king and had therefore committed treason.

The fall from grace of any trusted minister on charges of treason and his, at least impending, execution would certainly have been a huge event with serious impact throughout the Empire. The news of this event and the reason for it, namely that the first decree was illegitimately issued by Haman, would have spread like wildfire throughout the Empire, certainly no less speedily and widely than the mitigating second decree itself. Everyone in the Empire would have known that the decree to kill the Jews, although still in effect, was not really to be obeyed because its issuer had already been arrested for issuing it in the king's name and was, if not already executed, awaiting execution. Independent of the moral implications and social consequences of the mass murder of the Jews prescribed by this decree, even the allies and political appointees of Haman throughout the Empire would no doubt be scrambling at this point to distance themselves from him. Anyone with a shred of common sense would not attempt to carry out this first decree.

Nevertheless, the first decree would still technically be a decree with the seal of the king, which everyone would be duty-bound to obey. The genius of the second decree according to the Persian version is that it provided a reprieve not only to the would-be victims, the Jews, but also to any would-be killer, who would need a way out of carrying out a king's decree that everyone knew was not to be carried out. With Jews dressed up as Persians on that fateful day, any sensible would-be killer could feign an honest attempt to find Jews to kill on that day and conveniently fail, all the while protesting and feigning disappointment that there were just no Jews to be found; the would-be killer had obeyed the letter of the first decree.

If there were a would be-killer who (1) either did not have any common sense or wanted the Jews killed anyway, but (2) who knew from reading the second decree that his quarry were disguised as Persians, he could not with certainty distinguish Jews dressed as Persians from non-Jewish Persians. Since the would-be killer would not be allowed to kill other Persians, even in error, he would probably have opted on the side of caution and would have spared everyone he found that day. In addition, if the true second decree had been a combination of the second decrees according to both the Jewish and Persian traditions, he would have known that the Jews were armed, prepared, and permitted to defend themselves.

In all likelihood, however, any sincere attempt by a would-be killer to identify which people dressed as Persians were really Jews would probably be the exception rather than the rule. While the Jews would be pretending to be Persians, Persians would be pretending that they did not know any better, and everyone would rejoice this masquerade dance through the administrative loopholes opened up by the very inspired, clever second decree that rendered the ominous first decree innocuous.

6.5. Support for Persian Version of Second Decree in Jewish Tradition

Recall item 3 in the list in section 4 of currently understood theories of when Jews began to wear costumes on Purim. The authors of this article read Schauss's paragraphs as saying that the Purim holiday was first celebrated as going out to nature while masquerading, which would be a fair description of participating in a Sizdeh Bedar celebration while dressed, as required, in a Persian's best clothing. Certainly Schauss's description does not contradict the origin of the Purim celebration arising from the Persian version of the story of Purim. It looks as though Schauss had read or heard descriptions of the early celebrations without having read, heard, or known the Persian version of the story. Therefore, Schauss was compelled to report his findings as not well founded and not entirely satisfactory.

7. Possible Answer to the Question and Solutions to Problems

The authors believe that the Persian version of the story of Purim described in this article provides clarity to the Jewish tradition of Purim. Of course, the Jewish tradition's big military victory seems a better cause for a big celebration. However, the survival of the Jews by the decidedly simple Persian version's second decree is no less miraculous. The Persian version second decree is a particularly clever mitigation, which according to the Persian version, was Mordecai's invention.

The second decree according to the Persian version solves the three problems listed in section 3.

1. It explains why Jews have a tradition of wearing costumes to disguise themselves and to dress as non-Jews on Purim. On the day that Purim commemorates, the Jews dressed up as Persians, to pretend to be Persians and to celebrate a Persian holiday. Moreover, they dressed as non-Jewish Persians so that they could not be identified as Jews (i.e., so that no one would know who they really are).

2. It offers a second decree the obeying of which is far more likely to lead to the peaceful coexistence that followed the events that Purim celebrates.

3. It explains also the issue with the date attached to the decree. The Jewish tradition says that the date attached to the decree was the thirteenth of Adar. The Persian version says that the date attached to the decree was the thirteenth of Farvardin. Certainly, a Persian royal decree is far more likely to have specified the thirteenth of Farvardin than the thirteenth of Adar. Could the two dates have coincided? They clearly could not. Farvardin *starts with* the Spring Equinox, and the ceremonial outing of Sizdeh Bedar comes thirteen days later. The Babylonian Hebrew calendar is such that if a day is on or after the Spring Equinox, its date must be on or after the fifteenth of Nisan, the first day of Passover, which *must* be on or after the Spring Equinox.[26] The fifteenth of Nisan is the beginning of Passover and is one month and one day after Purim on the fourteenth of Adar. Thus the Persian date attached to the decree would be in Nisan by the Jewish calendar. In fact, in the year 474 B.C.E., suggested in section 6.1 as the year of the event, the thirteenth of Farvardin was the Sabbath day, the twenty-fourth of Nisan, *after* the end of Passover.

8. Source of the Persian Version of the Story of Purim

The story of how Arbab and Berry came to write this article is instructive: Several years ago, when Berry visited Arbab in

Amsterdam on a date that happened to be near the Purim holiday, Berry asked Arbab if he, Arbab, an Iranian, knew how Jews celebrate Purim. Arbab said that he did not know all the details. Berry then asked Arbab to explain the details that Arbab knew. Arbab explained the Persian version as described here. When Berry heard about the Persian version's second decree, he knew that he had just learned the solution to one of Judaism's heretofore unsatisfactorily answered questions, "Why do Jews wear costumes to celebrate Purim?" Just to be sure, Berry asked Arbab if he knew that Jews celebrate Purim by dressing in costumes. Arbab said that he did; however, he knew about the Persian version in Iran before he came to the United States to study, and he learned about Jews celebrating Purim by wearing costumes only later, in the United States while studying there. Thus, Arbab knew about the Persian version long before he learned that Jews celebrated Purim by wearing costumes, having learned the Persian version in elementary school. Moreover, to his memory, while Jews in Iran dress up nicely for Purim, as they do for other holidays, they do not dress in outlandish or disguising costumes, as he saw that Jews in the United States do. Arbab was surprised to learn from Berry that Jews outside of Iran know nothing of the Persian version of the second decree. He had assumed that Jews everywhere naturally knew what he and some other interested Iranians knew. Arbab and Berry realized that they had to write this article.

9. How Purim Is Celebrated by Iranian Jews and More on the Source of the Persian Version

Karmel Melamed, an Iranian Jewish attorney and writer about Iranian Jewish affairs, told the authors by e-mail that Iranian Jews do not wear costumes to celebrate Purim. He said, "From my knowledge and expertise, no. This is a european/ashkenazi [sic] tradition."[27] Melamed wrote:

> "Even though Purim is for all Jews around the world, we as Jews living in Iran feel particularly close to Purim," said Parviz Yeshaya, national chairman of the Jewish Council in Iran. "Especially since the tombs of Esther and Mordechai[28] are here in Iran."
>
> Iran's Islamic regime does not discourage the celebrating of Jewish holidays, including Purim, Yeshaya said. Still, the tone of the

holiday is quite different than [sic] in other countries. The Jewish community in Iran has embraced the long-standing religious aspects of Purim rather than the light-hearted festivities that characterize American observance.

"The most important part of celebrating Purim in Iran starts with the fast, which is 24 hours, and the reading of the megillah in synagogues during the fast," Yeshaya said. "We give gifts here, but not as many, and we don't have carnivals like the Ashkenazim. But children in their Jewish school conduct their own plays of the Purim story."

Melamed adds:

[Amnon] Netzer [an Iranian Jewish Scholar] did, however, have an explanation of the more subdued, religious nature of the holiday's observance. Jews in Iran have always been cautious in their celebrations of Purim, he said, because the Book of Esther contains unflattering depictions of non-Jewish Persians and also includes the tale of a slaughter of non-Jews.

"If you read the book [M'gillat Esther] itself you will see that it says the Iranian Jews were permitted actually to massacre a lot of Iranians on a certain day and King Ahasuerus, also known as Xerxes, is pictured as a stupid king," Netzer said. "So these factors actually made Iranian Jews extremely careful not to have high-profile celebrations for Purim."

Consistent with the observation that for Iranian Jews, Purim is more religious than festive, Schauss mentions that Iranian Jews observe the Fast of Esther as strictly as they observe the Fast of Yom Kippur.[29]

Julie G. Fox confirmed: "For Iranian-American Jews, Purim is a serious day . . . Wearing costumes is not a Persian custom, but emissaries and educators who arrived in Iran from Israel brought the notion, and Persian children in America today do enjoy dressing up."[30]

This situation is the ultimate opposite in the so-called holiday of opposites. In Iran, where some people know about the Persian version second decree, Jews do not wear costumes to celebrate Purim, and Jews believe that the custom is a tradition introduced outside of Iran. Outside of Iran, Jews wear costumes to celebrate Purim, they do not know about the Persian version second decree, and they are *uncertain* about the origin of costume wearing. The authors are mystified about this inversion as indeed they are about the evident lack of written record about the Persian tradition. They can only speculate as to the reasons for them.

In the Zoroastrian religion, Sizdeh Bedar, which is as old as the Persian civilization and predates Islam, originally was an exaggeratedly jovial celebration to exhort the angel of rain and rainwater to defeat the demon of drought. After the Arab conquest of Iran was sealed with the fall of the Sassanid Empire in 651 C.E., the Arab Muslim rulers generally suppressed all non-Islamic traditions. Almost overnight, the Zoroastrian majority found itself severely persecuted and its traditions strongly suppressed. The Muslim Arab rulers considered Zoroastrianism as paganism and Zoroastrians as infidels that had to be converted to Islam.

On the other hand, the Muslims *tolerated* Judaism as an Abrahamic faith, and the Jews, as the people of the book, were allowed to practice their religion. Jews, in their precarious position as a tolerated minority under Islamic rule, found it prudent to distance themselves from Zoroastrian practices such as Sizdeh Bedar. Thus, Persian Jews had every reason to at least appear to expunge from Purim celebrations and traditions any link to Sizdeh Bedar and to stick to what is written in *M'gillat Esther*, which is part of the book that Jews were the people of. So it is not surprising that there are few if any Iranian Jewish *writings* that mention the link between Sizdeh Bedar and Purim.

At the same time, the non-Jewish Persians, Muslim or otherwise, were trying to preserve their cherished ancient culture and traditions under Islam. They managed to neutralize enough of the Zoroastrian religious aspects of their culture and of many of their traditions, including those of Noruz and Sizdeh Bedar, to be able to continue to celebrate them, albeit in what appeared to the Muslim rulers as nonreligious, national events. This suppression of the religious aspects of Sizdeh Bedar would include disassociation of Sizdeh Bedar from the Purim holiday celebrated by another religious group, even though the group itself and its own celebrations might have been tolerated. Thus, it is not surprising that there are few if any non-Jewish Iranian *writings* that mention the link between Sizdeh Bedar and Purim.

What *is* surprising and somewhat miraculous, is that the story of the connection between Sizdeh Bedar and Purim, the Persian tradition of this paper, has survived to this day, albeit apparently primarily among non-Jewish Iranians, solely by verbal transmission. Perhaps this back-channel verbal transmission is yet another miracle of Purim. It is no less a miracle than the survival of Jewish tradition strictly by oral transmission from generation to generation among Crypto Jews.[31] Finally, it seems to these authors that Schauss, in his characterization of Purim as being derived from a nature festival, is alluding to some verbally transmitted traditions.

Why does this verbal transmission seem to exclude Iranian Jews? Since Jews celebrating Purim in Iran feel that they are walking on eggshells and have to mute the celebration because Purim is about an utter defeat and slaughter of the Persians, they do not talk with non-Jews about Purim. Non-Jews return the favor and do not talk with Jews about Purim either. Each tacitly assumes that the other knows what it knows when, in fact, the other does not.

Author Berry visited the Nessah Synagogue, the largest Persian Jewish congregation in Los Angeles one Sabbath in June 2009. No one that he asked, even among the older generation, claimed to have any knowledge of the Persian version of the story of Purim. For them, Purim was as described by *M'gillat Esther*. At the time, Berry was surprised. However, in retrospect, this lack of knowledge would be a clear result of suppression of any written record of Purim's connection to Sizdeh Bedar and of the lack of verbal transmission among Jews of the same.

In fact, the *Comprehensive History of the Jews of Iran: The Outset of the Diaspora* by Habib Levy is disappointing as a source of information for this article. It devotes only one sentence to the holiday of Purim, saying only, "From this time forward, Jews throughout the world have celebrated the 14th and 15th of the month of Adar as 'Purim.'"[32] This sentence is preceded by a summary of the *M'gillat Esther* version of the story of Purim, and there is no discussion of any other version of the story.

10. Conclusion

A Persian version of the events of Purim complements the Jewish traditions about some events of Purim by explaining some details that have long been mysterious. In particular, the Persian version provides the simplest answer to the question of why Jews wear costumes when celebrating Purim, and specifically why Jews are to dress as non-Jews on Purim. The Persian version says that the second decree was an order to Jews to dress as Persians on the day that they were to be killed so that the killers would find no Jews to kill.

Note that this article is itself an example of the resolution of two traditions leading to better understandings of both traditions. The two authors come from two different traditions, neither knew about the other's traditions about Purim, and each had assumed that there was no difference in the two traditions. They had to resolve their traditions and in doing so, came to an understanding that led to this article's writing.

The authors believe that in order to understand the truth behind such a complex phenomenon that happened so long in the past, it is essential to juxtapose deep understandings of multiple cultures, traditions, histories, and narratives, and look for real answers to questions, while assuming that the people back then were inherently just as reasonable, competent, intelligent, capable, and rational as they are today, albeit, operating in less informed, less technologically advanced societies, with somewhat different norms and structures. Very few people have approached the topic of this article in this way.

The authors thank Behnaz Changizi, Rabbi Lori Cohen, Leah and Simcha Goldin, Rav Izak Lifshitz, Jair Jehuda, Shmuel Katz, Eli Ben Yosef, Karmel Melamed, Jason Mokhtarian, Ali Niknafs, Behrooz Parhami, Nahid Pirnazar, Shaul Shaked, Shahram Siman, Shahram Esmaeilsabzali, and Judith Romney Wegner.

Notes

To find a .zip file containing a .pdf file preserving the contents of each of the cited Web pages as of its date viewed, please go to http://se.uwaterloo.ca/~dberry/FTP_SITE/tech.reports/ArbabBerryPurimPaperCitedWebPages.zip.

1. F. Arbab and D. M. Berry, "Why Jews Wear Costumes on Purim" (technical report, Cheriton School of Computer Science, University of Waterloo, 2011), http://se.uwaterloo.ca/~dberry/FTP_SITE/tech.reports/ArbabBerryPurimFullPaper.pdf.

2. *JPS Hebrew-English Tanakh* חנ"ך (New York: Jewish Publication Society, 1999).

3. N. Mindel, *Complete Story of Purim, Compiled from The Book of Esther, Targum, Talmud and Midrash*, 7th ed. (Brooklyn, NY: Merkos L'Inyonei Chinuch, Inc., 1961).

4. Ibid., 17.

5. Ibid., 15.

6. B. D. Wallfish, *Esther in Medieval Garb: Jewish Interpretation of the Book of Esther in the Middle Ages* (Albany, NY: State University of New York Press, 1993); K. M. Craig, Jr., *Reading Esther, A Case for the Literary Carnivalesque* (Louisville, KY: Westminster John Knox Press, 1995); L. Day, *Esther* (Nashville: Abingdon, 2005); J. Carruthers, *Esther through the Centuries* (Malden, MA: Blackwell, 2008).

7. D. Medwin, "Who knows why we're all dressed up today? [Purim!!]," http://tx019.urj.net/DM_purim.pdf (accessed August 1, 2011).

8. H. Schauss, *The Jewish Festivals, From Their Beginnings to Our Own Day* (Cincinnati: Union of American Hebrew Congregations, 1938); E. Segal, *Holidays, History, and Halakhah* (Northvale, NJ: Jason Aronson, Inc., 2000).

9. Being Jewish, "Why Do People Dress in Disguises and Costumes on Purim?" http://www.beingjewish.com/yomtov/purim/costumes.html (accessed August 1, 2011).

10. E. Kitov, *The Book of Our Heritage*, vol. 2 (Jerusalem: Feldheim Publishers, 1973), 90.

11. Segal, *Holidays, History, and Halakhah*, 116.

12. K. ben Kalonymos (ק. בן קלונימוס), *Touchstone* (in Hebrew) (אבן בחן [*Even Bochan*]) (Tel Aviv: Machbaroth Lesifrut Publishing House, 1956), 30.

13. Ibid., 31.

14. M. Steinschneider, "Purim und Parodie," in *Monatsschrift* (1903), 46, 47.

15. H. Malter, *The Jewish Encyclopedia*, s.v. "Purim," ed. I. Singer (New York: Funk and Wagnalls Company, 1905).

16. Schauss, *The Jewish Festivals*, 318, 215.

17. It is curious that "nature festival" occurs in the index entry but not in the referred-to text. Perhaps the translator from Yiddish to English had correctly translated the index entry, but inadvertently dropped one phrase (e.g., "of being out in nature") from the long list of aspects of the "festival."

18. Mindel, *Complete Story of Purim*.

19. A. M. Shulman, *Gateway to Judaism: Encyclopedia Home Reference*, vol. 1 (Cranbury, NJ: Thomas Yoseloff, 1971).

20. Whenever a Persian word is given in parentheses as the original for an apparently English word of Persian origin, the

pronunciation of the Persian word is given enclosed in brackets, using Latin letters according to English pronunciation rules, with two exceptions: "kh" stands for a guttural sound similar to that of the "ch" in the German "ach" or the "J" in the Spanish "Javier," and "gh" stands for a sound similar to that of the French or German "r."

21. Even Jewish tradition heaps all condemnation on Haman and none on the king. Therefore, Jewish tradition seems to recognize that the only real villain in the story is Haman and that the king was probably at most an ignorant fool in trusting Haman.

22. E. L. Daniel and A. A. Mahdi, *Culture and Customs of Iran* (Westport, CT: Greenwood, 2006); M. Saadat-Noury, "Outdoor Moments of Sizdah Bedar," http://www.iranian.com/main/blog/m-saadat-noury/outdoor-moments-sizdah-bedar (accessed August 1, 2011); Wikipedia, s.v. "Nowruz," http://en.wikipedia.org/wiki/Nowruz (accessed August 1, 2011).

23. The Persian association of bad luck to the number thirteen is thought by some to come from the fact that ancient Persians believed that the twelve constellations of the Zodiac controlled the twelve months of the year. Each constellation ruled the earth for a thousand years, and at the end of twelve thousand years, the sky and earth collapsed into chaos. Thus, the number thirteen is unlucky.

The Zoroastrian Heritage Institute offers an explanation of the Zoroastrian religious significance of Sizdeh Bedar that touches on the unluckiness of the number thirteen and of the day:

> While the superstitious may associate the 13th day with bad luck, there is no such notion in Zoroastrian traditions. Perhaps the myth that it is unlucky to stay at home on the thirteenth was created to give the house-bound added incentive to leave their homes and appreciate the spring-time unveiling of nature's beauty.
>
> In the Zoroastrian calendar, Sizdah-be-dar falls on Tir (the 13th) day in the month of Farvardin, April 2. The name Tir is a modern and short form of the Middle Persian (Pahlavi) Tishtar and Avestan Tishtrya, the Zoroastrian Avestan name for the brightest star Sirius as well as the guardian angel of rain and rain water. Zoroastrians therefore make a special effort to spend the day beside a river or a lake. The devout will recite passages from the Tir Yasht.
>
> For Zoroastrians, this day also celebrates the unfolding bounty of nature and life (gaya). Sizdah Bedar provides an opportunity for Zoroastrians to enjoy what nature has to offer while renewing their covenant to protect or enhance the environment, and not defile any of the seven aspects of the corporeal creation (gaiety): fire, air, water, earth, plants, animals and human beings.

K. E. Eduljee, "Nowruz: The Outdoors and Sizdah-Bedar," Zoroastrian Heritage Institute, http://heritageinstitute.com/zoroastrianism/nowruz/nowruz3.htm#sizdeh_bedar (accessed October 1, 2011).

24. Remember that these events predate Islam; so, there was no prohibition against drinking alcohol.

25. E. M. Reingold and N. Dershowitz, *Calendrical Calculations, the Millennium Edition* (Cambridge, UK: Cambridge University Press, 2002), chapter 14; E. M. Reingold and N. Dershowitz, "Calendar Applet," Calendrical Calculations Web Site, http://emr.cs.iit.edu/home/reingold/calendar-book/Calendrica.html (accessed August 1, 2011).

26. Reingold and Dershowitz, *Calendrical Calculations*, chapters 7 and 14.

27. K. Melamed, "For Iranian Jews, Purim Is the Real Thing," http://www.jewishjournal.com/iranianamericanjews/item/for_iranian_jews_purim_is_the_real_thing/ (accessed August 1, 2011).

28. The tombs of Esther and Mordecai exist to this day next to each other in a mausoleum in the center of the city of Hamadan in western Iran. The present mausoleum was built in the thirteenth century and most likely replaced an older one, containing more ancient tombs. It has the Islamic architecture of the period, with an entrance, a vestibule, a sanctuary, and a sitting area. Under the mausoleum's simple brick dome are two exquisite wooden tomb boxes. The older box has an inscription in Hebrew, and there are some Aramaic and some more Hebrew inscriptions, including that of the Ten Commandments, on the plaster wall.

29. Schauss, *The Jewish Festivals*.

30. J. G. Fox, "For Iranian-American Jews, Purim Is a Serious Day," http://www.jewishworldreview.com/0301/purim.iran.asp (accessed August 1, 2011).

31. Wikipedia, s.v. "Crypto-Judaism," http://en.wikipedia.org/wiki/Crypto-Judaism (accessed October 1, 2011).

32. H. Levy, *Comprehensive History of the Jews of Iran: The Outset of the Diaspora* (Costa Mesa, CA: Mazda, 1999), 70.

The "Man" as "Fool-King": Alexander the Great and the Wisdom of Women

Admiel Kosman

Alexander of Macedon . . . went [on his campaigns of conquest] to a land named Kartigna, that was inhabited entirely by women. [Some of the women] came out to meet him and said: "If you wage war against us and defeat us, you will be known in the world as having destroyed a land of women. And if we wage war against you and defeat you, again, you will not be able to face any kings [due to your embarrassment]." When he [Alexander] left there, he wrote on the city gate: "I, Alexander of Macedon, I was a fool-king, until I came to Kartigna, and I learned wisdom from the women."

—*P'sikta de Rav Kahana* 9[1]

This short tale raises many questions, which can be resolved with the modern tools of gender studies. The male and female components of everyday life are usually intertwined, while this vignette presents an extreme situation of total separation between the two. Alexander the Great, who clearly represents the male element, is confronted by a land without any men at all, only women (this might be a midrashic adaptation of the Greek story of the Amazons, with Kartigna being Carthage).[2]

Why does the midrash select Alexander the Great to represent the male dimension? The answer seems evident: if we assume that the most direct characteristic of masculinity is expansion, the need to "be more" in every way possible—stronger, richer, smarter, and even more righteous—then we could ask for no better example of this than Alexander, the great conqueror, of whom the midrash declares elsewhere that "he left no place that he did not conquer."[3]

ADMIEL KOSMAN currently holds the chair for Rabbinic Studies at the University of Potsdam, and is the academic director of Geiger College in Berlin.

Alexander in this midrash is therefore a sort of hidden code for the male trait of conquest.[4] Obviously, this attribute is not characteristic only of military leaders who set out to war. Rather, this basic component of the male character is present in everyone (even among women who possess male character traits). The import of this quality is the inner inclination to conquer—in our self-image—more and more "lands."

This, then, is the significance of the "phallus" (in the Freudian/Lacanian conception; as are many of the terms appearing in this article): To be "Alexander" means to be immersed in doing in the external world in order to expand our self-image in the "more" dimension, that of infinite expansion. Paradoxically, even regarding seemingly positive efforts—like each person's inner struggles to be a decent, honest, or virtuous person—if the comparative inclination ("to be more than") is involved, then it is a distinctly Alexandrian propensity.

Then what in this narrative does femininity teach masculinity of the latter's hidden nature? The women's main argument against Alexander's need to conquer their city seems to be this: Since your primary concern, Alexander, is not the conquered entity itself, but consists solely of proving your ability to conquer, proving your masculinity, of being "known in the world," then what will you gain by conquering Kartigna? If you defeat us, "you will be known in the world as having destroyed a land of women," and you will be derided, since your excessive masculinity will be cast in a ridiculous light. And if we prevail over you, then certainly "you will not be able to face any kings," you will no longer be able to appear as a "man" before "men," other conquerors, out of shame (the "castration" argument).[5]

We see, therefore, that the obsessive need of the "male" for conquests does not ensue from any positive necessity. The "male," in all his conquests, makes only a single statement, in different ways: "I am not a female!"[6]

The need to continually "penetrate" does not result from any real interest in the sites of his conquests, for otherwise he would not be drawn into a never-ending series of attacks (another obvious example of this is the "Don Juan" type, who hops from one woman to another in an unending string of conquests). Simply put, his very existence as a "man" is a fiction, a product of the imagination that he must support over and again lest it fall (like an erection). He therefore suffers from continuous and hidden anxiety, that if he were to rest for a moment, he would, all of a sudden, be perceived as "castrated," as being "feminine," and "being penetrated."

At this juncture, what can we say about the other aspect of the psyche, its feminine side, which is represented in the narrative by the land of women? The women who face Alexander do not truly fear him, for they unerringly identity the weak point of masculinity; and when Alexander acknowledges this, he thanks them for teaching him wisdom.

Just what is this female wisdom? The narrative does not go into detail on the nature of this discernment, since the wisdom of women is merely that of reflecting—helping others to see themselves. If this had been a story of a wise "male," we would certainly find a portrayal of the city or land's sage, who, through his military counsel, with its special cunning and sophistication, would find some way of overcoming the enemy, of defeating him, of making him an object of scorn and derision. This is not the way of femininity. It has no interest in defeating the Other. The women's reflective wisdom in this tale is expressed solely in their ability to become a mirror.

Freud was critical of this ability, and declared that it was based in its entirety on the woman's being castrated. But it would be more correct to state, as the theory was amended by Nancy Chodorow, that women are more familiar with the experience of Being, while men are closer to Doing.[7]

In either event, the women in this narrative very simply reflect for the Alexander who stands before them the emptiness and nullity inherent in his need to conquer.[8] They thereby reflect for the male the fact that no sincere motive stands behind this need, except for the male apprehension of being perceived as a "female."

The narrator adds, ironically, that Alexander expressed his male needs at the end of the story in a subliminal manner, as someone who cannot end an argument without having the last word: He inscribes on the city gate the testimony that he has just learned new words of wisdom.[9] This inscription is patently a surrogate for penetration (into the city). Alexander leaves his name imprinted forever on—and in—the entrance to the city, in a manner visible to all.

The ironic narrator winks to us, the readers, behind the back of Alexander the Great, and says: if only all conquerors would always be satisfied to inscribe their name on the city gate, and in this way give us respite from their stormy urge to conquer.

This feminine interpretation of masculinity is therefore one of peace, and is presented to Alexander the conqueror from a most surprising perspective, to the extent that even he, Alexander the Great, is amazed by it, since it frees him, at least for the moment, from the obsessive male need to "conquer"—which, in the final analysis, is a burden that weighs heavy.

When, however, all is said and done, such a feminine interpretation of the narrative also releases the story itself for us, its readers, from its initial chains to masculinity and femininity as innate biological traits, and allows us the possibility of seeing these basic attributes as mingled, to whatever degree, within each of us.

Notes

1. Bernard Mandelbaum, ed., *Pesikta de Rav Kahana*, (New York: The Theological Seminary of America, 1987), vol. 1: 148. See also BT *Tamid* 32b.

2. A later transformation of the story in *Sefer Josippon*, ch. 12, speaks explicitly of the land of the Amazons. On Alexander's encounter with the Amazons, see Elizabeth Baynham, "Alexander and the Amazons," *Classical Quarterly* 51, no. 1 (2001): 115–26.

3. Solomon Buber, ed., *Midrash Aggadah* on the Pentateuch (*Agadischer Commentar zum Pentateuch*) (Vienna, 1894), Gen. 26:34, p. 67.

4. See the extensive discussion in Admiel Kosman, "Rereading the Story about Alexander and His Visit in Katzya in the Midrashic Tradition," *Sidra* 18 (2003): 73–102 (Hebrew).

5. This rhetorical argument was known and accepted in the Greek world. See E. A. Halevi, *The Gates of the Aggadah* (Tel Aviv, 1982), 128 n. 3 (Hebrew).

6. My contention here was influenced by several of the ideas set forth by Judith Butler, "Critically Queer," in *Bodies That Matter: On the Discursive Limits of "Sex"* (New York: Routledge, 1993), 223–42.

7. See Nancy Chodorow, "Being and Doing: A Cross-Cultural Examination of the Socialization of Males and Females," in Vivian Gornick and Barbara K. Moran, *Woman in Sexist Society: Studies in Power and Powerlessness* (New York: Basic Books, 1971), 259–91.

8. "The Greek does not fight only for bread, but mainly for glory" (see the citation in Halevi, *Gates*, 128).

9. On the gate and the door as a female symbol in Rabbinic expressions, such as women "whose doors are locked," see Jacob Nacht, *Symbolism of the Woman: A Study in Folklore with Reference to Jewish and World Literature* (Tel Aviv, 1959), 94–95 (Hebrew); and on the gate in early literature as also symbolizing the passage to a secret mysterium, see, e.g., John 10:9 (the city gates were apparently of iron; see Acts 12:10; Samuel Krauss, *Antiquities of the Talmud*, vol. 1 [Berlin-Vienna, 1924], 356 n. 1 [Hebrew]).

Sh'ma Echad

David L. Kline

One of my favorite midrashim is an imaginative linking of *Sh'ma Yisrael* to the deathbed scene at the end of Genesis. At the hour when Yaakov our patriarch was passing from the world, he called for his twelve sons and said to them: "Listen. Is the God of Israel [Who is in the Heavens] your father? Perhaps there is division in your heart regarding the Holy Blessed One?" They said to him: "Listen Israel our father, just as there is no division in your heart regarding the Holy Blessed One, so in our heart there is none. To the contrary, *Adonai Eloheinu Adonai echad!*" From here, the Rabbis conclude, Israel merited to recite the *Sh'ma*. (*B'reishit Rabbah* 98:3.) (Please note that instead of endnotes this article includes an appendix with supporting documents, illustrations, excerpts, quotes, and thoughts.) Rabbi Elazar ben Achui, the author, was a fourth century Palestinian Amora.

This midrash, over the years, helped me talk about the *Sh'ma*. A rabbi could count on every Jew knowing by heart what used to be called "the watchword of our faith," making *Sh'ma* a handy peg from which to hang a sermon on monotheism and universalist ethics. Talking about *Sh'ma* was almost too easy an exercise in sermonizing.

Almost but not quite, for two obstacles present. First, the syntax of Deuteronomy 6:4 in the Masoretic text does not make a meaningful declaration. Second, in its context, the line cannot refer to monotheism (and the same can be said about the above midrash). This article addresses the theological and linguistic difficulties, arriving at a revised reading of the words that, I think, is faithful to the intent of the author.

RABBI DAVID L. KLINE (C62) retired with his wife, Barbara, from congregational and university work to West Roxbury, Massachusetts. He keeps busy fulfilling *sabba* duties, teaching Bible in Brandeis University's lifelong learning program, and reworking *Tanach* narratives into readable and tellable English.

Let's turn first to the matter of monotheism. A classic strand of teaching makes Abraham the first monotheist, with later genera-tions falling from his lofty logic or inspiration. Preachers, be they Jews or Christians, keep alive the Genesis 12 story of his hearing God's call to go forward. Telling a story as if it were revealed and historical counts as *p'shat* (simple), the entry level to homiletics, midrash (seeking). Midrash is the usual method by which rabbis teach *Tanach*.

Critical method, however, reigned in history and *Tanach* courses at Hebrew Union College. I accept that monotheism similar to what we hold today was introduced by Deutero Isa-iah, probably during the Babylonian exile, in the sixth century. To grasp what the *Sh'ma* meant in the seventh century we must review some premises of the Documentary Hypothesis as taught for the past couple of centuries. II Kings 22:8 relates that in the course of cleaning and repairs to the Holy Temple, by royal order in 622 B.C.E., the workers are said to have found a scroll. Offi-cials read it and declared it a previously unknown and unheard of *sefer Torah*. The critics think this scroll was Deuteronomy and that it was authored in the seventh century by priests who had survived the destruction of the northern kingdom, Israel, by the Assyrians in 721 B.C.E. Deuteronomy interprets the destruction as divine punishment for idolatry (e.g., Deut. 4:25). The north-erners had worshiped at two sanctuaries featuring golden calves (I Kings 12:28–29). The scroll warns Judah not to anger *Yah* in the same way and thereby meet the same fate. Hence the major foci in Deuteronomy: proper worship as opposed to idolatry, and punishment for the latter. The author wrote dialogue so as to cast the work in the mouth of Moses, the better to communicate the teachings.

Lacking documentary authentication we have to be chary of bib-lical history, but it would seem that our early ancestors, while they may have claimed a national deity, were either avowed polythe-ists or at least broad-minded about worshiping a variety of gods that might be found in the local culture. Critical readers ascribe the quasi history books, Joshua, Judges, Samuel, and Kings, to the Deuteronomic historian, an individual or school carrying on the teaching that worshiping other gods is the sin most certain to bring on punishment. In these books we find this retribution as a key literary motif as the consistent explanation for disasters—political, military, economic. And the writings mention more or less ongoing improper worship.

Divine fury also characterizes the thinking and the accusations of the eighth century prophets. Hosea in particular issued vivid warnings of destruction as punishment for unfaithfulness. And there are the tantalizing statuettes, mini idols, unearthed by archaeologists from various *tels* in the land. (See appendix.)

We are left with two possibilities. Either the *B'nei Yisrael* were supposed to have been monotheists since Abraham (or, say, Moses) but were tempted into sin by indigenous peoples, as Deuteronomy "warns" and "predicts" (e.g., 7:1–6; 31:16–17). Or they were accustomed from the start—whenever that was—to a world of deities, with different names, shapes, and functions. Prior to Deuteronomy, they saw nothing wrong in worshiping their own *Yah(veh)* in the form of a Golden Calf. Not only did they have the Canaanite gods, Baalim, Ashtarot, etc., but by the eighth century the Assyrian presence imposed worship of Shamash, Ishtar, and Ashur. II Kings 23 describes the purge of a long list of newly, officially, improper worship practices.

Hosea spoke of *Yah* as feeling like a rejected husband when Israel went whoring after Baal and others, but he was a poet and prophet. Deuteronomy drops that image and frames exclusive worship of *Yah* as a covenant (ברית, *b'rit*) article. The issue is not denial of other gods as in the words Deutero Isaiah put into God's mouth: "I am first and I am last and apart from Me there are no gods" (Isa. 44:6). Rather, as Deuteronomy puts it in the second commandment, "You shall have *no other gods before* Me." And furthermore, "You shall not make a statue, any image from the sky above, the earth below, or the water beneath the earth. You shall not worship them or serve them for I, *Yah* your God, am a jealous deity, visiting the guilt of the fathers upon the children to the third and fourth generation of them that hate me, though I show covenantal love to the thousands of My lovers who keep My commandments" (Deut. 5:7–10). *Yah* jealous? (A nod to Hosea!) Of whom? Of others His stiff-necked people might worship along with Him or even before Him. Apparently what the authors of Deuteronomy had in mind was not monotheism but henotheism, which the *Random House Dictionary* defines as "the worship of a particular god, as by a family or tribe, without disbelieving in the existence of others."

I learned this term from my mother who taught confirmation class but, for a long time, what should have been obvious, that our ancestors were essentially polytheists, was occluded by midrash that takes up the Deuteronomy message. For rabbis, beginning with our predecessors the Pharisees, monotheism alone is legitimate and virtuous. Anything else is alien and condemned as in the *Tanach* history books. It occurred to me somewhere in the middle of my pulpit career that critical reading of *Tanach* offers teaching moments just as relevant as midrash and, I think, makes better sense than the deliberate misreading sometimes necessary to make a point. So when I come to *Sh'ma*, I see polytheism/henotheism in process of evolution to monotheism and to who knows what.

As for the midrashic twelve sons reassuring their dying father about their theology, what Rabbi Elazar may have had in mind was defining Judaism in contrast to the ever expanding and developing Christianity, which had just had its First Council of Nicea (325). The Nicean creed speaks of Jesus as coexisting with God the Father, "begotten, not made, being of one substance with the Father." The good rabbi found it useful to misread the verse so as to combat emerging Trinitarian thinking.

The point is: the words in Deuteronomy aim not at polytheism or compound godhead but simply and powerfully at loyalty to *Yah*. Israel must worship *Yah* to the exclusion of all others.

Now let's have a look at the syntax of *Sh'ma*. Here's Deuteronomy 6:4 with its Masoretic punctuation:

שְׁמַע יִשְׂרָאֵל יְהֹוָה אֱלֹהֵינוּ יְהֹוָה | אֶחָד:

Sh'ma Yisrael: Adonai Eloheinu, Adonai echad

Consider some translations, all of which begin with "Hear, O Israel":

1. the Lord our God, the Lord is One. (*Union Prayer Book* of my childhood, Jewish Publication Society 1917)
2. the Lord is our God, the Lord is One! (*Gates of Prayer* 1975)
3. the Eternal is our God, the Eternal is One! (*Mishkan T'filah* 2004)
4. the Lord is our God, the Lord alone. (Jewish Publication Society 1985)

5. the Lord our God is one Lord. (King James Version 1611, Douay-Rheims 1609)

6. κύριος ὁ θεὸς ἡμῶν κύριος εἷς ἐστιν (Septuagint, third century B.C.E.)

7. Dominus Deus noster Dominus unus est (Vulgate, late fourth century C.E.)

Substantial differences, that is, not merely stylistic tendencies, alert us to disagreement, if not confusion, regarding the text.

One relatively simple challenge to the translator is where to insert "is." The first two words make up a clear imperative clause or sentence: Hear, O Israel. The following four Hebrew words lack a verb to make a forceful declaration. Since the verb "be" in present tense is understood rather than expressed in Hebrew, the first phrase, "Adonai Eloheinu," can be correctly understood either in apposition (1, 5, 6, 7) or as a declarative (2, 3, 4). The same holds for the second pair but here we have a more substantial difference: What does it mean to say that the Lord is one? (Not two? Not nine? Could not the same be said of Zeus?) What does "one Lord" mean? How can the word for "one" be stretched into "alone?" I think these are all imaginative measures on the part of translators to make sense of "Adonai echad."

Note that in the third century B.C.E. Greek Septuagint the verb *estin* (is) comes at the end of the verse and thus means either "Lord is one" or "is one Lord." The fourth century Latin copies the form. The avowedly Catholic Douay, considered a translation of the Latin, reads "is one Lord," and the Protestant KJV agrees.

A more pertinent challenge: What about the substitution of "Lord" ("κύριος," "Dominus," "The Eternal") for the Tetragrammaton, the four letters that spell the personal name commonly used in *Tanach* for God? This appears to be a convention by which to avoid speaking the name of God. Reading "Lord" where the text says "Yah" makes it harder to get to the meaning of any passage in *Tanach*, and I think this is particularly true with regard to the *Sh'ma*.

The matter of how to pronounce the name falls outside the scope of this article. I am comfortable and confident in speaking "Yah," its pronunciation clearly indicated in *Tanach* (e.g., Exod. 15:2, עָזִּי וְזִמְרָת יָהּ, *ozzi v'zim'rat Yah*, "Yah is my strength and song"). The first two letters serve as a short form, a nickname. I acquired this habit from my teacher Reb Zalman. A recent brief statement of his is appended.

In the eighth century, scholars in Palestine studied manuscripts and fixed what was to become the authorized Hebrew version, the Masoretic text, and they inserted the diacritical marks that serve as vowels. They, the Masoretes (from *masar*, pass down) wrote the Tetragrammaton with the vowels of *Adonai* ("my Lord," plural form as in *Elohim*). I long accepted the common teaching that the Masoretes followed a practice dating back at least to the third century B.C.E., based on the evidence of *Kyrios* (Lord) for the name in the Septuagint. The usual expanation—lacking early documentation—is either that the sound of the name had become too holy for common usage or that pronouncing it would violate the third commandment. Rather than profane the holy or break the commandment, we don't take the name at all. This would follow the principle of *siyag* (fence), a precautionary distancing ("Make a fence for Torah," attributed to the members of the Great Assembly, as early as Ezra, fifth century B.C.E.).

Two arguments point to a later, Talmudic (see appendix) start for avoiding speaking the name. First, *Mishnah B'rachot* 9:5 presents a formula for greeting:

> A person should seek the welfare of his friend with the name שׁוֹאֵל אֶת שְׁלוֹם חֲבֵרוֹ בַּשֵּׁם, as it is said: "And here Boaz comes from Bet Lechem and said to the harvesters: 'Yah (YHVH) be with you.' And they replied to him: 'Yah bless you.'" (Ruth 2:4)

No hesitation here in speaking the name in ordinary usage, a fortiori in sacred usage.

The second is speculative and indirect, based on the distinction between substituting and translating. The Greek-speaking Jews who made the Septuagint may have considered *Kyrios* (Lord) a translation of the name, based perhaps on the frequent use of:

$$\text{אֲדוֹן כָּל־הָאָרֶץ}$$

Lord of all the earth (Josh. 3:11, 13; Zech. 4:14, 6:5; Pss. 97:5, 114:4)

There are also several occurances of *Yah Adonai* (אֲדֹנָי), in apposition, and the clause:

$$\text{אָמַרְתְּ לַיהֹוָה אֲדֹנָי אָתָּה}$$

"Yah, You are *Adonai*" (Ps. 16:2; cf. Pss. 109:21, 140:8, 141:8).

Note also: *Kyrios* simply means "Lord," not "my Lord" as in *Adonai*, and, of course it is singular. Connecting *Kyrios* to a supposed but undocumented practice of avoiding pronouncing the name is a weak assumption. Rather, the authors chose a characteristic of divinity to convey their understanding of the divine name. Ironically, most translations appear to reflect the Greek text rather than the Hebrew.

By intent similar to that of the Septuagint, the modern authors of *Mishkan T'filah* chose to render the name as "The Eternal." They follow Moses Mendelssohn's 1811 Torah translation:

Der Ewige, unser Gott, ist ein einiges, ewiges Wesen.
the Eternal, our God, is a unique, eternal Being.

Mendelssohn, prophet of enlightenment, picked a suitable characteristic of God to use in place of the name. (My colleague and friend Tovia Ben-Chorin kindly transliterated Mendelssohn's German-in-Hebrew into Latin characters, properly spelled.)

One other translation catches my attention:

Hashem is our God, *Hashem* the One and Only (ArtScroll 1984)

ArtScroll speaks for the Orthodox who say *Hashem* (The Name) in place of *Yah* in all non-ritual usage. *Hashem* has the virtue of referencing the original rather than the interpretive substitution or translation, *Adonai*. The ArtScroll *Sh'ma* translation, as a whole, comes close to what strikes me as the intent of the text. It would come closer still were it to call our God "*Yah*."

A further obstacle to comprehension is that we read the *Sh'ma* according to musical tropes that serve as punctuation. These tropes were inserted, also, by the Masoretes. The verse includes three combinations. The words *Sh'ma Yisrael* are marked *tipchah/etnachtah*, the equivalent of a clause ending with colon. *Merchah/tipchah*, the most common of combinations, joins *Adonai Eloheinu*. *Adonai Echad* concludes with *merchah/sof pasuk*, signing the end of a verse. (In the verse as shown above the tropes are difficult to read and the *sof pasuk*, a small vertical line just left of the *kamatz* in *echad*, is lacking.) A literal rendition of the Masoretic reading would thus have three word groups:

Hear Israel: *Adonai*—our God   *Adonai*—one.

All the translations I have cited flow from this division, and so do the various melodies to which the words are recited. The usual understanding of *Sh'ma* results from what might be an idiosyncratic division of the text. For critical readers of *Tanach*, the Masoretic spin on the ancient manuscripts is subject to challenge, as herewith. Suppose we were to read the Hebrew:

Sh'ma Yisrael: Adonai! Eloheinu Adonai. Echad!

The opening words would remain *tipchah/etnachtah*. *Adonai* would have what A. W. Binder calls an "extraordinary" sign, setting it apart from the rest of the words (see, e.g., *Biblical Chant*, p. 38, *shalsheles*, a disjunctive). *Eloheinu Adonai* would become *merchah/tipchah*. *Echad* remains *sof pasuk*.

Note the *pasek*, the vertical line between *Adonai* and *echad*. The tropes each indicate a melisma, a phrase of several notes sung to one syllable. *Pasek* is a rest, separating between words. The article on *pasek* from online *Encyclopedia Judaica* appears in the appendix. The explanation there does not adequately describe our case. I think the Masoretes were hinting that the last two words were simply not a clause or even a phrase. They are to be read separately.

In English I would read:

Hear O Israel: *Yah*! Our God, *Yah*. One!

This is not a statement, a declaration, or a theological limitation. It is a dramatic exclamation. It is a hortatory call to associate with God, and a poetic statement about oneness, unity. Actually, this reading enables what I have for years been teaching as the meaning of *Sh'ma*, but now the meaning flows from the words and their syntax rather than in spite of the words and their syntax.

This reading also fits into the seventh century context. First, it emphasizes connection to *Yah*, our God, *Yah*. The chapter proceeds to command love (*v'ahavta*) for *Yah*. Second, the word *echad*, standing alone, suggests rather than defines. Henotheism could be the point here, or it might be "the one and only" as seen by the ArtScroll editor. If it does not stand for monotheism, it yet foreshadows that development. Third, we find similar dramatic rhetoric in *Tzedek! Tzedek tirdof* ("Justice! Justice, pursue") (Deut. 16:20) and *Adonai! Adonai El rachum* ("*Yah*! *Yah* merciful God") (Exod. 34:6).

Finally, there is Zechariah's remarkable response to *Sh'ma*. The prophet lived in the sixth century B.C.E., following the return to Palestine of some of the Babylonian exiles. He paid attention to the monotheism taught by Deutero Isaiah in that diaspora context. The national community struggling to revive itself faced difficult conditions. "One day . . .," the prophet said, "*Yah* will be king over all the earth. On that day *Yah* will be one and his name One!" (Zech. 14:9) (בַּיּוֹם הַהוּא יִהְיֶה יְהֹוָה אֶחָד וּשְׁמוֹ אֶחָד). Like the Deuteronomy verse, these words hint at an ideal.

Monotheism hints at unity in the world and oneness in human experience. Different peoples have different names for deity. Each culture has its own way of thinking about God. For some there is no God. The concept of monotheism transcends diversity. If there is truly One, it must be beyond what we call religions. If *Sh'ma*, written for the ancient world, is to bridge to the twenty-first century, then *echad* must reference the oneness of at least a galaxy. I use a personal name for God as part of my spiritual practice. The name *Yah* is subjective, that is it belongs to a Jew, more specifically to me as an individual Jew, rather than to the object of my thought. Someday I may advance to skipping the name in favor of the *echad*.

וְנִהְיֶה אֲנַחְנוּ וְצֶאֱצָאֵינוּ, וְצֶאֱצָאֵי עַמְּךָ בֵּית יִשְׂרָאֵל, כֻּלָּנוּ יוֹדְעֵי שְׁמֶךָ,
וְלוֹמְדֵי תוֹרָתֶךָ לִשְׁמָהּ:

APPENDIX

This appendix contains the primary sources and the background material for the above article. The citations follow the order of the points made in the article. I chose this form over endnotes for two reasons: (1) Initiated readers will recognize the sources without endnotes and the uninitiated might not find the Hebrew of interest; and (2) The collected material itself makes for a worthwhile read on its own. For ease, each section concludes with a horizontal line.

ג הקבצו ושמעו בני יעקב, רבי ברכיה זימנין אמר לה בשם רבי חייא וזמנין אמר
לה בשם רבנן דתמן, מכאן שהיו מפוזרין וירד מלאך וכינסן, אמר ר' תנחומא
מכאן שהיו מפוזרין וכינסן ברוח הקודש, ושמעו אל ישראל אביכם, רבי יודן
ורבי פנחס, רבי יודן אמר שמעו לאל ישראל אביכם, ורבי פנחס אמר אל הוא
ישראל אביכם, מה הקב"ה בורא עולמות אף אביכם בורא עולמות, מה הקב"ה
מחלק עולמות אף אביכם מחלק עולמות, אלעזר בן אחוי אמר: מכאן זכו

ישראל לקריאת שמע, בשעה שהיה יעקב אבינו נפטר מן העולם קרא לשנים
עשר בניו. אמר להם: "שמעו, אל ישראל שבשמים אביכם? שמא יש בלבבכם
מחלוקת על הקב"ה? א"ל: (דברים ו) "שמע ישראל אבינו, כשם שאין בלבך
מחלוקת על הקב"ה, כך אין בלבנו מחלוקת, אלא ה' אלהינו ה' אחד." אף
הוא פירש בשפתיו ואמר ברוך שם כבוד מלכותו לעולם ועד, רבי ברכיה ורבי
חלבו בשם רבי שמואל הדא הוא שישראל משכימים ומעריבים בכל יום
ואומרים שמע ישראל אבינו ממערת המכפלה אותו דבר שצויתנו עדיין הוא
נוהג בנו ה' אלהינו ה' אחד.

(*B'reishit Rabbah* 98:3, with my added punctuation)

Note the creative reading of Genesis 49:2b, "Listen to Israel, your father." By inserting *shebashamayim* after Yisrael, the word *el* (אל), which means "to" in Genesis, becomes "God" in the midrash and the line becomes a question rather than a wish. In their reply, the sons insert *avinu* after *Sh'ma Yisrael*, turning Deuteronomy 6:4 into a reassurance to their father. Homiletic license.

In the Hebrew transliteration, we have broken away from the conventional use of *Adonai* (Lord) for the Tetragrammaton (four-lettered name), Y-H-V-W, the unpronounceable name of God. Instead we have chosen to represent the name in English letters as you see here. When this must be read aloud, we recommend replacing it with the name *Yah*, "Being," which is used at various times in this book. For *Yah* is a part of the divine name and participates in its power and immediacy, but the letters *yud-heh* are not connected to the prohibition on pronunciation. Moreover, *Yah* is not an exclusively masculine name but has both masculine and feminine attributes, making it even more palatable for use by both men and women today.

(Zalman Schachter-Shalomi, *A Heart Afire*
[Philadelphia: Jewish Publication Society, 2009], xiv)

מכאן את למד שהרגו בשם המפורש

Tanchuma (Warsaw edition) *perek* 10: Moses killed the Egyptian with the Shem Hamforash (ninth century collection with references to a fourth century source)

---

by the transcription Ιαουαι/ε in Clement of Alexandria Stromata 5:6,
34 (Baudissin 2:116f : Ganschinietz in Pauly-W. 9:700: Ιαου); . . . by
the transcription Ιαβε in Field on Ex 63 (Baudissin 2:222f)

(Article on *YHVH, Hebrew and Aramaic Lexicon,
Old Testament, BibleWorks* 8)

Note that the Clement, an early Church Father, was a contemporary of Y'hudah HaNasi. (Thanks Wikipedia.) The transliteration,
Yaouai/e may tell us how the name sounded in Greek ears. I have
no idea about the Field reference, but the transliteration is *Yave*.
Beta represents a voiced bilabial fricative by the first century C.E.,
when it is used regularly to transliterate the Latin u (v). It develops
gradually into a labial dental fricative [v]. (Doctor Francis T. Gignac,
professor of Biblical Studies at the Catholic University of America,
Washington, D.C.) I received this and much other technical help
from my Catholic colleague and friend, Rev. Patrick J. Madden,
Ph.D., director, Greco Institute, Shreveport, Louisiana. We continue,
via Skype, weekly Bible study that has lasted twelve years.

κύριος [υ⁻], α, ον, and ος, ον: (κῦρος):
   I. of persons, having power or authority over, lord or master of, c.
   gen., Pind., Att.:- κύριός εἰμι, c. inf., I have authority to do, am entitled to do, Aesch., etc.; κυριώτεροι δοῦναι better able to give, Thuc.
   2. absol. having authority, authoritative, supreme, κ. εἶναι to
   have authority, Plat.; τὸ κύριον the ruling power in a state, τὰ
   κύρια the authorities, Soph., Dem.
   II. not of persons, authoritative, decisive, dominant, supreme,
   δίκαι Eur.; μῦθος κυριώτερος of more authority, Id., etc.
   2. opp. to ἄκυρος, authorised, ratified, valid, νόμοι, δόγματα Dem.;
   κ. θέσθαι or ποιεῖσθαί τι to appoint by authority, Soph., Dem.
   3. of times, etc., fixed, ordained, appointed, Hdt., Eur., etc.;-so,
   τὸ κύριον the appointed time, Aesch.:-at Athens, κυρία ἐκκλησία
   a regular or ordinary assembly, opp. to σύγκλητος ἐκκλησία
   (one specially summoned), Ar.
   4. *legitimate, regular, proper,* Aesch.
   5. of words, *authorised, vernacular,* Lat. proprius, Arist.
   B. as Subst., κύριος, ὁ, *a lord, master,* Lat. dominus, of gods, Pind.,
   Soph., etc.: *the head* of a family, *master* of a house, Aesch.,

etc.:-later, κύριε was a form of respectful address, like our *sir*,
N.T.

2. κυρία, ἡ, *mistress* or *lady of the house,* Lat. domina, Menand., etc.

II. ὁ Κύριος, *the LORD,* = Hebr. *JEHOVAH,* LXX.; in N.T. esp. of
CHRIST. Hence κυριότης

(Lidel-Scott Greek Lexicon, online)

T'murah 3b bottom of page:

אלא למאי אתא למקלל את חבירו בשם, ואימא: למוציא שם שמים לבטלה? מי
גרע מקלל את חבירו בשם, ממוציא שם שמים לבטלה? אנן הכי קא קשיא לן:
אימא, מוציא שם שמים לבטלה תיסגי ליה במלקות, אבל מקלל חבירו בשם,
כיון דקעביד תרתי, דקא מפיק שם שמים לבטלה, וקמצער ליה לחבריה לא
תיסגי ליה במלקות!

But why not say that the text refers to one who pronounces the Lord's
name for no purpose?— Is then one who curses his fellow with the
Name less culpable than one who pronounces the Lord's name for no
purpose?—Our question is really this: Why not say that for one who
pronounces the Lord's name for no purpose the punishment of lashes
will suffice, but if one curses his fellow with the Name, since he commits two [forbidden things], first in pronouncing the Lord's name for
no purpose and then in vexing his fellow, therefore punishment with
lashes should not be sufficient? (Soncino translation)

One who pronounces The Name by its letters . . .

Thanks to my colleague and friend Rifat Soncino's "God Doesn't
Need a Name" (*CCAR Journal* [Fall 2010]: 111) I found *agadic,* i.e.,
legendary/speculative references (as opposed to halachic, legal
declarations) in Mishnah and Talmud. The Mishnah passage is the
well-known statement of who has and has not a portion in *Olam
HaBa* (The World to Come).

א כָּל יִשְׂרָאֵל יֵשׁ לָהֶם חֵלֶק לָעוֹלָם הַבָּא, שֶׁנֶּאֱמַר (ישעיה ס) וְעַמֵּךְ כֻּלָּם צַדִּיקִים
לְעוֹלָם יִירְשׁוּ אָרֶץ נֵצֶר מַטָּעַי מַעֲשֵׂה יָדַי לְהִתְפָּאֵר. וְאֵלּוּ שֶׁאֵין לָהֶם חֵלֶק לָעוֹלָם
הַבָּא, הָאוֹמֵר אֵין תְּחִיַּת הַמֵּתִים מִן הַתּוֹרָה, וְאֵין תּוֹרָה מִן הַשָּׁמַיִם, וְאַפִּיקוֹרוֹס.
רַבִּי עֲקִיבָא אוֹמֵר, אַף הַקּוֹרֵא בִסְפָרִים הַחִיצוֹנִים, וְהַלּוֹחֵשׁ עַל הַמַּכָּה וְאוֹמֵר
(שמות טו) לָךְ הַמַּחֲלָה אֲשֶׁר שַׂמְתִּי בְמִצְרַיִם לֹא אָשִׂים עָלֶיךָ כִּי אֲנִי ה' רֹפְאֶךָ.
אַבָּא שָׁאוּל אוֹמֵר, אַף הַהוֹגֶה אֶת הַשֵּׁם בְּאוֹתִיּוֹתָיו:

(Mishnah Sanhedrin 10:1)

אבא שאול אומר אף ההוגה את השם באותיותיו וכו׳. אנת: ובגבולין,
ובלשון עגה. (TB Sanhedrin 10:1:)

אתיוהו לרבי חנינא בן תרדיון, אמרו ליה: אמאי קא עסקת באורייתא? אמר
להו: כאשר צוני ה׳ אלהי. מיד גזרו עליו לשריפה, ועל אשתו להריגה, ועל בתו
לישב בקובה של זונות. עליו לשריפה, שהיה הוגה את השם באותיותיו. והיכי
עביד הכי? והתנן, אלו שאין להם חלק לעולם הבא: האומר אין תורה מן
השמים, ואין תחיית המתים מן התורה אבא שאול אומר: אף ההוגה תא השם
באותיותיו! להתלמד עבד, כדתניא: (דברים יח) לא תלמד לעשות אבל אתה
למד להבין ולהורות. אלא מאי טעמא אענש? משום הוגה את השם בפרהסיא
[דהוי]. לעו אשתו להריגה, דלא מיחה ביה. מכאן אמרו: כל מי שיש בידו
למחות ואינו מוחה נענש עליו. (TB vodah Zarah 17:18)

All Israel have a portion in the *Olam HaBa*, as it is said (Is 60:21)
"Your people, all of them righteous, shall forever inherit the land.
They are the shoot I planted, My handiwork for glory." And
these have no portion in *Olam HaBa*: One who says revival of
the dead is not from the Torah, and Torah is not from Heaven,
and an *apikoros* ("disbeliever"). Rabbi Akibah says, also one who
reads Apocrypha and one who whispers over a wound, saying
(Ex 15:26) "Every disease I set on the Egyptians I shall not set on
you for I, Yah, am your healer." Abba Shaul says: also one who
pronounces The Name by its letters.

Abba Shaul says: also one who pronounces The Name by its letters. It has been taught: This applies in the country (not the Temple) and in the sense of *aga* (Samaritan blasphemy).

They then brought up R. Hanina b. Teradion and asked him,
"Why hast thou occupied thyself with the Torah?" He replied,
"Thus the Lord my God commanded me." At once they sen-
tenced him to be burnt, his wife to be slain, and his daughter to
be consigned to a brothel. The punishment of being burnt came
upon him because he pronounced the Name in its full spelling.
But how could he do so? Have we not learnt: The following have
no portion in the world to come: He who says that the Torah is
not from Heaven, or that the resurrection of the dead is not taught
in the Torah. Abba Saul says: Also he who pronounces the Name
in its full spelling?—He did it in the course of practicing, as we
have learnt: Thou shalt not learn to do after the abominations
of those nations, but thou mayest learn [about them] in order to
understand and to teach. Why then was he punished?—Because
he was pronouncing the Name in public. His wife was punished
by being slain, because she did not prevent him [from doing it].

From this it was deduced: Any one who has the power to prevent [one from doing wrong] and does not prevent, is punished for him. (Soncino translation)

5.3.3.3.1. Signs for Pause and not for Melody. (Paseq; maqqaf)

Paseq. The sign | (a vertical line between words; originally a small line ')—פסק (Aramaic: cutting off), פּסק (Aramaic: cut off); a symbol for pause only and not for melody. It occurs only after conjunctive accents and indicates a pause. One should consider it an additional improvement in the systems of accentuation, for it is a sign used to complete the punctuation system after the system of the melody was stabilized. With regard to its phonetic influence upon the pronunciation of the word it is also like a disjunctive in that it voids the fricative nature of בגדכפ"ת at the beginning of the following word; that is, it cancels the fricativeness which is caused by the conjunctive accent near it. A distinction should be made between a *paseq* which is wont to occur after any one of the conjunctives as opposed to the similar sign which goes with one of the disjunctives: *shalshelet, munah legarmeh, shalshelet gedolah, azla' legarmeh, mahpach legarmeh*. With these disjunctives the sign is part of the system of accentuation. To distinguish between the two kinds, the masoretes arranged lists of the *paseqs* (פּסקתא) found in the Bible. The lists are not identical, but in general the number of *paseqs* reaches about 400. Already in *Dikdukei ha-Te'amim* a few rules for *paseq* were enumerated, and in effect it was possible to explain most of the *paseqs* in the Bible with the aid of a list of rules. Yet these rules did not always work, and one cannot explain why they were not applied in every instance. The *paseq* as a means of perfection fulfills two main needs:

(1) a phonetic need for the correction of pronunciation—
  (a) to separate between equal consonants or similar ones at the boundaries of adjacent words e.g. לגלים | מעון תנים והיבבה בבל (Jer. 51:37);
  (b) to separate between a pair of identical or similar words, e.g., יום | יום (Gen. 39:10), המול | ימול (Gen. 17:13);
(2) a punctuational need to correct the understanding of a verse—
  (a) to separate between words, one of which is a name of God, which should be joined according to the context, but

their conjunction is liable to allow for a different under-standing, in which God's name would be profaned, e.g. אם תקטל אלוֹהּ‖ רשע (Ps. 139:19)–"if Thou shall kill, O God, the wicked," not "if you kill the wicked God";

(b) to separate words which should be separated according to the context, but for which the accentuation did not find the proper disjunctives. This refers mainly to an additional division of the hemistichs of the smallest disjunctives—*pazer, telisha' gedolah* and sometimes *geresh*—which cannot be divided further with accentuation signs: e.g. תשא אתי רוח‖ הארץ ובין השמים‖ (Ezek. 8:3). The above, though, are not rules for the placement of the *paseq*, but categories according to which one can classify and understand most of the *paseqs* of the Bible. Yet there are many places in the Bible which come under this classification and a *paseq* is not found there. A relatively small part of the *paseqs* are not explained even according to this classification, and there is no doubt that hidden explanations and exegetical homilies played a part in the placing of the *paseq*, as with the accentuation signs.

(Encyclopedia Judaica, Masorah, online)

My colleague and friend Harvey Tattelbaum shared with me his homiletic spin: *Adonai Eloheinu echad* tells us that *YHVH* and God are one and the same, tribal and universal have come together.

Book Reviews

Early Modern Jewry: A New Cultural History
by David Ruderman
(Princeton, NJ: Princeton University Press, 2010), 326 pp.

Jewish scholars and their students have frequently indulged in the convenient but delicate task of periodizing Jewish history. Periodization in its broad strokes is an artificial construct. The challenge of periodization requires definition of terms like "classical," "medieval," or "modern." It also requires establishing clear criteria for assigning a unifying title or theme to an era. Without a careful, thorough approach, periodization tends to mask the ebb and flow of change as though it were uninterrupted, smooth, or sharply delineated.

David Ruderman (HUC-NY, 1971) has grappled with periodization, its definitions and processes, for at least the past fifteen years. In this regard, he has expressed two hopes:

> Whereas the early modern period in general European history has been considered a major watershed politically, economically, socially, and culturally, it has appeared in patently dissimilar terms in Jewish historiography . . . I hope to return to the question of periodization of early modern Jewish history in a future study.[1]

Ruderman's second hope stems from his desire to hone the periodization of modern Jewish history: "I hope to problematize the notion that Jewish strategies of coping with modernity originated exclusively under the aegis and in the pattern of the Berlin Haskalah."[2] In expressing his two hopes, Ruderman is suggesting the inadequacy of a periodization that jumps precipitously from the medieval to the modern eras. He intends, as well, to show that, contrary to assigning the beginning of modernity to the early German Haskalah, Jews were compelled to respond even earlier to nascent forces and issues of modernity.

In *Early Modern Jewry: A New Cultural History*, Ruderman fulfills his previously stated hopes in a thoroughly researched and elegant analysis culminating in what truly could be called his magnum opus. This work of incisive thought and clear language is, in part, a synthesis of Ruderman's treatment in his earlier books on Kabbalah and Sabbateanism, the decline of rabbinic authority, and the Converso diaspora. Indeed, he combines and connects social history and intellectual history to demonstrate the unique facets of those three centuries that follow the expulsion from Spain up to Emperor Joseph II's Edict of Toleration of 1782.

These three centuries comprise for Ruderman the early modern period of Jewish history. He asserts they are shaped and characterized by five elements:

1. Increased mobility of Jews, and a concomitant increase of contact among Jews of different backgrounds
2. A strengthening in various Jewish communities of a sense of communal cohesion
3. A widespread explosion of knowledge, both secular and sacred, due to the invention and dissemination of the printing press
4. A crisis in rabbinic authority across Europe
5. The blurring of religious identity due to Conversos returning to the community, the presence of Sabbateans, and interaction with Christian Hebraists

These five trends touched Jews from Amsterdam to Istanbul, from Poland to the Italian peninsula. Ruderman admits his five characteristics may not be exhaustive, but

> undermine once and for all a view long entrenched in modern Jewish historiography of an inevitable one-dimensional and one-directional path from servitude to emancipation, from communal solidarity to disintegration, from ghettoization to citizenship, and from normative tradition to radical assimilation.[3]

The early modern period that Ruderman delineates is a continuum stretched between the poles of the medieval and modern Jewish experience with characteristics of both overlapping.

A nuanced understanding of the early modern period helps us to see how it differs from the modern period. Ruderman reminds us of ingredients that are particularly part of the post-Berlin Haskalah landscape of modernity. These include the two great revolutions in America and in France, absolutism and the centralization of political power, and emancipation and the rise of nationalism. Haskalah was a programmatic movement, but there is much more to modernity, including a radically different political and social reality from the early modern centuries.

Ruderman's conceptual framework of the interconnectedness of social, cultural, and religious trends over time and across regions is the powerful glue that binds and defines the early modern period. There are two other substantial sources of strength in this work. First, Ruderman presents an extended historiographical discussion of the work of other scholars in this period. He presents the approaches of those who influenced him, including his teacher Jacob Katz. He credits historians Jonathan Israel, Jerry Bentley, and Sanjay Subrahmanyam, who have employed "connectedness" in addressing a culture and a period. Disagreements with the views of Robert Bonfil, Moshe Rosman, Gershon Hundert, and Yosef Kaplan are aired for the sake of achieving greater understanding. This discussion is enhanced by a tone of openness, modesty, and respect for colleagues.

The second strength of this work is its prodigious scholarship. Most of Ruderman's footnotes are extensive and function as a guide to his thought as well as a mini-bibliography on any given point of discussion. The "Bibliography of Secondary Sources" covers thirty pages and is wide-ranging. Had we not been previously familiar with the integrity and thoroughness of Ruderman's earlier work, they are apparent in this latest book.

As one who received his Bachelor of Arts degree in history, I confess I enjoy the study of history for its own sake. I love to read about the challenges of human interaction, discovery, and development. Yet, there is more within the covers of *Early Modern Jewry*. It reveals a preview of so much Jews are still confronting today: a knowledge explosion more vast and intense even than the arrival of the printing press; mobility and interaction among Jews over thousands of miles and across oceans; a fluidity of identity, boundaries, and gateways both into, out of, and within Jewish communities; and a yearning for mystical/spiritual solutions to our post-modern ennui.

Though much has changed in Jewish life and history since 1782, *Early Modern Jewry* provides us with a context for the beginning of what Jews have experienced since 1492 and, in a number of contemporary ways, continue to experience. Ruderman's *Early Modern Jewry*, a vital resource for reflection, teaching, and preaching, is a study I highly recommend.

Notes

1. David Ruderman, *Jewish Thought and Scientific Discovery in Early Modern Europe* (Detroit: Wayne State University Press, paperback, 2001), 6, 6 n. 14.
2. David Ruderman, *Jewish Enlightenment in an English Key* (Princeton, NJ: Princeton University Press, 2000), 3.
3. David Ruderman, *Early Modern Jewry: A New Cultural History*, 204.

RABBI PAUL J. CITRIN (C73) is retired in Albuquerque, New Mexico.

Wisdom of the Heart: The Teachings of Rabbi Ya'akov of Izbica-Radzyn
by Ora Wiskind-Elper
(Philadelphia: Jewish Publication Society, 2010), 240 pp.

The Przysucha (p'SHICH-sa) school of Chasidism is arguably one of the most creative, heretical, and contemporary of them all. Focusing on spiritual autonomy, free will, personal integrity, intellectual rigor, and serious study, it traces its origins from Jacob Isaac Rabinowitz, the "Holy Yehudi," to Simcha Bunam of Przysucha and Menahem Mendl Morgenstern Halperin of Kotsk. It includes Hanokh of Alexander, Isaac Meir Rotenberg-Alter of Ger and, of course, Mordecai Yosef Leiner of Izbica (Izh-bitz).

Mordecai Yosef Leiner began as a colleague and disciple of Kotsk. But, after what Chasidim call "The Incident" (in which the Kotsker either touched the Sabbath candles, knocked them over, or actually said: "*Layt din, v'layt dayan* [There is no judgment and there is no Judge!]") in 1839, he left for Izbica to found his own community. His teachings were compiled after his death (1854) in *Mei HaShiloah*. It is clearly radical, antinomian, and probably heretical. For Leiner, human freedom is an illusion.[1]

Leiner's son, Ya'akov (d. 1878) continued in his father's intellectual footsteps. His teachings were assembled by his son, Gershon Hanokh Henikh Leiner of Radzyn (d. 1891) in the four, very big volumes of *Beit Ya'akov*. They are the primary focus of Ora Wiskind-Elper's *Wisdom of the Heart*.

Hanokh Henikh also, by the way, claimed to have identified the Mediterranean mollusk from which the dye for *t'chelet* (the tallit's thread of blue) is made. (Last time I bought a set, they went for $25.)

Notwithstanding its poetically inviting title, *Wisdom of the Heart* is not a popular book. There are fifty pages of footnotes. The language is often opaquely scholarly. (What, for example, is a "paradoxical valence," a "minor modality," or being "devalorized by the diurnal mind"?) There are only four stand-alone chapters whose titles and subheads unfortunately are equally poetic but not very helpful as descriptive waypoints. In fairness, if Wiskind-Elper's overview of Ya'akov Leiner's *Beit Ya'akov* sometimes seems scattered or unorganizable, it is much more a reflection of the original text rather than Wiskind-Elper's analytic skill. The reader feels that Professor Wiskind-Elper has channeled Rabbi Ya'akov Leiner; she is effectively his contemporary amanuensis. Drawing on the work of sages such as Emanuel Levinas, D. W. Winnicott, and Charles Taylor, and, above all, her own insights, she invites us to consider the *Beit Ya'akov* as an important contribution to theology, psychology, and philosophy.

And yet, for its occasionally bewildering language and structure, this is an important and rewarding monograph. With grace and insight, it touches on virtually every dimension of Jewish spirituality: religious determinism, freedom of spirit, antinomianism, sin, resurrection, birth, God's hiddenness, ego annihilation, self and other, the illusion of personal autonomy, and God's plan for our world and ourselves. Indeed, the *Beit Ya'akov* and *Wisdom of the Heart* speak wisely and convincingly about nothing less than the purpose of creation and human life.

It is not customary in such a short review to list breakout quotations. But, in this case, I can think of no more economical a way of communicating the often astonishing breadth of Yaakov Leiner's thoughts and Wiskind-Elper's insights into them. Certainly, for those in the preaching/teaching business, each one is the touchstone for another High Holy Day sermon. I list but a few here in order of their appearance:

EGYPTIAN BRICKS: "Each [brick] was transformed into a stone of sapphire. Truly, all that is holy comes to be only through forgetting—the deeper the oblivion into which they sank, the greater was the holiness awarded to them in the end." (p. 13)

WOMEN: "As long as [Adam] remained awake, the feminine aspect of humankind . . . was indiscernible. Only after God casts him into deep sleep could the feminine emerge." (p. 17)

SUFFERING: "Every trouble a person suffers, in body or in soul—when one realizes that in that very suffering is God Himself, only in concealed form—as soon as one sees this, the concealment is taken away and the suffering ends, and with it all one's persecutions." (p. 49)

AUTONOMY: "When the human will acts in isolation, as an autonomous ego, it can achieve nothing of real value." (p. 56)

T'SHUVAH: "The baal teshuvah . . . cannot know, during the time of concealment, that God is with him. But when he repents with all his heart, then he sees how, from beginning to end, everything that happened to him was 'the words of the living God'" (p. 102)

FAILURE: "The flaws of rejected attempts are never really forgotten. Not only does something of them linger; they become an integral part of the work that finally pleases its creator." (p. 119)

AROUSAL: "The world was created for you. Everything depends on you...on your soul's willingness to be aroused to question. The world exists for the sake of that arousal." (p. 125)

CONCEALMENT: "All of Creation is possible only through concealment, through the illusion that the world is separate from God . . . That way, people may imagine they are autonomous beings." (p. 135)

CHILDREN: "Our children reveal some precious essence hidden deep within us: Through them, our own identity or 'root' can become 'clear,' evident, and cherished by ourselves and others." (p. 143)

SPOUSE: "Ezer ke-negedo . . . means that God so wills it that an individual's aid and help should stem from things that oppose one." (p. 177)

BROKEN TABLETS: "Originally, [Adam's] being filled the whole world . . . Similarly, on the first Tablets, the word 'and' was not written . . . Thus, each commandment expanded endlessly; no room was left for the next one . . . And so the first Tablets [had to be] broken." (p. 178)

ADAM'S SIN: "God, finally, will make it clear that, in truth, Adam ate the good part [of the tree] alone. There was no sin. It only seemed so to Adam." (p. 181)

Marriage: "Since, at first, [Eve] had been together with him in a single body, if deficiency is in her, [Adam] realized, it must be his as well . . . If not, if he were wholly good, how could something bad ever emerge from him?" (p. 183)

Resurrection: "One suffers from [birth deficiencies] all the days of one's life, and recalls [them] continually...[Thus] if the dead were to arise in perfect form, they would not recognize themselves." (p. 193)

Ora Wiskind-Elper's *Wisdom of the Heart: The Teachings of Rabbi Ya'akov of Izbica-Radzyn* gives us the keys to one of Chasidism's most important and fecund traditions. Indeed, had she only shared with us her translations, *dayeinu*! We are all in her debt.

Note

1. Readers more interested in Mordecai Yosef Leiner's *Mei HaShiloah* and his philosophy of divine will may wish to consult two earlier works: Morris M. Faierstein, *All Is in the Hands of Heaven: The Teaching of Rabbi Mordecai Joseph Leiner of Izbica* (New York: Yeshiva University and Ktav, 1989); and Shaul Magid, *Hasidism on the Margin: Reconciliation, Antinomianism, and Messianism in Izbica/Radzin Hasidism* (Madison, WI: University of Wisconsin Press, 2003).

RABBI LAWRENCE KUSHNER (NY69) is the Emanu-El Scholar at Congregation Emanu-El, San Francisco. His most recent book is *I'm God; You're Not: Observations on Organized Religion and Other Disguises of the Ego* (Woodstock, VT: Jewish Lights, 2010).

Religious Toleration: Political Theory and Practical Arrangements—A Review Essay

Marc Saperstein

Reviewing

Divided by Faith: Religious Conflict and the Practice of Toleration in Early Modern Europe by Benjamin J. Kaplan (Cambridge: Harvard University Press, 2007/paperback: 2010), 415 pp.

The Hebrew Republic: Jewish Sources and the Transformation of European Political Thought by Eric Nelson (Cambridge: Harvard University Press, 2010), 229 pp.

These two books, recently published by Harvard University Press, both challenge the commonly accepted narrative that toleration of religious diversity came as the result of secularism and Enlightenment. Yet they differ fundamentally in their approach to the subject.

Benjamin J. Kaplan, professor of Dutch History at the University of Amsterdam, has written an extremely impressive work, exploring how post-Reformation Europeans with radically different religious commitments were sometimes able to live together in the same village, town, or city, if not in friendship then in peaceful coexistence, thereby accommodating religious diversity in strong tension with their own religious doctrine.

His focus is on Christians, with the status of Jews and Muslims consigned to one forty-page chapter near the end. We might assume that following the Reformation, toleration of Jews was a greater problem for Christian majorities than toleration of minority Christian groups. But that is not the case. A tradition originating with St. Augustine justified the continued existence of Jews observing their own religious traditions within a Christian Commonwealth. But both Catholic and Protestant leaders believed that Christian deviance from their own orthodoxy was heresy, and allowing a minority group to observe its aberrant ways was a sinful affront to the one true faith. Another long tradition, also originating with St. Augustine, justified force against heresy.

Thus peaceful coexistence for different expressions of Christianity was not the norm; it was fundamentally problematic and usually deemed illegitimate. Many examples of persecution are provided in the first section of the book, ranging from religious wars (which continued well into the eighteenth century) to violent attacks on a parade of monks, part of a Catholic minority protected by imperial law, carrying crosses through the center of the officially Lutheran city of Donauwörth. Yet in addition to chronicling these expressions of intolerance, Kaplan shows how modes of coexistence were indeed developed.

Minority religious groups were sometimes permitted to reside alongside the majority, though not permitted the open exercise of their faith. In late sixteenth-century Vienna, for example, Protestants were expected on Sunday mornings to proceed outside the city limits (a practice called *Auslauf*) to an estate where they could worship and hear the Bible read and a sermon delivered in accordance with their own religious convictions. Another option was unofficially sanctioned clandestine churches. In seventeenth-century Amsterdam, there were twenty clandestine Catholic and six Mennonite churches, concealed from the public domain in the upper stories of private homes (p. 174).[1] In German Augsburg, following 1648, Catholicism and Lutheranism were legally permitted, with each religious community governing its affairs autonomously, but no other Protestant denomination was allowed (p. 243).[2]

Such arrangements certainly fail by our understanding of toleration. Yet Kaplan argues that such arrangements should be judged not by nineteenth- and twentieth-century standards, but rather from the perspective of the previous period and realistic alternatives at the time, which included execution, violent attack, emigration, or dissimulation (p. 300). Arrangements such as *Auslauf* or clandestine churches provided opportunities for people of different religious faiths to live together and interact economically and even to some extent socially.

Alongside this older model of toleration based on recognized groups with authority to impose uniformity among their own members, a newer model based on individual decisions also emerged. Kaplan's prime example for this is Amsterdam, where individual members of churches were free to decide to what extent, if at all, they would attend weekly services or take communion. A fascinating example of productive coexistence in this environment is depicted in Rembrandt's 1662 painting *The Syndics*, presenting five men with hats (and one servant) supervising the standards for cloth sold in the city. Kaplan informs us (though without explaining how this is known) that the five officials represented four confessions (Catholic, Calvinist, Mennonite, Remonstrant), working together in an arena where people would be judged by their talents and skills and religious differences had little significance (pp. 237–39).

One weakness of the book is the documentation in the endnotes, with rare exceptions limited to identifying the source for direct quotations. Fascinating detailed information about communities and events is provided without any indication of the basis for what the author is reporting.[3] When he turns to the Jewish material, it seems as if Kaplan's confidence in his narrative voice has been lost, and he falls back on direct quotations from secondary works, some of them clichés.[4] The section on "Further Reading" is useful, but does not fill the lacuna of abundant information lacking guidance to its source.

Eric Nelson, an associate professor of Government at Harvard, has written a different kind of challenge to widely accepted explanations of the origins of modern progressive democratic thinking about kingship, its role with regard to the redistribution of private property, and its commitment to religious toleration. He argues that the rejection of long-standing medieval traditions was driven not by a secularist repudiation of religious authority, but rather by a new reading of the Hebrew Scriptures, facilitated by the accessibility of Rabbinic and medieval exegetical Hebrew texts to a group of European Christian Hebraists. Thus the assertion, implied by the book's subtitle, that European political thought was transformed, through the influence of Jewish sources, toward an acceptance of progressive values that we identify with the modern democratic state.[5]

As this claim should be extremely appealing to rabbinical readers, I will examine his arguments at greater length. Focused not on how people lived but on the thought of scholars and intellectuals, yet written in an engaging and accessible style, the book shows wide reading in the Latin works of such European Hebraists as Wilhelm Schickard of Germany, Peter Cunaeus and Hugo Grotius of Holland and John Selden of England, as well as influential writers who drew from their works—James Harrington (author of the controversial *Commonwealth of Oceana*), Milton, and Hobbes. The author's facility with the Jewish sources is evident. Its jacket is adorned with glowing encomia by Anthony Grafton and Michael Walzer, both highly respected academics. Yet I found the book's central argument unconvincing. I am not competent to evaluate the accuracy of the startling assertion that Christian texts studying the *respublica Hebraeorum* in light of newly recovered Rabbinic materials became "perhaps the most dominant genre of European political writing over the next [i.e., the seventeenth] century" (p. 17). I can however, speak to the sources themselves and their relationship to the ideas they were used to support.

The first chapter traces a new attitude toward kingship. The regnant theme of European political thought before the transformation was "constitutional pluralism": the idea that monarchy, aristocracy, and democracy were all potentially legitimate forms of government. This view is then challenged in favor of a position that Nelson calls "Republican Exclusivism": that monarchy is by its nature sinful (p. 3).[6]

Responsible for this radical change, according to Nelson's argument, is one reading of the well-known passage where Samuel responds negatively to the Israelite elders' request or demand to appoint a king who will judge them, and God instructs him to appoint the king, as their desire is not a repudiation of Samuel but of God Himself (I Sam. 8:4, 22).

Now this would appear to be a rather weak foundation for the position that according to the Bible kingship is inherently sinful for European countries, as the narrative informs us that God indeed endorses the request to have a king. And of course, appointing a king is presented in Deuteronomy 17:14–17 without any indication of divine disapproval. The Talmudic discussion (BT *Sanhedrin* 20b), later codified by Maimonides, indicates that the appointment of the king is a divine commandment, and Nelson notes that this view, normative in Jewish thought, was used by royalists to buttress the claim that God not only permitted but commanded kingship for Israel (p. 35).

The Hebraist antimonarchists, however, seized upon a passage in *D'varim Rabbah* (on Deut. 17:14), which Nelson presents as expressing a radically different view. Thus Milton, responding to the monarchist Hebraist Salmasius (who acknowledged the existence of the midrashic text), wrote, "you freely admit that some of their rabbis deny that their fathers should have recognized any king but God, though such a king was given to punish them. I follow the opinion of these rabbis" (p. 40).

Nelson concludes that "Milton's derivation of an exclusivist commitment to republican government from a set of rabbinic materials would have profound and long-lasting consequences" (p. 50). But the only Rabbinic materials attributed to Milton by Nelson in this context are the passage in *D'varim Rabbah* and a midrash on Nimrod as the first king, whose name is connected with *mered* (rebellion) (p. 49).[7] Moreover, Nelson fails to report that in the same work against Salmasius, where a statement from Josephus is more useful for his polemical purposes, Milton writes that Josephus was "infinitely preferable to a thousand obscure ignorant rabbins."[8] This does not suggest a thinker deeply influenced by Rabbinic texts, but rather a polemicist who would use such texts, among many others, where they fit his purpose.

Nelson's second chapter traces the idea that economic inequality among the citizens is improper, unethical, or unjust, and should be rectified by government policy leading to a redistribution of wealth. Focusing on the issue of land holdings, Nelson asserts that meditation by certain political thinkers on biblical land law seen through the prism of Rabbinic commentaries convinced a new generation of republican writers to reexamine their traditional antipathy toward governmental limitations on the size of private land holdings (pp. 59, 62–63).

The cause of this change, he argues, was a decision by the Dutch Hebraist Peter Cunaeus to characterize the biblical narratives of land distribution in Canaan and the laws of Jubilee in Leviticus 25 as "agrarian law." Roman writers, including Cicero, had lambasted government attempts to distribute land among the ordinary people as unjust expropriations of private property. But if God had ordained agrarian laws guaranteeing that land would not accumulate in the hands of the wealthy, then these Roman writers must have been wrong (p. 64). Cunaeus made the connection between biblical law (as expanded by the Rabbis and codified by Maimonides) and the Roman debate, "and in so doing he knew full well that he was forcing a dramatic reconsideration of the republican inheritance" (p. 75).

Turning to texts by English writers, Nelson maintains that through Harrington's extraordinary influence, from 1660 on, agrarian laws would remain permanently at the center of republican political thought, producing a consensus that republics must legislate limits on private ownership (p. 86). Yet in the final paragraph of the chapter, he informs us that in the eighteenth century, "the Biblical warrant for agrarian laws disappeared from view," and those who argued for redistribution did so without reference to the "divine landlord" (p. 87). This honest concession undermines the thesis that a new exposure to Jewish sources was an enduring influence on modern political thought.

While nonbiblical sources (Maimonides' *Code*) are mentioned, nothing in the use of the Hebraic agrarian laws by the writers cited depends on a unique insight of newly discovered postbiblical material. And, unlike the Roman legislation, the Jubilee law provided no mechanism for governmental enforcement or implementation. Indeed, Nelson notes that according to the Rabbis, the Jubilee legislation—if indeed it was *ever* actually enforced—was abolished at the time of the Assyrian exile of the northern tribes (BT *Arachin* 32b; 69). Perhaps this was a reason why the biblical legislation became irrelevant to eighteenth-century thinkers.

A further indication that the Rabbinic sources did not transform political thinking to the extent claimed can be seen in the paradoxical relationship between the argument in chapter 1 and the material in chapter 3, entitled "Hebrew Theocracy and the Rise of Toleration."

The thesis here is that the modern idea of religious toleration is derived not from the doctrine of separation between "church and state"—that the state has no right to interfere in the religious behavior of its subjects—but from an earlier antithetical doctrine associated with the sixteenth-century Swiss theologian known as Erastus, who held that religious bodies should have no coercive power (such as excommunication), and that the civil magistrate of the state must have jurisdiction over religious behavior, to be regulated by the state for the common good. The model claimed for this view was the Hebrew commonwealth.

The "Jewish source" most relevant to this chapter is Josephus, who wrote that ancient Israel had a unique political system, a "theocracy."[9] By this he meant that all sovereignty and authority was in the hands of God, who (in the Erastian reading) entrusted administration of His law to the supreme civil magistrate: Moses, Joshua, Judges, and then a long series of kings. Hugo Grotius, a leading exponent of this view, held that this authority entrusted to kings and then to the Sanhedrin as supreme civil magistrate, included the authority to suspend or change religious law, without challenge from independent religious authorities.

Note that there appears to be a blatant contradiction between this view and the view analysed in the first chapter, which cited a Jewish source to hold that kingship is by its very nature a sinful rebellion against God. Here the Jewish sources are employed to assert that the kings of Judea were appointed by God as civil magistrates with total authority to determine the law. But this presentation overlooks a crucially important component of biblical politics: the challenge to kings by prophets who claimed that they (the prophets) were the ones authorized to articulate God's rule at present. Sometimes this claim is recognized by the kings (Samuel and Saul, Nathan and David), sometimes not (Elijah and Ahab, Jeremiah and Zedekiah), but it is a major problem for an Erastian political philosophy rooted in an absolute link between God and the civil magistrate.

What does this have to do with toleration? While it removes coercive power from the religious institutions, it enhances the power of the state to impose conformity. Yet Nelson finds in this theory the origins of modern religious toleration because the coercive power of the state pertains only to the realm of behavior, not to the enforcement of uniform doctrine or belief. Thus the right of the individual conscience remains beyond the reach of both church and state (e.g., Harrington, cited in Nelson, p. 122).

Except that this freedom of conscience had significant limits for most of the writers cited. It did not include atheism, for example, or (according to Grotius) a deistic view that God is unconcerned with human affairs (p. 105). Harrington, brought as a firm supporter of this new doctrine of toleration, held that no religion contrary to or destructive of Christianity should be tolerated in the ideal state (p. 120). In short, the freedom of belief and conscience protected under this view is a rather limited basis for the insistence that the free exercise of religion must be beyond the interference of the State.

It is a shame that some of the Jewish sources that might indeed be considered relevant to modern progressive thinking are not mentioned by Nelson because they did not seem to be used by Christian Hebraists. Especially noteworthy is Don Isaac Abravanel's systematic reinterpretation of early biblical narratives based on the assumption that the original state of nature was one in which there was no private property and nothing superfluous to human life.[10] And Maharal of Prague's stirring condemnation at the end of his *Be'er ha-Golah*—two generations before Milton's *Areopagitica*—of any attempt to stifle the free exchange of ideas through censorship.[11]

Much as we might like to believe that postbiblical Jewish sources had a transformative impact on progressive western thought, Nelson's case that a new knowledge of these sources changed the minds of serious thinkers remains weak, and Kaplan's account of change implemented less by intellectuals arguing in Latin texts than by practical exigencies on the ground seems more compelling.

Notes

1. Many synagogues in other locations were also of this nature, pp. 188-90.
2. One eighteenth-century visitor observed (perhaps facetiously?) that there were separate pigsties, one used by the Lutherans and one by the Catholics.
3. E.g., pp. 214, 253, 269–70, 282–84, 307–8.
4. In 1391, "when a third of Spanish Jewry had been massacred and another third 'dragged forcibly to the baptismal font,'" citing Jonathan Israel's book that covers a period beginning in 1550; "Other Conversos remained true 'sons and daughters of Israel,'" endnote: "Phrase adapted from Renee Levine Melammed, *Heretics or Daughters of Israel?*"; "Ferdinand and Isabella had to ensure that Jews would no longer 'attract and pervert [New Christians] to their damned faith and opinion,'" reference to an article by Haim Beinart, though the phrase actually comes from a translation of the Edict of Expulsion. And so it continues.
5. This in addition to an assertion tossed off in the Introduction without any evidence or documentation, that the proliferation of Christian scholars who were capable of reading Hebrew texts in the sixteenth and seventeenth century "transformed European literature and criticism, medicine and science, theology and ecclesiology, and philosophy and law" (p. 16). Traditional Hebrew texts transformed European medicine and science in this period?! That is truly an original academic claim.
6. It is somewhat jarring to encounter in contemporary academic literature the use of "pluralism" as a negative and "exclusivism" as a positive value.
7. Nelson acknowledges, in note 94, that this Hebrew derivation of Nimrod is also in Augustine, so that it was not an innovation of seventeenth-century Christian Hebraists.
8. "A Defence of the People of England in Answer to Salmasius's Defence of the King," in *The Prose Works of John Milton*, 3 vols. (London: Henry G. Bohn, 1848), 1:34. A few pages later, Milton dismisses an argument by his antagonist as "grounded upon this worse than an old wife's tale, that is, upon a rabbinical fable." Id., 1:44.
9. *Against Apion*; this is apparently the first recorded use of this term.
10. See especially his commentary on the Eden story and on the Tower of Babel, translated in part in Ralph Lerner and Muhsin Mahdi, eds., *Medieval Political Philosophy: A Sourcebook* (Ithaca, NY:

Cornell University Press, 1983), pp.255-259.; B[enzion] Netan-yahu, *Don Isaac Abravanel: Statesman and Philosopher* (Philadelphia: JPS, 1968), 150–94.

11. See the passage cited in Hayim Hillel Ben-Sasson, "The Reforma-tion in Contemporary Jewish Eyes," *Proceedings of the Israel Acad-emy of Sciences and Humanities* 4, no. 12 (1971): 310–11.

RABBI MARC SAPERSTEIN (NY72) is professor of Jewish History and Homiletics at Leo Baeck College, London.

Sacred Treasure—The Cairo Genizah: The Amazing Discoveries of Forgotten Jewish History in an Egyptian Synagogue Attic
by Mark Glickman (Woodstock, VT: Jewish Lights, 2011), 288 pp.

There can be little doubt that the two most momentous discoveries of Jewish manuscripts in the last 125 years were the Scrolls found in the caves of Qumran and the manuscripts uncovered in the Ben Ezra synagogue in Fustat, Cairo.

Of the two it is the Dead Sea Scrolls that have hitherto achieved primacy in the public consciousness and have a shrine dedicated to them at the Israel Museum in Jerusalem; yet it might well be argued that the documents from the Cairo Genizah, hundreds of thousands in number and covering a period of many centuries' duration, have even greater importance.

Rabbi Solomon Schechter, the Romanian born Cambridge ac-ademic whose name will forever be associated with the Cairo Genizah, owed his discovery of this trove of treasure to two re-markable lay scholars, the independently wealthy sisters Mar-garet Gibson and Agnes Lewis. The two women, about whom a fascinating book has been written by the academic Janet Soskice, came upon some scraps of text in the Cairo market and brought them back to show to Schechter, with whom they were close friends.

The first piece of text that they showed him turned out to be from the hitherto unknown Hebrew text of the apocryphal book Ecclesiasticus, and this text led Schechter to travel to Egypt in 1896 to see what else might be found. It was a journey well worth mak-ing, for he brought back to Cambridge a lifetime's worth of texts, which was to become after his death the Taylor-Schechter Genizah Research Unit housed at the University Library.

The story of the Cairo Genizah and its manuscript treasures has fascinated many generations of scholars, and its hold on the imagination of Rabbi Mark Glickman is part of that tradition.

For *Sacred Treasure*, Glickman was able to trace the journey of Schechter to the Ben Ezra Synagogue as well as going to the Genizah Research unit, taking his son Jacob along for what turned out to be an exhilarating ride. Glickman writes with passion in an engaging style, and he draws in the reader whether aware or ignorant of the Genizah and its importance.

Sacred Treasure is divided into eleven chapters with an introduction and conclusion, telling the story of Schechter himself, the discovery of the Genizah by him and by other scholars both before and after him, and then of the work that has taken place on the texts since Schechter moved to America in 1902 and the later scholars who have studied and written about them—such as Jacob Mann, Shlomo Dov Gotein, and Stefan Reif.

Glickman also details the other places where manuscripts from the Cairo Genizah may be found, and although the largest quantity of them are at Cambridge, sizable numbers may be found at the British Library in London, the Bodleian Library in Oxford, the John Rylands Library in Manchester, and the Jewish Theological Seminary in New York, with varying small quantities of texts spread across the world from Tel Aviv to Los Angeles and Vienna to Toronto.

Sacred Treasure is a determinedly populist book in style, which will doubtless bring the existence of the Genizah to the attention of many readers who would eschew a more serious academic work; the author's passion about the subject shines through, as well as his wonder at some of the Genizah's contents, particularly material bearing the handwriting of Moses Maimonides himself and the texts that have no parallel in Jewish literature, such as a piece of sheet music by Ovadiah ha-Ger.

Rabbi Mark Glickman has created a fine, highly readable, and entertaining monument to Solomon Schechter's greatest discovery and his most significant contribution to Jewish scholarship and to the Jewish literary tradition.

CHARLES H. MIDDLEBURGH, Ph.D. (Leo Baeck College, 1986) is director of Jewish Studies at Leo Baeck College and congregational rabbi in Wales.

Poetry

Waking

Daniel F. Polish

*[Waking] is the riskiest moment . . . If you can manage to get through it
without being dragged out of place, you can relax for the rest of the day.*
—Franz Kafka, *The Trial*

Babies, they say,
Do not want to be born
Sameichim b'chelkam
At one with their watery world

And I, no newborn,
Separate from my sleep
Only with resistance—
Embrace the new day
With no joy

Still, in dawning wakefulness
Tradition voices through me
Praise that would not have
Tumbled from my tongue
On its own
Modeh ani l'fanecha . . .
She'hechezarta bi nishmati

DANIEL F. POLISH is the rabbi of Congregation Shir Chadash of the Hudson
Valley, Lagrange, New York. He is a member of the editorial board of this journal
and the editor of its section "*Maayanot*: Primary Sources," a published poet, and
the author, most recently, of *Talking about God* (Woodstock, VT: SkyLight Paths
Publishing, 2007).

Yom HaDin

Daniel F. Polish

From the minute they tell you
"It needs to be biopsied"
To the time they call with results
You are dead

A *goses*
Walking and acting
But gone
Already in the other world
Not this

The phone rings
The doctor's call,
"I think I have some good news for you"
Benign
T'chiyat hameitim
Returned to life
Your place is among the living still

On Yom Kippur we are told
we are
judged,
in danger,
deemed dead

By *N'ilah*, when we hear
salachti kidvarecha,
we are returned to hope,
our lives restored

To Make Sacred

Reeve Robert Brenner

You ask what desecration means.
That lampshade at Yad Vashem
of tawny amber parchment
torn from a torah scroll
whose skin testifies to sizzling flesh,
once illuminated the thighs
of an ubermensch und frau,
once cast, flickering,
the holy tongue upon their
compounding frames,
their frankfurt, furth and fulda
flaying limbs,
once flung filigreed letters
of redemptive writ,
obedient Hebrew script,
to march and retreat across
shifting sweaty nazi spines
as on keeled carapaces,
rippling wavy corrugated words
in shadows
enlarging with their heavings,
fleeting with each thrust,
once projected silhouetted shapes:
thou shalt
thou shalt not.
and we,
still shaken by that shade,
might make love
in the holy city
in the holy tongue
my quill stenciling torah tropes
upon your holy of holies

RABBI DR. REEVE ROBERT BRENNER (NY64) serves Bet Chesed Congregation, Bethesda, Maryland, and is the retired Sr. Staff Chaplain of the National Institutes of Health. His pieces of "SportSculpture" have been exhibited in a number of international museums including the Museum of Modern Art Design Department and The Israel National Museum in Jerusalem, and are now on permanent display at the Boston Children's Museum.

a wholly holy act,
and therewith
discomfit Jerusalem's profaners
and soften the sacrilege.

Dance Lessons from My Sister

Reeve Robert Brenner

A New York suburban wind
now slants, now shuffles
the single hardened rose box-stepping
beside my sister's grave. So very still;
the no longer soft loam holds fast
in the stomp of winter's sway.

When we were young
we watched cardinals, catbirds, and grackles
like those feathery wings moving rhythmically
over her stone
providing secret names for them
as did Adam and Eve
in their garden and supervised
our monument-maker dad
chiseling lambs and candlesticks
pitchers for layvees
and priestly fingers
out of rock-of-ages
barre granite slabs
like this
delivered very nearly raw
from Vermont quarries.

 Full skirted my sister
swirled in the glowing effulgence
of Chanukah lights singing Jerusalem verses
and golden oldies
. . . till the end of time
. . . till the mountains disappear . . .

 Chana, she taught me to guide her
steps from the lawn
to the bungalow
our parents chose for our summers
that my feet would know
what they were doing
when I would one day ask her
to dance at her wedding.

Chana, she leads my steps still.

Yom Kippur

Kendrah Raye Whyte

A day so solemn, even the flowers weep,
If our collective pleas for forgiveness,
Were all heard at once,
The very stars would blink in amazement,
But, Eternal One, Your mercy covers us like a tallit,
And tomorrow, we shall arise as newborns.

KENDRAH RAYE WHYTE is an artist, as well as a poet. She lives in West Roxbury, Massachusetts, with her cat, Dena. She dedicates this poem to Michael (z"l) and Rabbi Emily Gopen Lipof.

אהיה אשר אהיה
I am that I am
I am that I will be

Alison Burchett

Poland.
I am colder than cold and empty.
I am with my best friend, but I am alone.
He is alone, so I must be alone.
I am watching as he is watching his history. Separated by clear
glass from them. Their life. Their Death.
I am watching as he is watching his history. Blue and white,
tattered and torn from pain, death, suffering, horror.
Horror.
It is silent.
I am watching as he is watching his history. Hills of hair. His
mother's hair, his daughter's hair, his grandmother's hair,
his grandmother's mother's hair, his grandfather's wife's, his
grandfather's wife's mother's
mothers
nieces
daughters
wives
menorahs. Enough for 1,800 days of light. But there is no miracle here.
I am watching as he is watching his history. What does he see?
I am colder than cold and empty.
I am alone. He is alone.
I am watching. I am a voyeur, a perpetrator, a seer, a Christian
who did not see, a Christian who did not know how to see, a
Christian who does not see, a Christian who does not know how
to see.
I am colder than cold and empty.
I am alone.

ALISON BURCHETT, a native of the Pacific Northwest, graduated in 2011 from
Pacific Lutheran University in Tacoma, Washington, where she studied English
Literature and Religion. She is currently pursuing a Master's in Divinity at
Princeton Theological Seminary in Princeton, New Jersey.

I am 7 years old. I am in Mrs. Clark's Sunday school class at
Westminster Presbyterian Church. I am very good at painting
wooden crosses. I have perfect Sunday school attendance.
I am 7 years old. I am being chauffeured by my mom to youth
group at a Baptist church. I am going to meet my friend. I am
singing songs about Jesus with guitar music. I am trying to find
the organ. I am listening to the pastor and I am going to hell
because I haven't accepted Jesus Christ as my personal Lord
and Savior.
I am 7 years old. I am competitive. I am going to ask Jesus to
save me and then I am going to learn the bible verses and I am
going to recite them and I am going to get a sticker in my
handbook and I am going to get a pin for the uniform that I am
going to get and then I am going to make my mom buy me a
zippered carrying case for my bible, and then I'm going to be
the best Christian ever and I am going to go to heaven.
First, though, I am going to learn the membership verse.
By grace I am going to be saved by faith and not by myself, for
grace is a gift from God, not earned or bought by works, lest
any man should boast.
And then I will get my sticker and my pin and my uniform and
my bible case, and my . . .

At the top of Yad Mordechai I am squinting to see Gaza. I am
looking out at the hot, dead, iron men on the kibbutz. I am in
the line of fire. I am asking the rabbi a question. I am right.
Good girl.
He asks just to make sure. I am raising my hand in response. I
look around. I am the only one raising my hand. I am the only
not a Jew.

I am not here on birthright. I am not here because I have family
here. I am not here to make *aliyah*. Why am I here? I am not a
Jew.

I am 21 years old. I am a single female traveling alone in Egypt.
I am an American woman with hair, with white teeth, with skin,
with a camera, with money, with courage, with chutzpah. I am
cornered by a waitstaff on the boat.
Egypt tells me about Jews. The bad Jewish people who must die.
Egypt tells me and I feel othered and I know
Egypt tells me
I am a Jew.

I am pimply, insecure, hormonal. I am a senior in high school.
I am sitting in English class, listening silently as my mother
dies at home. Listening, listening, listening for something, for
nothing. Gasping, choking, a seizure, a scream, a head knocked
against a bedpost, a retching, a silence. Again. I am sitting in
English class. Listening. I am watching as the teacher throws a
bible into a garbage bin. I am listening. A gasp. A choke. A
silence. My knee jerks, responding to the prompt. It writes. I
read: "Screw Authority."
I am walking down the hall, my best friend behind, catches
up. I am confronted by her and another. "Do you call yourself
a Christian?" My best friend, who isn't listening as our mother
dies at home. Gasping, choking, a seizure, a scream, a head
knocked against a bedpost, a retching, a silence.
I am hearing nothing.

Sitting in an art gallery, a town hall, a holy place, a house, we
are listening to Ben-Gurion declare the nation. ישראל We are
moved, the Jews and I.
"Ay-men" one man shouts. Rookie Goy mistake, I think.
I have done my research. I know better.
Ah-main
I am not exposed.
We are moved, we are crying, we are standing. I am watching as
everyone stands, listening as they sing.
I am not singing.
I am not able.
I do not know
I am not one
I am not a Jew.

I am learning Hebrew. I am singing silently the *alef-bet*. I am
wanting not to be the only one, the only not a Jew. I am wanting
to be accepted, not by grace, but by them.

I am walking toward the exit of the Jewish Diaspora Museum in
Tel Aviv. I am approached by an older man from my tour group.
It's "Ay-men" from the other day.
I am asked whether I knew that Christians had done such ter-
rible things to Jews.
I have been outed as the Goy and now I will always be asked
whether I know about what Christians have done to Jews. I am
the token Goy, responsible for the suffering.
I am tempted to ask whether he knows that Jesus was a Jew,

whether he knows anything about Judaism even.
I am annoyed.
Yes, I learn about this in school.
I am the representative of a Lutheran education. I am the
representative of Liberal Protestantism. I am Luther. I am
Calvin. I am Christendom.
I am outed as the Goy.
I am also the only person who follows kashrut.

I am at my father's retirement party. I am approached by a
couple he must work with. They ask how school is, what I'm
majoring in. I am studying English and Religion. Religion? Why
religion? What do I want to do with that? I am honest. I am
trying to get rid of fundamentalism of hate of the gospel of John
in America.
"Why would you say such a thing?" He screams. He does not
understand. He is a Christian who does not see. A Christian
who does not know how to see. A bystander, a perpetrator. How
can I make him see?
I am 22 and a heretic. I am being prayed for. But I am going to
hell.

I am 20 years old and I am walking to the Vatican. I pass the
homeless, pitiful beggars as I walk through massive marble
arches. Vatican employees in jester costumes guard the papal
walls. Inside, gold leaf is being reapplied to the magnificent
gates of St. Peter's Basilica. Outside, a woman shakes a paper
cup for change. Inside, born-again virgins weep for Peter's
bones. Outside, women die from AIDS after being raped by
patriarchy, by the omnipotent Gods the Fathers.

I am 8 years old in the back seat of a minivan on my way home
from church watching a haze of weeds whir by. I am wondering
what will happen if my parents aren't right about god. I don't
ask. I already know. They aren't.

I am 17 years old and my mother will die. I am in charge of my
sister while my parents visit the hospital.
My father has forgotten how to cook, but there is hot food to-
night. There is hot food every night. The spaghetti and brownies
on the table are better than anything my parents ever make.
Some women from the church brought it.
I am 17 years old and our mother has died. What would we like
in the service on Sunday?

The grey-haired congregation grasps hands, a chain, with ours,
and sings.
I am blessed by the tie that binds
Our hearts in Christian love;
The fellowship of kindred minds
Is like to that above.

I am at the Kotel, listening. I am at the Kotel and Rambam's
grave and in Compostella, Spain, and at the Vaticano. I am
watching thorns go by at Notre Dame. I am
Sick. Idolatry, I diagnose.

In a shopping complex in London with my beloved. My David.
I am in a bad mood. I am angry. I am horrible. I am lashing out.
"The stereotypes must be true," I am hearing myself say. "We
could never date because we couldn't even eat together.
Vegetables would be too expensive!"
I am the daughter of American anti-Semitism. But I am not
excused.

I am walking around a church in Wittenberg, looking for the
door. It's snowing.
Germany is colder than cold and empty.
I am alone.
I go inside the unheated room. I am sitting next to an old
woman.
I am unable to read the German, but I know what is going on.
The pews are cold.
Candles are lit and people process. I am taking the cup then I
am taking a hand. I am at home and warmed despite the fact
that Germany is colder than cold and empty.

I am 22 years old driving home in the rain and thinking about
writing this poem. I am thinking about who I am. I am crying. I
am the daughter of a father who lets me question, who lets me
fight, who throws his hands up and accepts that I am what I am.
That I am what I will be. I am a daughter without a mother. I am
lonely. I am lost. I am anxious.
I am listening.
I am hearing nothing.
I am a Christian without a Christ
    a Lutheran without a heritage
    a Presbyterian without condemnation
    a Jew without a lineage or a homeland or a tragedy or a people.

The wipers beat the windshield. I am having trouble seeing. I
am almost home.
אהיה אשר אהיה
I am that I am.
I am that I will be.

The Man in the Picture

Sinéad Mac Devitt

The man in the picture was selling bread.
The man was just selling bread.
Sirens filled the air and arms were raised
because the man was selling bread.

A man that could sell bread in Kovno
could have been a politician or a rabbi.
He became a famous warrior
because he had the courage to sell.

The man in the picture stopped selling bread.
The man in the picture vanished.
The man in the picture was shot
because he broke *their* law.

The man from the Polish ghetto died.
No funeral service was held.
No words in Hebrew were uttered.
No one blessed his name forever.

SINÉAD MAC DEVITT is from Ireland. Her poems and stories have been published in various periodicals in Ireland, and she also teaches Creative Writing to children. Her poem refers to an article in "Fighting for Dignity: Jewish Resistance in Krakow" published by the Holocaust Education Trust Ireland, www.hetireland.org.

Naso and *Nisuin*

Nancy S. Abraham

It is not about the registries
numbers of porcelain place settings,
quantities of sterling silver serving pieces,
but lifting our heads as we walk together
receiving the Priestly Benediction each mundane day
each holy day—
they can be one and the same.

It is not about the cut crystal water goblets,
the kind that sing when tapped,
the damask table cloths and raw-silk sofa fabrics,
but, combining our riches for living,
to make a path together through
the wilderness of suburbia,
city formations, cosmopolitan caves.

It is not about the famous photographer and his images,
the seating arrangements and abundance of pale-pink peonies,
it is about the long way to
the Promised Land of vowed togetherness.
It is not the Nazarite vow of abstinence
but an intoxication in the moment
and a glistening string of moments ahead,
a letting down of the hair or a trimming of locks
as we become locked into a partnership.

It is not about the up-do and strappy satin sandals,
eyes lined by kohl,
but the way we were fashioned to walk side by side
cutting through fields of illusion, our hearts open,
in step with the other,

NANCY S. ABRAHAM is an administrator, teacher, and *b'nei mitzvah* tutor in the Religious School of Westchester Reform Temple, Scarsdale, New York. Her poetry appears in the new *Women's Torah Commentary* and several of her many *nigunim* are included in the URJ's *Nigun Anthology II*.

as we seek lives of beauty and truth,
revealing them from the eye-mind,
the worthy hand
the soul space
the heart song
the place even beyond the soul.

It is about lifting our heads,
walking hand-in-hand,
shadows overlapping
counting ourselves as blessed
for being brought together in the Tent of Meeting
surrounded by Israel
strugglers, as we are,
where everyone counts
where trend and tradition intersect to form eternity.
It is about registering as a couple,
guided by pillars of light and fire
as we journey through
the great wilderness of life.

Surcease

Michael A. Meyer

Sing a song of worldly splendor,
Dance the mighty Lord's defeat.
Gather on the windswept mountain
Where triumphant rebels meet.

Whirl in circles corybantic,
Don't look up but glance around.
Grasp the moment, fear no vengeance.
Where' 's the thunder—not a sound!

Revel on without cessation
Till a sudden, fearful thought:
Is there then no God above us?
Can our lives be built on nought?

MICHAEL A. MEYER is Adolph S. Ochs Professor Emeritus at HUC-JIR, Cincinnati, and international president of the Leo Baeck Institute. This is his first published poem since he was a graduate student.

A Midrash on Deuteronomy 6:5

Norman Hirsh

V'ahavta—You shall love
Family, friend and neighbor

With all your
Mind,
Aware what to do,
And not to do

With all your
Soul,
Only the soul
Can find the soul

With all your
Strength,
Overcome what is dark within,
Act generously.

With all, all, all

NORMAN HIRSH (C58) is a retired rabbi living in Seattle, Washington. He is the author of a book of poetry: *God Loves Becoming*.

Call for Papers: *Maayanot*

The CCAR Journal: The Reform Jewish Quarterly is committed to serving its readers' professional, intellectual, and spiritual needs. In pursuit of that objective, the Journal has created a new section to be known as *Maayanot* (Primary Sources). The new rubric will have its debut in the Spring 2012 issue.

We invite the submission of proposals for translations of significant Jewish texts, accompanied by an appropriate introduction and annotations and/or commentary. These texts can represent fresh approaches materials from any period of Jewish life that would be of interest to our readers. When appropriate, we will include the original document in the published presentation.

Please submit your ideas and proposals to *Maayanot* editor, Daniel Polish, dpolish@optonline.net.

Along with submissions for *Maayanot*, the *Journal* continues to welcome the submission of scholarly articles in fields of Jewish Studies, as well as other articles, poetry, and book reviews that fit within our Statement of Purpose.

The CCAR Journal: The Reform Jewish Quarterly
Published quarterly by the Central Conference of American Rabbis.

Volume LIX, No. 2. Issue Number: Two hundred thirty-two.
Spring 2012.

STATEMENT OF PURPOSE

The CCAR Journal: The Reform Jewish Quarterly seeks to explore ideas and issues of Judaism and Jewish life, primarily—but not exclusively—from a Reform Jewish perspective. To fulfill this objective, the Journal is designed to:

1. provide a forum to reflect the thinking of informed and concerned individuals—especially Reform rabbis—on issues of consequence to the Jewish people and the Reform Movement;

2. increase awareness of developments taking place in fields of Jewish scholarship and the practical rabbinate, and to make additional contributions to these areas of study;

3. encourage creative and innovative approaches to Jewish thought and practice, based upon a thorough understanding of the traditional sources.

The views expressed in the Journal do not necessarily reflect the position of the Editorial Board or the Central Conference of American Rabbis.

The CCAR Journal: The Reform Jewish Quarterly (ISSN 1058-8760) is published quarterly by the Central Conference of American Rabbis, 355 Lexington Avenue, 18th Floor, New York, NY, 10017. Application to mail at periodical postage rates is pending at New York, NY and at additional mailing offices.

Subscriptions should be sent to CCAR Executive Offices, 355 Lexington Avenue, 18th Floor, New York, NY, 10017. Subscription rate as set by the Conference is $75 for a one-year subscription, $125 for a two-year subscription. Overseas subscribers should add $36 per year for postage. POSTMASTER: Please send address changes to The CCAR Journal: The Reform Jewish Quarterly, c/o Central Conference of American Rabbis, 355 Lexington Avenue, 18th Floor, New York, NY, 10017.

Typesetting and publishing services provided by Publishing Synthesis, Ltd., 39 Crosby Street, New York, NY, 10013.

The CCAR Journal: The Reform Jewish Quarterly is indexed in the *Index to Jewish Periodicals*. Articles appearing in it are listed in the *Index of Articles on Jewish Studies* (of *Kirjath Sepher*).

ISBN: 978-0-88123-181-6

GUIDELINES FOR SUBMITTING MATERIAL

1. The *CCAR Journal* welcomes submissions that fulfill its Statement of Purpose whatever the author's background or identification. Inquiries regarding publishing in the CCAR Journal and submissions for possible publication (including poetry) should be sent to the editor, Rabbi Susan Laemmle, in electronic form via *Laemmle@ usc.edu*. Should problems arise, call 323-939-4084.

2. Other than commissioned articles, submissions to the *CCAR Journal* are sent out to a member of the editorial board for anonymous peer review. Thus submitted articles and poems should be sent to the editor with the author's name omitted. Please use MS Word format for the attachment. The message itself should contain the author's name, phone number, and e-mail address, as well as the submission's title and a 1–2 sentence bio.

3. Books for review and inquiries regarding submitting a review should be sent directly to the book review editor, Rabbi Laurence Edwards, at *LLE49@comcast.net*.

4. Inquiries concerning, or submissions for, *Maayanot* (Primary Sources) should be directed to the *Maayanot* editor, Rabbi Daniel Polish, at *dpolish@optonline.net*.

5. Based on Reform Judaism's commitment to egalitarianism, we request that articles be written in gender-inclusive language.

6. The *Journal* publishes reference notes at the end of articles, but submissions are easier to review when notes come at the bottom of each page. If possible, keep this in mind when submitting an article. Notes should conform to the following style:

   a. Norman Lamm, *The Shema: Spirituality and Law in Judaism* (Philadelphia: Jewish Publication Society, 1998), 101–6. **[book]**

   b. Lawrence A. Hoffman, "The Liturgical Message," in *Gates of Understanding*, ed. Lawrence A.Hoffman (New York: CCAR Press, 1977), 147–48, 162–63. **[chapter in a book]**

   c. Richard Levy, "The God Puzzle," *Reform Judaism* 28 (Spring 2000): 18–22. **[article in a periodical]**

   d. Lamm, *Shema*, 102. **[short form for subsequent reference]**

   e. Levy, "God Puzzle," 20. **[short form for subsequent reference]**

   f. Ibid., 21. **[short form for subsequent reference]**

7. If Hebrew script is used, please include an English translation. If transliteration is used, follow the guidelines abbreviated below and included more fully in the **Master Style Sheet**, available on the CCAR website at *www.ccarnet.org*:

   "ch" for *chet* and *chaf* "ei" for *tzeirei*

   "f" for *fei* "a" for *patach* and *kamatz*

   "k" for *kaf* and *kuf* "o" for *cholam* and *kamatz katan*

   "tz" for *tzadi* "u" for *shuruk* and *kibbutz*

   "i" for *chirik* "ai" for *patach* with *yod*

   "e" for *segol*

   Final "h" for final *hei*; none for final *ayin* (with exceptions based on common usage): atah, Sh'ma, <u>but</u> Moshe.

   Apostrophe for *sh'va nah*: b'nei, b'rit, Sh'ma; no apostrophe for *sh'va nach*.

   Hyphen for two vowels together where necessary for correct pronunciation: *ne-eman, samei-ach,* <u>but</u> *maariv,* Shavuot.

   No hyphen for prefixes unless necessary for correct pronunciation: *babayit, HaShem, Yom HaAtzma-ut.*

   Do not double consonants (with exceptions based on dictionary spelling or common usage): *t'filah, chayim,* <u>but</u> *tikkun,* Sukkot.